Rorty and the
Mirror of Nature

'The book is clearly written and fair-minded throughout, just the sort of work one would want as a guidebook for reading an important and difficult book. In this sense, it seems clear about its audience and will be useful for a sophisticated study of Philosophy and the Mirror of Nature and also of interest to those who already have a good deal of background and familiarity with Rorty.'

David Hiley, *University of New Hampshire, USA*

'This is well-written, clear, accessible, sharp and pitched at the right level. It strikes the right balance between the detailed exploration of particular arguments, and setting Rorty's book in a wider intellectual context.'

Matthew Festenstein, *University of York, UK*

Richard Rorty is one of the most influential, controversial and widely-read philosophers of the twentieth century. In this guidebook to *Philosophy and the Mirror of Nature* Tartaglia analyses this challenging text and introduces and assesses:

- Rorty's life and the background to his philosophy
- the key themes and arguments of *Philosophy and the Mirror of Nature*
- the continuing importance of Rorty's work to philosophy.

Rorty and the Mirror of Nature is an ideal starting point for anyone new to Rorty, and will be essential reading for students of philosophy, cultural studies, literary theory and social science.

James Tartaglia is Lecturer in Philosophy at the University of Keele, UK.

ROUTLEDGE PHILOSOPHY GUIDEBOOKS

Edited by Tim Crane and Jonathan Wolff,
University College London

Plato and the Trial of Socrates Thomas C. Brickhouse and Nicholas D. Smith

Aristotle and the Metaphysics Vasilis Politis

Rousseau and The Social Contract Christopher Bertram

Plato and the Republic, Second edition Nickolas Pappas

Husserl and the Cartesian Meditations A.D. Smith

Kierkegaard and Fear and Trembling John Lippitt

Descartes and the Meditations Gary Hatfield

Hegel and the Philosophy of Right Dudley Knowles

Nietzsche on Morality Brian Leiter

Hegel and the Phenomenology of Spirit Robert Stern

Berkeley and the Principles of Human Knowledge Robert Fogelin

Aristotle on Ethics Gerard Hughes

Hume on Religion David O'Connor

Leibniz and the Monadology Anthony Savile

The Later Heidegger George Pattison

Hegel on History Joseph McCarney

Hume on Morality James Baillie

Hume on Knowledge Harold Noonan

Kant and the Critique of Pure Reason Sebastian Gardner

Mill on Liberty Jonathan Riley

Mill on Utilitarianism Roger Crisp

Wittgenstein and the Philosophical Investigations Marie McGinn

Spinoza and the Ethics Genevieve Lloyd

Heidegger on Being and Time, Second Edition Stephen Mulhall

Locke on Government D.A. Lloyd Thomas

Locke on Human Understanding E.J. Lowe

Derrida on Deconstruction Barry Stocker

Kant on Judgement Robert Wicks

Nietzsche on Art Aaron Ridley

Rorty and the Mirror of Nature James Tartaglia

Routledge Philosophy Guidebook to

Rorty and the Mirror of Nature

James
Tartaglia

Routledge
Taylor & Francis Group

LONDON AND NEW YORK

First published 2007
by Routledge
2 Park Square, Milton Park, Abingdon, Oxon OX14 4RN

Simultaneously published in the USA and Canada
by Routledge
270 Madison Ave, New York, NY 10016

Routledge is an imprint of the Taylor & Francis Group, an informa business

© 2007 James Tartaglia

Typeset in Aldus and Scala by
Book Now Ltd, London
Printed and bound in Great Britain by
TJ International Ltd, Padstow, Cornwall

British Library Cataloguing in Publication Data
A catalogue record for this book is available from the British Library

Library of Congress Cataloging in Publication Data
A catalog record for this book has been requested

ISBN10: 0–415–38330–7 (hbk)
ISBN10: 0–415–38331–5 (pbk)
ISBN10: 0–203–94600–6 (ebk)

ISBN13: 978–0–415–38330–1 (hbk)
ISBN13: 978–0–415–38331–8 (pbk)
ISBN13: 978–0–203–94600–8 (ebk)

CONTENTS

1   Rorty   1

2   The Mirror of Nature   25

3   The origins of the Mirror   41

4   The Antipodeans   71

5   The origins of philosophy   100

6   Linguistic holism   112

7   Naturalised epistemology: psychology   134

8   Naturalised epistemology: language   147

9   Science and pluralism   177

10 The power of strangeness   203

    NOTES   231
    BIBLIOGRAPHY   241
    INDEX   252

1

RORTY

It is a miserable story: man seeks a principle through which he can despise men – he invents a world so as to be able to slander and bespatter this world: in reality, he reaches every time for nothingness and construes nothingness as 'God,' as 'truth,' and in any case as judge and condemner of *this* state of being.

Friedrich Nietzsche, 1888
(Nietzsche 1967: 253)

OVERVIEW: PHILOSOPHY AND TRUTH

It is sometimes said as a criticism of someone's views that they 'cannot see the wood for the trees', meaning that they have focused so narrowly on a particular issue that they have failed to see the significance of that issue within a wider context. This is certainly not a criticism ever likely to be levelled at Richard Rorty, philosophy's self-professed specialist in 'great big pictures' (Rorty 1982: xl), whose frame of reference is more likely to be the entire history of Western thought than the latest hot topic of debate within the professional journals. That is not to say that Rorty does not go in amongst the trees to debate the fine detail of particular philosophical positions. On the contrary, that he has done so consistently throughout his career is what provides his work with its content and power.

Nevertheless, whenever Rorty takes sides in philosophical debates, he is sure to have one eye securely fixed on a grand narrative that contextualises the debate for him, and which provides the motivation for his continual efforts at 'breaking the crust of convention' (379), at shaking up received views in the hope of instigating new and more fruitful lines of inquiry. The two received views he has done the most to challenge are, characteristically enough, amongst the biggest themes available to a philosopher: philosophy itself and truth. These themes are deeply connected within Rorty's thought, and by beginning with an overview of what he has to say about them, we can approach *Philosophy and the Mirror of Nature* (henceforth *PMN*) as Rorty approaches philosophy: with an eye to the big picture.

Rorty wants to undermine the confidence philosophers have in their subject as an autonomous discipline with its own subject-matter and its own methodology for dealing with that subject matter. Unlike history, geology, biology, and a whole host of other standard academic subjects, Rorty thinks that philosophy is deeply suspect. On a fairly neutral conception of the subject, philosophy studies our most basic and general ways of understanding the world by attempting to overcome perennial problems that can arise whenever those ways of understanding are reflected upon. The philosopher investigates the nature of mind, knowledge, and time, to take some prime examples, but does so in full generality, as opposed to investigating minds of particular people, instances of knowledge, or historical eras. Since philosophy is a problem-based subject, the way into these investigations is to address problems for understanding the world in such terms, problems like finding a place for minds alongside physical objects, or securing human claims to knowledge from sceptical challenges, or explaining the elusiveness of the temporal present. Throughout the long history of the subject, philosophers have developed methods for solving these problems, or at least in the hope of making progress towards solutions. One of the most complex and thorough methods ever developed was that of Immanuel Kant, a method which Kant hoped would place philosophy on the 'secure path of a science' (Kant 1933: Bxiv). This is a phrase Rorty loves to quote, for it encapsulates everything he does not want for philosophy. Rorty's aim, in stark contrast to Kant's, is to keep philosophy well away from the 'secure path of a science'.

Kant's ambition for philosophy to become a scientific enterprise has resurfaced in all the main philosophical movements since his time, and it manifests itself as strongly as ever in the highly specialised work which predominates in philosophy today, at least in the English speaking world. Rorty is against this sort of technical, professionalised philosophy not because he thinks there are better ways of making progress on the central problems of philosophy. Rather, he is against it because he thinks progress in philosophy is impossible, and that a scientific approach obscures this. For Rorty, the 'perennial problems' I mentioned above are little more than historical aberrations, outdated ways of thinking which it is a mistake to perpetuate. Philosophical problems are to be ignored. They are to be put aside and forgotten rather than solved, just as problems which interested mediaeval scholars, such as how best to understand the nature of angels, were never solved, only forgotten. While philosophy remains on the 'secure path of a science', however, Rorty thinks it will be able to continually renew itself. The old problems will be forever recycled in new formulations, which will in turn spin off technical side-issues that only specialists can debate. As the technicality increases, encouraged by the dream of piecemeal scientific progress, philosophical research becomes increasingly detached from the intuitive problems that first attracted its practitioners, and increasingly irrelevant to the rest of culture. And the more philosophers are required to specialise to understand the latest research, the less likely they are to have the synoptic and historical vision required to question their own research programmes and recognise old debates resurfacing in contemporary jargon. In short, once on the 'secure path of a science', Rorty thinks that the degeneration of philosophy is self-perpetuating. And that is why he wants to break 'the crust of convention', to disrupt 'normal' philosophical activity.

These are views *on* philosophy rather than *in* philosophy, and hence Rorty's work is distinctive in being primarily metaphilosophical rather than philosophical, where a metaphilosophical position is a position on the nature of philosophy, rather than on the nature of mind or knowledge or some other topic in philosophy. Rorty does have views *in* philosophy too – as already mentioned, he goes in amongst the trees as well as surveying the woods – but his philosophical views are generally adopted for metaphilosophical purposes, namely to make traditional lines of philosophical inquiry appear uninteresting, and thereby to persuade conventional philosophers to try something new. Rorty is not proposing a view of the nature of philosophy in any conventional sense, however, since he denies that philosophy has any autonomous subject-matter, and hence that it has any specific nature. This is what led him to say that '"the nature and function of philosophy" is a pseudo-topic' (Rorty 1998: 317), on the face of it, a rather surprising denouncement of metaphilosophy from the man widely regarded as its premier exponent. But consider the parallel case of eliminative materialism, the view that minds do not exist. If we insisted on a narrow conception of 'philosophy of mind', we might deny that this is a view in the philosophy of mind. But it would be misleading to do so. Likewise, it would be misleading to deny that Rorty holds views on the nature of philosophy. He has a metaphilosophy, just a negative one.

It is, in fact, multiply negative. As Donald Davidson has succinctly put it, 'Rorty sees the history of Western philosophy as a confused and victorless battle between unintelligible scepticism and lame attempts to answer it' (Davidson 1990: 137). It is this view of the history of the subject which lies behind Rorty's scepticism about normal philosophical research: he thinks philosophy was designed for dubious purposes, and that it has had no success in fulfilling those purposes anyway, despite trying for a very long time. History provides Rorty with a tool for dismantling philosophy and a motivation for wanting to do so. By showing the questionable origins of issues and ideas now taken for granted, he hopes to undermine the confidence of philosophers inclined to think of their work as akin to science, and hence as largely ahistorical. But Rorty has at times gone much further than just trying to inject some historical circumspection into philosophy to keep it off the 'secure path of a science': he has suggested that even philosophers of his own disruptive ilk should aim to work themselves out of a job (Rorty 1991b: 86), and has expressed the hope that his brand of 'antiphilosophy' might lead to a 'post-Philosophical culture' (Rorty 1982: xl). This sounds like a call to bring philosophy to an end once and for all. That, however, is not necessarily the idea. What he certainly wants to end is philos-ophy-as-we-know-it, or as he used to say, Philosophy (with a capital 'P'). Rorty fully expects future generations to read the classic works of philosophy such as Descartes' *Meditations* and Kant's *Critique of Pure Reason*. He also expects the people who specialise in reading these texts to call themselves 'philosophers'. Nevertheless, he hopes that in the future, these texts will no longer be read in the same spirit, will no longer be taken literally. Instead, philosophy will be thought of as a vaguely demarcated genre of literature, and nobody will think of this genre as dealing with real and important problems, much less as contributing to an ongoing quest to unravel the funda-mental enigmas of human existence. He wants the great texts of philosophy to be thought of as just great texts.

Now if it were not for the connection between philosophy and truth, the other major theme in Rorty's work, then this negative metaphilosophy might easily be dismissed. After all, if the problem is that philosophy cannot make any progress, then it is not obvious why turning it into a form of literary study which does not even aim at making progress should have any great significance. Nor is it obvious that this transformation would make philosophy more inter-esting, as Rorty thinks, rather than simply more accessible. But the connection Rorty makes between philosophy and truth provides his attacks on philosophy with greater urgency than if he were simply calling out for members of his profession to stop deluding them-selves. The connection is that Rorty sees philosophy as the last respectable bastion of a certain conception of truth, one which he thinks is holding back progress in intellectual life. He thinks that the abandonment of this conception of truth is required for the complete secularisation of human thought, and that a transformation in philosophy might, in the long run, have a positive role to play in this much wider transformation.

The conception of truth in question here is that of objective truth, in the literal sense of a truth that that comes from objects, by contrast with the subjective truth which sentences such as 'I like liquorice' express: this may be true when I say it, but false when you do, indicating that its truth depends as much on the subject (me or you) as the object (liquorice).[1] Now one traditional way of under-standing objective truth is in terms of a relation of correspondence holding between our language and the world. So for instance, a sentence like 'some roses are red' can be used to say something objectively true, according to this view, because it is able to relate in the right sort of way – able to correspond – to certain real objects, i.e. real red roses. Of course, objective truths do not always relate so neatly to physical objects – consider the sentence 'house price inflation is getting out of control' – but even a sentence of this sort can be thought of as corresponding to some rather messier portion of reality, the 'object' of the sentence in an extended sense of 'object', which in this example might incorporate banks, houses, and people in some complex way. This idea of objective truth, then, may be summed up as the idea that whether or not the things we say, think or write are true, depends on whether or not they correspond to how the world really is.

This idea of objective truth may sound like an innocuous piece of common sense, as many philosophers and the vast majority of non-philosophers still think that it is, but Rorty thinks it is anything but innocuous. On his view, it is a residue of religious thought hidden deep down within our ordinary ways of thinking, a residue which philosophy has unwittingly helped to perpetuate. The explanation of how this situation came about, according to Rorty, is to be found in the Enlightenment movement of the eighteenth century.

Kant proposed as a motto for this movement: 'Have courage to make use of your *own* understanding!' (Kant 1996: 17), since the guiding idea was to cast off the authority of the church, the crown, and ancient texts, and to instead rely upon human reason for understanding the world. Rather than believing God had already revealed the truth through certain institutions, people should instead try to work the truth out for themselves by means of science and philosophy. These ideas made an unprecedented contribution to the secularisation of culture, but did not go far enough according to Rorty, for an element of religious thought remained that has prevented the secularisation process from reaching completion. This is because the notion of objective truth was left untouched. Belief in divine guidance was thereby simply displaced rather than discarded, for truth continued to be thought of as something forced upon us by a non-human agency. Faith in God was gradually transformed into faith in science, because with the religious conception of truth intact, the most we could do was progress from believing that the truth is dictated by God, to believing that the truth is dictated by an independent, objective world, i.e. by the 'way the world is' (Goodman 1972).

Rorty took this idea from Nietzsche, but he has long since made it his own. To see the force of it, consider how naturally acceptance of a 'way the world is' leads into the supposition that there must be a single form of description that can capture all of reality, i.e. a maximally correct description of 'the way the world is'. In the present age, science is the obvious place to look for such a description, and scientifically minded people do indeed often assume that the progress of science is bringing us ever closer to the final truth about the universe, to what some physicists call 'a theory of everything'. Thinking this way only requires extending the common-sense view of progress in science as consisting in the production of ever more accurate descriptions of reality. The only further assumption needed is that this process has an end point. Now according to Rorty, the fact that we are so inclined to think this way is the 'legacy of an age in which the world was seen as the creation of a being who had a language of his own' (Rorty 1989: 5). This is Rorty's explanation of why we so readily suppose that there must be one privileged description of the world. And Rorty is surely right to suppose that *some* explanation is needed of why it is so natural for us to think this way, given that human beings have developed many different ways of describing the world, and that there is no barrier to our developing many more. Of course, some ways of describing the world are much more useful than others, and scientific descriptions have proved extremely useful in the development of new technologies. But the question remains of why we should seek to explain differences in usefulness with the notion of objective truth. Rorty thinks there is no good reason, only an historical explanation.

A striking consequence of this view is that to be 'consistent' atheists (Rorty 1998: 62), people need to give up on realism, that is, on the belief that reality has its own intrinsic nature independently of how we describe or experience it, and about which there is an objective truth to discover. With this in mind, Rorty has put a new spin on the old atheist jibe that religious belief stems from a longing for permanent parental guidance: 'A lot of people now find belief in God immature, and eventually a lot of people may find realism immature' (Fosl 1999: 40). A culture that matures to the point of finally giving up on realism would, he thinks, realise that 'what matters is our loyalty to other human beings clinging together against the dark, not our hope of getting things right' (Rorty 1982: 166). In such a culture, the authority of non-human objectivity would be replaced by human solidarity, and forms of description would not be ranked according to their supposed ability to correspond to the true nature of reality, only according to their usefulness, something which varies from context to context. This could have far-reaching consequences. For example, it would remove any reason for thinking that 'quarks and human rights differ in "ontological status"' (Rorty 1998: 8), that the former are more real than the latter. Thus liberated, people would realise that there may be as much or more reason to believe in human rights than fundamental physical particles, since neither sort of belief is forced upon us.

RORTY'S CAREER

These themes of philosophy and objective truth run throughout and motivate Rorty's many and diverse writings. They are intimately connected, for Rorty sees philosophy as the guardian of objective truth: the academic subject which sets out to determine what objective truth is, and under which circumstances we can have access to it. Without objective truth and the cluster of ideas which revolve around it, Rorty does not think that philosophy as traditionally conceived makes any sense. So his views on truth clearly provide a motivation for his metaphilosophical agenda. Nevertheless, for the purposes of assessing Rorty's thought, it is his metaphilosophy that must take priority, since his views on truth derive from his reading of the history of philosophy, and from certain arguments within that history. As Rorty himself has often insisted, his case for breaking with the philosophical tradition stands on its own merits, regardless of the wider cultural benefits he hopes for from the abandonment of objective truth (Rorty 1991b: 6). And that is why *PMN* occupies such a crucial position within Rorty's work, for it is in this book that Rorty presents his case against traditional philosophy, a case which has not substantially moved on since then, though Rorty himself has. If that case is flawed, then philosophers may safely carry on with business as usual, ignoring Rorty's subsequent attempts to get to grips with life after objective truth. On the other hand, if that case can be sustained, then carrying on with business as usual might be a waste of time, or worse still, an actual hindrance to wider intellectual progress.

On its publication in 1979, *PMN* had an impact that was immediate and dramatic, and it is still at the vanguard of debate today, though the full extent of its influence is disguised by the perfectly understandable tendency – given the way Rorty writes – for philosophers to discuss the figures he discusses in the way he discusses them, rather than to discuss Rorty himself. *PMN* is a large-scale, uncompromising, occasionally venomous, and extremely ambitious book, with a long and detailed plot that works its way inexorably towards conclusions of the most substantial kind. It is the hub of Rorty's most influential ideas, and contrary to a popular misconception which Rorty has encouraged, his position has hardly changed at all since he wrote it. He did go on to widen his interests, discuss new figures, and talk more about politics, but aside from the politics, there is very little in his subsequent work which was not prefigured in *PMN*. Moreover, there are a number of surprising and highly original positions buried deep within *PMN* which have hardly seen the light of day, probably because Parts One and Two can be extremely hard going in places, unlike the far more accessible and better known Part Three.

What makes *PMN* unique is that it was not intended as a constructive contribution to philosophy at all, but rather as an attack on it. If it were not for *PMN*, Rorty might just be thought of as continuing in a tradition of radical philosophers who reject objective truth, one which goes back to Protagoras, who claimed that 'man is the measure of all things'. But by turning philosophy against itself, by employing analytic methods to undermine analytic philosophy, and by using the history of philosophy as an argument for the discontinuation of that history, Rorty challenged objective truth in a far more fundamental way: by challenging the wisdom of continuing to debate topics like truth.

The conclusions of *PMN* placed Rorty on a trajectory away from the philosophy departments and towards his current life as a professor of comparative literature. The fact that he was prepared to make such a move generates interest in his biography: what sort of philosopher ends up turning against philosophy? Well, one uncharitable answer that you often hear is: a philosopher who failed to make any progress on philosophical problems, and so set out to show that no-one else could either. This line came out recently in response to a review Rorty wrote of a book on the history of analytic philosophy (Rorty 2005). Its author, Scott Soames, concluded by celebrating the fact that philosophy 'has become a highly organised discipline, done by specialists primarily for other specialists', or as he might as well have said, that philosophy is now on the 'secure path of a science'. No prizes, then, for guessing the pitch of Rorty's review. In response, Soames dismissed Rorty's 'weary scepticism' as 'not so much the result of Olympian detachment as the disappointment of a true believer' (Soames 2005),[2] echoing Richard Bernstein's original charge that,

> There seems to be something almost oedipal – a form of patricide – in Rorty's obsessive attacks on the father figures of philosophy and metaphysics. It is the discourse of a one time 'true believer' who has lost his faith.
>
> (Bernstein 1991: 251)

A more enlightening version of this charge, however, came from Jürgen Habermas:

> [Rorty's] program for a philosophy that is to do away with all philosophy seems to spring more from the melancholy of a disappointed metaphysician . . . than from the self-criticism of an enlightened analytic philosopher.
>
> (Habermas 2000: 32)

This is more enlightening because if Rorty ever was a 'true believer', it seems to have been long before he joined the analytic establishment.

Richard McKay Rorty was born in New York City on October 4th, 1931, an only child born into a highly intellectual and politically active environment. His parents were well-known left-wing writers, advocates of Trotsky's socialism and vocal opponents of

Stalin, who both wrote books and articles on social reform, and whose house was a melting pot of left-wing ideas, visited by a constant stream of unionists and organisers, philosophers and poets. The philosophical hero of the house was John Dewey, with whom the family had loose connections. Dewey was one of the founders of Pragmatism, American's only home-grown philosophy, and was also a socially committed public intellectual, who Rorty remembers as 'the dominant intellectual figure in America in my youth . . . often called the philosopher of democracy, of the New Deal, of the American democratic intellectuals' (Borradori 1994: 105). This combination meshed perfectly with his parents' deep patriotism and political ethos. And the esteem in which Dewey was held clearly had a big influence on the young Rorty, since Dewey is to this day his main inspiration: he describes himself as a follower of Dewey (Rorty 1991a: 211), many of his central ideas are lifted directly from Dewey, and his career progression from academic philosophy into the public sphere has followed closely in Dewey's footsteps. Even 'breaking the crust of convention', Rorty's ever-present motivation, is a quote from Dewey.[3]

At the age of fifteen, Rorty was taken out of school and enrolled at a college for precocious youngsters at the University of Chicago – Dewey's old university – thereby finding himself a very young undergraduate in one of the most important philosophy departments of the time, the one where Rudolph Carnap was busy making logical positivism the mainstream philosophical approach in America. As Rorty was later to see it, logical positivists like Carnap who had fled Nazi Germany 'simply took over American philosophy departments' (Borradori 1994: 109), replacing what they regarded as the naïve, imprecise, and provincial tradition of American Pragmatism with a scientific approach to philosophical problems. This way of putting it, which is far from isolated within his writings, makes it hard to avoid the suspicion of a nationalistic motivation for Rorty's metaphilosophical agenda, but is nevertheless probably best regarded as a superimposition from his later political views. In any case, Rorty also says that he went along with the prevailing disdain felt for Pragmatists like Dewey as a form of 'adolescent revolt' (Rorty 1999: 9), and threw himself into traditional metaphysics: this, if anything, was his period as a 'true believer'.

The philosopher who dominated Chicago at the time was not Carnap, but Richard McKeon, a somewhat unique figure for the distinctively metaphilosophical and historical approach he took to the subject, seeking to provide taxonomies of the different ways of thinking that motivate philosophical views, rather than confronting those views directly (see McKeon 1990). This presence must have exerted its influence, but Rorty soon honed in on the most historically minded of all philosophers, Hegel; when he stayed on at Chicago for an MA, he wrote his thesis on the Hegelian philosopher A.N. Whitehead, supervised by an ex-student of Whitehead's, Charles Hartshorne. It was Whitehead who said that 'The safest general characterisation of the European philosophical tradition is that it consists of a series of footnotes to Plato' (Whitehead 1978: 39; Rorty 1999: xviii), a metaphilosophical position entirely in keeping with Rorty's own, though Whitehead's main concern, like Hartshorne's, was metaphysics of the most uncompromising variety. In the Preface to *PMN*, Rorty says of Carnap, McKeon and Hartshorne, three philosophers who could hardly have been much more different, that he 'treated them all as saying the same thing: that a "philosophical problem" was a product of the unconscious adoption of assumptions . . . which were to be questioned before the problem itself was taken seriously' (xiii). That he was able to hear them all this way suggests a distinctively Rortian approach to philosophy right from the start.

Rorty went to Yale for his PhD, where he continued to work on Whitehead. After his doctorate, there followed two years in the army (not through choice), and then three years at Wellersley College, before Rorty moved to Princeton University in 1961, where he was to stay for over twenty years. Any perception of Rorty as a regular analytic philosopher during this first period of his career, however, one who was later to 'lose his faith' or become 'disappointed', would require the support of some very selective quotation from what he was actually writing. The first sentence of his first published paper is:

Pragmatism is getting respectable again.

(Rorty 1961a: 197)

Wishful thinking at the time, perhaps, but Rorty was eventually to do more than anyone to raise the profile of pragmatism. The paper goes on to align pragmatism with the therapeutic approach to philosophy of Wittengenstein's *Philosophical Investigations*, just as he later did in *PMN*. His second paper, a review article called 'Recent Metaphilosophy', finds Rorty struggling to systematise metaphilosophical approaches, again showing quite clearly where his interests already lay.

Rorty first made his name with a 1965 paper called 'Mind–Body Identity, Privacy, and Categories', in which he argued that it was a consequence of physicalism (a.k.a. materialism[4]) – the view that everything which exists is physical – that mental sensations such as pains do not in fact exist. The term 'Eliminative Materialism' was coined to describe Rorty's position (Cornman 1968), but to the extent that this represented a regular contribution to analytic philosophy of mind, it was the contribution of easily its most controversial position. Constructive philosophers do still debate the pros and cons of various versions of eliminativism, but for Rorty, this seems rather to have been a stage on the way to the wholesale elimination of traditional philosophical problems undertaken in *PMN*, a useful tactic to be later applied across the board.

Rorty's work took on its more familiar shape in the seventies, in a series of classic papers eventually collected together as *Consequences of Pragmatism*. The collection begins in 1972 with 'The World Well Lost', which presents a complex argument, generated in typical Rortian style by weaving together various ideas from Quine, Sellars, and in particular Davidson, and which has 'Dewey's "naturalised" version of Hegelian historicism' emerging victorious at the other end. The hub of the paper is that given Davidson's argument for the impossibility of comparing radically different ways of conceptualising the world, an argument we shall examine in Chapter 8, there can be no prospect of assessing the accuracy of our own way of conceptualising the world by seeing how it measures up to 'the world itself'. This realist notion of the world is an 'obsession rather than an intuition', and hence is the 'world well lost' of the title. By this point in Rorty's career, his metaphilosophical preoccupations may not have changed very much, but he now had a plan: to deconstruct analytic philosophy with its own arguments.

As Dewey and continental philosophers like Heidegger and Derrida increasingly came to the forefront of his work, Rorty felt himself becoming estranged from the analytic establishment. This rift became public in 1979, when Rorty was the President of the Eastern Division of the American Philosophical Association at a time when the organisation was in a state of crisis. The crisis had built up because various types of non-analytic philosophers – pragmatists, idealists, continental philosophers, etc. – felt their careers had been sidelined by the dominance of analytic philosophy, thus depriving them of research funding and keeping them out of top jobs and journals. Organising themselves as the 'Pluralists', they flooded the APA elections, and voted in their own candidates to top positions, despite none of these candidates having been nominated by the official committee. The 'Analysts' looked to Rorty to overthrow the result, on the grounds that many of the votes had been illegally cast. Rorty refused.

1979 was also the year that *PMN* was published. Apart from its impact in philosophy, it became hugely influential in the humanities generally. This seems to have been a genuine surprise to Rorty, since the book was aimed squarely at professional philosophers. Nevertheless, its conclusions were plain enough for all to see, and appeared to legitimise new directions being taken in critical theory and literary, sociological and cultural studies, directions already taken by continental thinkers like Derrida and Foucault. By breaking down the hegemony of knowledge which natural science and philosophy had enjoyed over social science and literature, and by seeking to undermine any notion of a universal, atemporal truth, Rorty's book seemed to provide a theoretical sanction for the exploration of traditionally philosophical themes such as freedom, truth and power within the context of literature, contemporary culture, history and economics. Thus Rorty came to be seen as the principal English-speaking representative of postmodernism.

In 1982, Rorty moved to the University of Virginia to become a professor of humanities. His interests broadened accordingly, and he began making forays into the public arena with his political, ethical and cultural views. His brand of 'Postmodernist Bourgeois Liberalism' (Rorty 1991a: 197–202), which defended the 'bourgeois' liberal institution of a rights-based culture, whilst denying it any ahistorical legitimacy, led to him being denounced in the press as politically naïve, dangerous, or both. These ideas culminated in Rorty's second major work, *Contingency, Irony, and Solidarity*, in which he moves effortlessly between his old themes of philosophy and truth, and his new political and cultural ideas, to take in reflections on the novels of George Orwell, Derridean deconstruction, and much else besides. Since then, his career has been split between continued engagements with analytic philosophers, continental philosophers, and theorists of all descriptions, and life as a public intellectual, the world famous 'Man who Killed Truth', as he was dubbed in the title of a television documentary.[5] The year 1998 provides a revealing snapshot of this career, for he both moved to his current post in the Department of Comparative Literature at Stanford University, and published two very different books: *Achieving Our Country*, a defence of patriotism, and *Truth and Progress*, a volume of essays engaging recent work by analytic philosophers such as Crispin Wright, John McDowell, and John Searle.

Looking over his career, then, it is hard to see *PMN* as a product of dissatisfaction or disillusionment. Metaphilosophy, rather than problem-solving, was always Rorty's game, and this peculiarly singular vision seems to have guided him from the outset. Following that vision consistently, from criticising traditional philosophy to pioneering new approaches, has inevitably left Rorty with an ambiguous reputation amongst analytic philosophers. On the one hand, Rorty's association with postmodernism – though he has now disowned that label (Rorty 1999: 262–77) – and his efforts at breaking down the distinction between philosophy and literature, have understandably fuelled suspicions. On the other hand, philosophers doing serious work on mind and language cannot fail to notice that Rorty's views are very similar to those of his more conventional contemporaries, particularly Donald Davidson, Daniel Dennett and Hilary Putnam: if Rorty is to be believed, the only really substantial difference consists in their failure to follow through to his conclusions. Moreover, *PMN*'s challenge has already inspired two of the most interesting constructive efforts of recent philosophy, namely John McDowell's *Mind and World* and Robert Brandom's *Making it Explicit*. So there is circumstantial evidence on both sides. The only way for philosophers to be sure what to make of Rorty, however, is to assess the argument of *PMN*. If nothing else, he has at least provided an excellent opportunity for metaphilosophical reflection.

THE INTRODUCTION TO *PMN*

At the beginning of the introduction, Rorty says that philosophy takes itself to deal with 'perennial, eternal problems' (3), problems that characterise the human condition, and which consequently might occur to any person in any era, so long as they were to reflect in the right sort of way. That problems concerning mind and knowledge, which Rorty immediately singles out as the central philosophical problematics, do indeed strike us as perennial and eternal, is a consequence of the root problem with traditional philosophy: that it is 'an attempt to escape from history' (9), an attempt to substitute the particularity and happenstance of our lives for a universal and fail-safe understanding of what is going on based on an ahistorical objective truth. This aim conflicts with Rorty's commitment to historicism, the view that all human activities, including the ways we think, must be understood in terms of the particular historical epoch we find ourselves born into. On Rorty's view, there is nothing perennial or eternal about the central philosophical problems of mind and knowledge. They are rather a product of a certain period of history, in which a certain conception of mind seemed to provide the best available model for a foundationalist conception of knowledge.

To determine the foundations of knowledge is to determine exactly what it is that allows us to know. So, for instance, what allows me to know that there is a bottle on the table is that I can see it – my vision provides the foundation for that particular item of knowledge. The sense in which philosophy is a foundational discipline, however, is much wider than this, for it is concerned with the general foundations of knowledge, those most basic conditions which underwrite any case of human knowledge. If we could determine these conditions, then we could determine which sort of inquiries generate genuine knowledge, and which do not. Thus philosophy, in Rorty's view, seeks to play the role of a 'cultural overseer' (317), ranking different forms of activity according to their ability to make contact with the objective truth. So, for example, if we take experience as the foundation of knowledge, then we may rank science at the top of the cultural pecking order, astrology at the bottom, and Freudian psychoanalysis somewhere in between. If on the other hand we think that reason is more fundamental, as many traditional metaphysicians have, then we may place philosophy above science.

Philosophy sets itself up as foundational, according to Rorty, by seeking to adjudicate claims to knowledge on the basis of a special understanding of the foundations of knowledge, rather as a judge adjudicates claims to innocence on the basis of a special understanding of the law. By determining these conditions, philosophy attempts to 'eternalise' our best current understanding of the world, to 'ground' it in something that can never be overturned in the future, namely the objective truth. Now in order to adjudicate claims to knowledge, philosophy needed a special expertise, and according to Rorty, found it in the seventeenth-century idea of the mind as a repository of representations. Knowledge came to be seen as accurate representation of the world, that is, as the correspondence of a mental representation of the world to the objective truth about the world. Providing a 'general theory of representation' became the 'central concern' (3) of philosophy, because with such a theory it would be possible to determine exactly when our minds are accurately representing the world, and when they are not. So, for instance, philosophers could determine that science uses the right methods for generating accurate representations of 'the way the world is', but that astrology does not.

The mind was able to play the foundational role philosophers required of it, because it was conceived of as something that could be studied non-empirically, that is, by reflection and analysis rather than through experience. This immunised philosophical theories from history, since such theories were not based on observations of the world, which are always changing, but on reasoning about the ways in which we observe the world and come to know things. Rorty thinks that the idea of non-empirical reflection on the way in which we represent the world has dominated philosophy since the seventeenth century, simply changing format from the analysis of mind, to the analysis of language in the twentieth century, with all other issues in metaphysics and epistemology being in some sense spin-offs from this representation-based foundationalist agenda, an agenda which is itself simply a manifestation of the general urge to escape from history.

The particular representationalist direction which philosophy took in the seventeenth century was the result of latching onto and transforming something much older, namely 'Greek ocular metaphors', and it is with this historical contingency that Rorty explains the title of his book:

> The picture which holds traditional philosophy captive is that of the mind as a great mirror, containing various representations – some accurate, some not – and capable of being studied by pure, non-empirical methods.
>
> (12)

The 'Mirror of Nature' is the mind, and whether or not reflections in the mirror (i.e. representations in the mind) count as knowledge depends on whether they accurately reflect nature (i.e. correspond to the objective truth about the 'way the world is'). Philosophy is the non-empirical study of the 'mirror', which uses reason to determine the conditions in which the mirror is able to properly reflect nature. In this way, philosophy seeks to be foundational, to determine the conditions which any sort of inquiry would have to meet in order to generate knowledge, the ultimate aim being to put us in touch with the ahistorical objective truth so that we can 'escape from history'.

One major target of *PMN*, then, is the foundationalist project of trying to provide a theory of knowledge based on the notion of representation. Rorty's approach will be to reveal the dubious historical motivations which led to the entrenchment of this idea, and to show that recent arguments in analytic philosophy make any such project untenable. In this way, *PMN* aims to undermine all philosophical work which owes a debt to foundationalism and representationalism, broadly construed. He goes much further than this, however, because he also thinks that very idea of a separate and systematic subject called 'philosophy' is inextricably linked to its original foundationalist motivations. Consequently, he will also aim to discourage attempts to re-start philosophy on a non-foundationalist, non-representationalist basis.

Apart from running through the plot, the other important thing Rorty does in the introduction is introduce his three heroes: Wittgenstein, Heidegger and Dewey. This must have seemed a very provocative list of 'the most important philosophers of our century' (5) in 1979, but thanks to efforts made by Rorty and others at breaking down the divide between analytic philosophers like Wittgenstein and continental philosophers like Heidegger – in Rorty's case by treating them fairly indiscriminately, as he tends to treat all figures from all traditions and eras – Wittgenstein and Heidegger are these days fairly uncontroversial candidates, though the choice of Dewey still looks idiosyncratic. The clearest thing these three philosophers have in common, and hence the clearest reason for Rorty's selection of them – apart from their being, as he once said, 'the most romantic . . . the farthest-out, the most prophetic' figures he could find (Nizick and Sanders 1996: 113–14) – is that they are all opposed to representational conceptions of mind and knowledge, that is, to the 'Mirror of Nature' idea. There are many other thematic points of contact, however, especially in the case of Dewey where there is near thematic convergence, but fortunately the argument of *PMN* can be followed without even a basic understanding of these three major thinkers, only an understanding of certain self-contained arguments within analytic philosophy which can be explained as we go along. Nevertheless, it is good to at least be aware of the basic methodological influence which these philosophers had on the text of *PMN*.

The influence of Wittgenstein is to be found in Rorty's therapeutic conception of philosophy. In the later phase of Wittgenstein's career, which produced the *Philosophical Investigations*, one of his main methods was to show that 'philosophical problems arise when language *goes on holiday*' (Wittgenstein 1953: §38). The idea was that these problems are generated, and begin to puzzle us, when we isolate ways of talking from the ordinary situations which provide their *raison d'être*. Wittgenstein portrays the philosopher as someone who has entered into an abnormal linguistic practise and is behaving accordingly. So, for instance, he gives the example of a man thinking about the mind–body problem, clutching at his forehead and staring into empty space (ibid.: §412). The confusion he feels is not an appropriate response to a deep problem, according to

Wittgenstein, but rather part and parcel of a generally strange way of acting, as the man struggles to devise a way of talking which no real-life situation would ever require of him. The cure, or therapy, is to be reminded of the normal ways of using language which philosophy has deviated from, in order to lead the philosopher away from the linguistic traps laid by the tradition. The *Philosophical Investigations* is full of original analogies, disanalogies, and examples, to draw attention to the strangeness of philosophical language, and thus to persuade philosophers to put it aside. Rorty has his own examples in this vein (esp. 'The Antipodeans'), but on the whole his brand of therapy is 'parasitic': it is based on the arguments of constructive philosophers, which he uses to demonstrate the futility and undesirability of further constructive effort.

The influence of Heidegger is to be found in Rorty's method of historical deconstruction, or as Heidegger put it, 'destruction'. In his most influential work, *Being and Time*, Heidegger warned against an acceptance of philosophical tradition that 'takes what has come down to us and delivers it over to self-evidence' (Heidegger 1962: 43). This historicist advice is particularly important to Heidegger, since he thinks that the philosophical tradition has covered over and obscured 'the meaning of Being', leading human beings to fundamentally misinterpret their own existence. By 'destroying' the history of philosophy at the key stages which led to this misinterpretation, Heidegger tries to 'appropriate' that history – to give it some contemporary relevance rather than allowing it to become a source of dogma – and to thereby recover 'our first ways of determining the nature of Being' (ibid.: 44), an original understanding of reality which current ideas derive from but distort. There is, then, a negative and a positive aspect to Heidegger's historical agenda: uncovering past errors and recovering what has been lost. As far as the negative agenda goes, Heidegger, like Rorty, targets representationalist conceptions of mind and knowledge, which he thinks result from overemphasising a certain specialised and detached attitude to the world, and thereby overlooking the wider context in which such attitudes arise – a critique which resembles Wittgenstein's to the extent that the activity of philosophising is itself liable to induce this detached attitude. Heidegger, however, also has a positive agenda: to overcome today's technological and manipulative understanding of reality by recovering the ancient Greek ideas from which it derives. Now in many ways, *PMN* is a very Heideggarian book, since Rorty traces philosophical ideas right back to the ancient Greeks, and his main method is historical deconstruction. A crucial difference, however, is that Rorty is not trying to recover anything from the tradition (see Rorty 1991b: 27–49).

The influence of Dewey is to be found in Rorty's pragmatism. Dewey wanted to enact an 'emancipation' of philosophy from the problematic it had inherited from the tradition, because of doubts about 'the genuineness, under the present conditions of science and social life, of the problems' (Dewey 1917: 5). In *The Quest for Certainty*, Dewey traced traditional philosophy's lack of practical import, and thus its increasing irrelevance to the wider world, to the Greek idea that 'the office of knowledge is to uncover the antecedently real, rather than, as is the case with our practical judgements, to gain the kind of understanding which is necessary to deal with problems as they arise' (Dewey 1930: 20). This separation of knowledge from action, which Dewey explains in terms of the social conditions of ancient times and the influence of religion, led to both the idea of an atemporal, objective truth – an 'antecedently real' – and to a 'spectator theory of knowledge' (ibid.: 26). For Dewey, these ideas had long outlived their social relevance, turning the continued debate of traditional problematics into 'an ingenious dialectic exercised in professorial corners by a few who have retained ancient premises while rejecting their application to the conduct of life' (Dewey 1917: 58). Dewey's pragmatist remedy was to reconnect knowledge and action, so that beliefs would be evaluated by their usefulness within prevailing social circumstances, rather than by objective truth. And this, of course, is Rorty's agenda exactly. Quite apart from inheriting Dewey's overall motivation – as well as his intermediate targets of systematic philosophy, objective truth, and representational accounts of mind and knowledge – the strictly methodological influence of Dewey's pragmatism can be seen from the way in which Rorty evaluates philosophical ideas and distinctions according to their practical import, or lack thereof. Pragmatism can also be seen as a motivating factor for the whole format of *PMN*, since the use of contemporary analytic arguments was the approach most likely to persuade Rorty's target audience – contemporary analytic philosophers – of his Deweyan agenda.

OBSTACLES TO UNDERSTANDING *PHILOSOPHY AND THE MIRROR OF NATURE*

There are certain obstacles to a critical reading of *PMN*: to following the argument, and to doing so without being unduly sceptical or overly sympathetic. It is worth becoming aware of these before we move on.

The first and most obvious obstacle is that *PMN* makes unusual demands of the reader by drawing together numerous complex positions from throughout the history of philosophy in order to build its argument. Rorty's range of reference is notoriously vast – and daunting – and his presupposition of familiarity with all of these philosophical positions has excluded many interested parties from a first-hand acquaintance with his work: *PMN* was, after all, aimed at professional philosophers, and few of these can have picked up on every reference which Rorty breezes through. This book should be of help in overcoming the first obstacle.

The second obstacle, which can make readers unduly sceptical about Rorty's history, is the well known fact that his interpretations are very controversial: to get some idea of the extent of this, you need only note that there are scores of articles by Wittgenstein-, Heidegger-, and even Dewey-scholars, all disputing Rorty's interpretations, and that two of the key figures in *PMN*, W.V.O. Quine and Thomas Kuhn, personally disowned Rorty's use of their work. Now obviously we cannot go into even a representative proportion of these competing interpretations here: we would get bogged down immediately. However, for the purposes of critically engaging with *PMN*, there is really no need, just so long as Rorty's arguments do not depend on philosopher X or Y putting forward a view, rather than Rorty himself putting forward a view inspired by X or Y. The only time this distinction might be thought to make a difference is when Rorty is engaged in historical deconstruction. However, unlike Heidegger, whose appropriations really do force the words of other philosophers into the mould of Heidegger's own thought, Rorty's interpretations actually tend to be fairly conventional: much as he clearly admires appropriation and 'strong misreading' (Rorty 1982: 151), this is not obviously what he does. What he does do is 'purify' philosophers – leave out the bits he does not like – which can be intensely annoying, but is no great cause for concern. Consequently, there is no need to single Rorty's historical readings out for anything more than standard critical scrutiny, and no warrant for anything more than ordinary, healthy scepticism.

The third obstacle is the combination of Rorty's distinctive writing style and large-scale subject matter, which can come across as exciting and dramatic, making it easy to be uncritically carried along by Rorty's narrative, or else imprecise and evasive, making it just as easy to be uncritically dismissive of what can seem like endless sweeping generalisations. An early review, which took the latter perspective, described *PMN* as 'long on claims and polemic but short on argument' (Ruja 1981: 300), and it is not difficult to see how you might reach this conclusion, especially given Rorty's own widely reported negative comments about the value of argument (Rorty 1989: 8–9). Such comments, however, should be taken lightly – rather like his negative comments about metaphilosophy – since there is plenty of argument in *PMN* in the form of plausible considerations, objections, counterproposals, analogies, and all the other argumentative strategies normally employed in philosophy. Things only seem different in *PMN* because of the scale of the subject matter, which amplifies Rorty's claims and places greater burden on the arguments. Given that any historicist critique of philosophy would face similar difficulties of scale, however, and that the enterprise seems both valuable and legitimate, the critical reader must simply try to compensate accordingly: challenging when sub-stantive alternatives present themselves, and otherwise letting the narrative flow.

The fourth obstacle – by far the biggest one for readers without at least a degree in philosophy – is that *PMN* is designed to provide relief from philosophical puzzlement, and this can be of little interest to those not puzzled in the first place (cf. Malachowski 1990: 365–70). To appreciate Rorty's attempt at debunking the traditional philosophical picture, you must first have seen its power, and for this reason, the next chapter will provide a sympathetic overview of it which fills in some of the background that will be required later on. The brush strokes will be vast, of course, but that suits the subject-matter when dealing with Rorty, and in any case, the traditional picture is so compelling that it only requires minimal introduction to grasp how far from obvious Rorty's claims really are. If you already have a solid background in philosophy, and are much more sceptical about Rorty than you are about the traditional problems of mind, knowledge and language, then you may want to skip ahead to Chapter 3 at this point.

2

THE MIRROR OF NATURE

It surely needs no arguments to show that the problem, What can we know? cannot be approached without the examination of the contents of the mind, and the determination of how much of these contents may be called knowledge.

T.H. Huxley, 1887
(Huxley 1887: 49)

MIND AND KNOWLEDGE

Out of the window, I can see a woman walking past on the pavement below. My perception and background knowledge provide me with a certain unprivileged access to her consciousness. For a start, I know what it looks like to walk where she is walking, so I know how the various buildings look from roughly the angles she can see them from. In addition, I can hear the same traffic noises she can, though I know it would sound different at street level. I do not know how good her eyesight and hearing are, however, and I have almost no idea what she is thinking – she could be trying to remember the middle section of a song, working out what 15 per cent of her salary is, deciding what to say to somebody she is about to meet – I have no way of knowing. She, on the other hand, has privileged access to her consciousness: she is actually seeing the buildings, hearing the traffic, thinking the thoughts. This difference between my vague, uncertain, and incomplete unprivileged access, and her privileged access, reflects the difference between seeing her and being her. She knows her conscious experience by being the person whose experience it is, and I can only see her through the window. Moreover, what I see seems to confront me with a fact of transcendence, right there in the middle of the world, since her conscious experience transcends – goes beyond – the world I can see. It is not one of the things down there in the street for me to look at, not an object like a car, or a lamp-post, or even a woman. Neither is it a property of one of those objects, or at least not an ordinary property like velocity, density, size, or colour. Her consciousness is, rather, what it is like to be the particular physical object that she is.

Subjectivity is the traditional explanation of privileged access. To say that consciousness is subjective is to say that it is by its very nature something which only exists from a particular point of view. This offers a *metaphysical* explanation of the *epistemological* fact of privileged access: the special subjective *nature* of consciousness explains the way in which it is *known*, i.e. in a privileged way if you are the subject of the conscious experience (if you are the woman with the pavement panning out in front of you, the traffic noises to your left, the issues on your mind) and in an unprivileged way if you are not (if are watching her through the window, or using the latest psychological techniques to interrogate her, or scanning her brain). If we accept that consciousness is subjective, however, then we are landed with the mind–body problem. The problem is that our objective conception of the world as a collection of physical objects with a size, shape, and internal constitution, conflicts with our subjective conception of consciousness as a point of view on those objects. On the one hand, we think that planet Earth is a large physical object, and that all the various people who inhabit it are smaller ones. On the other hand, we think that there is something it is like to be certain objects, namely humans and animals, although there is nothing it is like to be a table or a television set. The mind–body problem, then, is the attempt to resolve this conflict between the objective and subjective ways we have of thinking about the world.

The two traditional positions on the mind–body problem are dualism and physicalism. Dualists believe that objectivity and subjectivity split reality in two. Thus according to substance dualism (Descartes's view), minds are non-physical subjective things which are connected to the physical world but not a part of it, and according to property dualism (the standard view until the 1950s), everything is physical, but some physical things have non-physical, subjective properties. These days almost everybody in the debate is a physicalist: it is generally accepted that subjective consciousness is ultimately just another part of objective, physical reality. The question is how to explain this. After all, knowing that the woman's subjective experience is just her brain is not much help in fitting her experience into the objective street scene, since we already know how her brain fits in: it is a grey organic object inside her skull. Thus physicalists need to explain the connection between our subjective and objective ways of conceiving of the world. Physicalist philosophers (and neuroscientists) are split over this issue in roughly the same way dualists and physicalists used to be split. One group thinks that given our current scientific understanding, we cannot even begin to imagine what an answer to the mind–body problem would be like; thus Thomas Nagel's wistful observation that,

> some day, long after we are all dead, people will be able to observe the operation of the brain and say, with true understanding, 'That's what the experience of tasting chocolate looks like from the outside.'
>
> (Nagel 1998: 338)

The other group thinks that we already know everything we need to know, and that the problem is either illusory (Loar 1997), or else a residue of old-fashioned, Cartesian ways of thinking (Dennett 1991).

The mind is of course the 'Mirror of Nature' of Rorty's title, although if conscious experience is indeed analogous to a mirror, then it is clearly a lot harder to understand than any ordinary mirror. Rorty's view, however, is that we should not even try to understand it, because the whole idea is an historical confusion to be recognised and discarded. The mind–body problem is nevertheless only one of Rorty's subsidiary targets, because it is the mind's function of representing the world which caused it to take centre stage in the history of philosophy. The reason for this is that once you think of the mind as representing (or 'mirroring') nature, then it becomes the obvious focus for an epistemology, or theory of knowledge; the mind will seem to provide our only epistemic point of contact with the world, since all knowledge ultimately derives from experience and thought, and experiences and thoughts are states of mind. By trying to understand the mind, then, philosophers have sought to ascertain the conditions under which we are able to represent nature correctly, and hence the general conditions under which knowledge is possible. Such a theory would tell us which methods of inquiry are to be trusted, thereby vindicating or debunking competing claims about the world.

The view that science is the best way of acquiring knowledge is a recent development in the 150,000 year history of *Homo sapiens*; it began to take hold less than 400 years ago. It is an epistemological view, as opposed to a scientific view about particles, human evolution, etc., and it was once one of the most contentious issues in European intellectual life. The issue arose because the 'New Science' developed by Galileo and others presented a challenge to the combination of Aristotelian science and Biblical teachings, known as Scholasticism, which had previously provided the bedrock of serious inquiry. The New Scientists used quantitative and mathematical methods for the first time – they found ways to measure nature – and they advanced their theories on the basis of systematic observation. From the Scholastic point of view, these theories and observations could at best be *technē*, a kind of practical knowledge or craft, as opposed to *epistēmē*, the more substantive kind of knowledge. It was against this backdrop, then, that Descartes and later Locke devised two very different forms of foundationalist epistemology, rationalism and empiricism, both of which were designed to establish the legitimacy of the New Science. In doing so, they enacted a division of labour between science and philosophy which was to become the basis of the clear demarcation we understand today; before then, the boundaries had been considerably more blurred.

An epistemological view is described as foundationalist if it holds that knowledge is ultimately justified by reference to self-evident truths, as in the case of rationalism, or self-justifying mental states, as in the case of empiricism. Both proposals share the same two basic motivations. The first is that the explanation of knowledge has to stop somewhere: there must be some basic foundation which is beyond question. Otherwise, the process of justification could go on indefinitely, generating an infinite regress and hence no explanation at all, just as an infinitely long set of directions would never explain to you how to reach your destination. The second is that anything built upon untrustworthy foundations is itself untrustworthy. So, for instance, if there is no connection between stars and destiny, then there is no reason to trust your horoscope, and if 'the weaker the dosage, the stronger the effect' is not a sound medical principle, then there is no reason to expect your homeopathic pills to work. Epistemological foundationalism proposes to isolate and systematise the foundation of all human knowledge, past, present and future, which is why Rorty describes it as ahistorical. Nevertheless, when the building blocks are as general as 'experience' or 'reason', this is not a self-evidently unreasonable aim.

Descartes's epistemology was based on methodological scepticism, on 'putting aside everything which admits of the least doubt' as if it had been discovered to be 'absolutely false' (Descartes 1985: 16). By employing this method, he found that sensory experience was unable to provide the foundation for knowledge he was looking for, since the senses sometimes deceive us, most notably at night when we dream. The one thing he could not doubt, however, was that he was thinking. From this starting point of inner certainty in his own mind and its operations, Descartes attempted to show that the true nature of the world could only be known by the intellect, not the senses, and that such knowledge must ultimately derive from innate ideas implanted in us from birth by God, and which are thus guaranteed to be true. In this way, Descartes hoped to provide a philosophical foundation for his own mechanistic physical science based on the innate idea of extension (being geometrically extended into space). Epistemology was thus 'first philosophy' for Descartes: the certain basis for all other forms of inquiry to build upon.

Though Locke followed the epistemological turn Descartes brought to philosophy, his own empiricist version of foundationalism was prefaced by a rejection of God-given innate ideas, since despite his belief that the existence of God was 'the most obvious Truth that Reason discovers' (Locke 1979: IV.10.§1), Locke thought

that there was good empirical evidence to deny that there is anything which everybody knows, and hence good reason to deny there
is anything we are all born knowing. This meant abandoning the
certainty Descartes had offered, and adopting a more modest
metaphilosophy: rather than providing a 'first philosophy' as a
foundation for the New Science, Locke saw his task as that of an
'Underlabourer' for scientists, employing similar observational
methods in order to describe the actual process of the acquisition of
knowledge. The purpose of this was to determine exactly what it is
possible for us to know, thereby clearing away the 'rubbish' (ibid.:
10) which stood in the way of the New Science, namely what Locke
saw as the empty disputes generated by the overambitious expecta-
tions of Aristotelianism and Cartesianism.

The central tenet of Locke's empiricism was that all knowledge
derives from experience, experience dividing into the ideas we derive
from the five senses, such as yellow, loud, etc., and the ideas we
derive from the operations of our minds, such as thinking, wanting,
etc. These 'simple ideas' are the building blocks of all human knowledge, for Locke, and the bulk of his system is taken up with elabo-
rate attempts to demonstrate his atomistic, empiricist thesis that,

> even the most abstruse Ideas, how remote soever they may seem from
> Sense . . . are yet only such, as the Understanding frames to it self, by
> repeating and joining Ideas, that it had either from Objects of Sense, or
> from its own operations about them.
>
> (Ibid.: II.12.§8)

This thesis still has great appeal today, unlike Descartes's. Nevertheless, by relying on the Cartesian idea of inner certainty in the mind,
and hence accepting that the mind 'perceives nothing but its own
Ideas' (ibid.: IV.4.§3), Locke ended up with an account of knowledge
that was internal to the mind, a matter of how our ideas relate to
each other. This is a surprising result, given that knowledge is naturally thought of as a relation between ideas and the world, and the
fact that Locke's apparently straightforward empiricism seemed to
have this consequence has generated some of the central problems
of philosophy.

The problems arise because Descartes and Locke both insisted on the *immediacy* of the mind: Descartes defined thought as 'everything that is within us in such a way that we are immediately aware of it' (Descartes 1985: 56), and Locke followed suit with his conception of an idea as 'the immediate object of Perception, Thought, or Understanding' (Locke 1979: II.8.§8). The flip-side of this immediacy, however, is that the world which causes our ideas can only be known mediately. Thus, for example, if the woman and I both look at the same car, then she is immediately aware of her experience, I am immediately aware of my experience, and we are both only mediately aware of the car. To think about perception in this way is to adopt some form of indirect realism, which is a combination of the realist view that the world exists independently of consciousness, and the epistemological view that we can only ever know the world indirectly through our own individual consciousness.

Once we start to think of perception as indirect, however, then we are landed with the 'veil of perception' problem, it being as if a 'veil' of ideas has between drawn between us and the physical world. This is a classic problem of epistemological scepticism, of knowledge claims apparently exceeding their evidential basis, for as Locke put it, 'the having the idea of anything in our mind no more proves the existence of that thing, than the picture of a man evidences his being in the world' (ibid.: IV.11.§1). Moreover, just as it would be impossible to determine whether a portrait provides a good likeness of a man if we never saw the man, so it seems impossible for us to determine whether our ideas accurately represent the true nature of the world if we only have access to the ideas, and cannot 'see reality plain, unmasked, naked to our gaze', as Rorty once put it (Rorty 1982: 154). There is a memorable play on this idea in a painting by the Belgian surrealist René Magritte called 'The Treachery of Images'. The painting shows a pipe with a caption below it reading 'Ceci n'est pas une pipe' ('This is not a pipe'): and of course, what you are looking at is not a pipe at all, but rather a representation of a pipe. Magritte's point generalises completely, however, if the veil of perception problem cannot be overcome, for we would then have to accept that we are never aware of pipes, or tables, or people, and are only ever aware of our own mental representations of these things.

STRUCTURE AND LANGUAGE

The epistemological problem of bridging the gap between know-ledge of our own minds, and knowledge of the outside world, inspired a metaphysical response in the shape of Kant's transcendental idealism. Kant held that in order to confirm that our thought about the world conforms to the world itself, we would have to know what it is about reality and about our minds that makes representation possible, i.e. what it is that allows the two to fit together. Now on Locke's indirect realist picture, we cannot know this in principle: to represent the relation between our representations and reality would require us to occupy a position outside of our representational capacities. But this was because Locke, like all other philosophers before Kant, had 'assumed that all our knowledge must conform to objects'. The alternative, which circumvented the problem, was to 'suppose that objects must conform to our knowledge' (Kant 1933: Bxvi). This was Kant's 'Copernican Revolution' in philosophy: Copernicus argued that the Earth revolved around the sun, rather than *vice versa*, with the apparent movement of the sun explained in terms of how we represent it, i.e. from the point of view of a rotating Earth. Likewise, transcendental idealism explains our knowledge of an apparently independently constituted reality in terms of our representational capacities, by showing that our way of representing the world must conform to the world itself on the grounds that if it did not, we would be oblivious to it.

To make this move, Kant needed to introduce a new, transcendental level of reflection, and hence distinguished between the world as it is for us – the empirical world of everyday life – and the unknowable (for us) things-in-themselves, the world as it would be with no minds to represent it. Transcendental reflection operates at the interface between the empirical and the transcendent, delimiting the scope of reason to determine the most general, structural features of representation which anything we are able to experience must conform to. It was ignorance of this distinction of levels which generated the veil of perception problem, according to Kant, because failing to distinguish the everyday world from the world as it is in itself made knowledge of the everyday world seem problematic. In terms of the 'Mirror of Nature' idea, then, we might say that Kant's idea was to work out how exactly mirrors work, in order to show that all objects reflected in mirrors must conform to our conceptions of those objects, since the objects would not otherwise be reflected at all.

A representative sample of Kant's method in action is provided by the so-called 'Refutation of Idealism', in which Kant's target is external world scepticism of the veil of perception variety (ibid.: B275–92). In the barest outline, the reasoning is as follows. The veil of perception problem assumes that we begin with the Cartesian premise that only mental states are immediately known, and then must try to move to knowledge of an external world on the basis of knowledge of our mental states. But Kant argues that empirical self-consciousness, our awareness of our own mental states, already presupposes the existence of an external world. This is because without the permanent presence provided by physical objects, and without immediate awareness of these objects changing in space, we would be unable to represent time. If we were unable to represent time, however, we could not even be aware of our own mental states, since introspective awareness is temporal. Therefore, awareness of our mental states, the starting point of the veil of perception problem, already presupposes that we have immediate awareness of outer objects, the very thing which was supposed to have been rendered problematic. In this characteristic argument, we see an appeal to general structural features of representation (time, space, permanence, change) as presuppositions of our being able to make any sense of experience at all.

Now in putting forward his theory of transcendental idealism, Kant made a number of technical distinctions which were to become a mainstay of subsequent philosophy, and in doing so, he facilitated an account of the history of philosophy which portrayed his Copernican Revolution as the culmination of the rationalist and empiricist traditions, fusing together what was best in each whilst overcoming their individual limitations; this is crucial to Rorty's critique in *PMN*, since he thinks that Kant effectively invented philosophy in the process.

Kant's starting point is that rationalism and empiricism recognised only two sorts of judgements (or claims to knowledge): necessary *a priori* and contingent *a posteriori*. *A posteriori* (empirical) judgements are made on the basis of experience, and are contingent because experience can only establish what happens to be the case, not what must be the case. *A priori* (non-empirical) judgements are made on the basis of reasoning, and according to the standard rationalist view, are necessary because they ultimately derive from logical principles. Empiricist philosophy was based on the former, rationalism on the latter. To show the inadequacy of both approaches, Kant introduced a new distinction between what he called 'analytic' and 'synthetic' judgements. An analytic judgement is one for which the predicate is contained within the subject, e.g. 'a vixen is a female fox'. Such judgements do not extend our knowledge, but rather draw out and make explicit something already implicitly there, i.e. within the definition of the subject ('vixen'). A synthetic judgement, by contrast, is one for which the joining of subject and predicate requires a synthesis, a 'something else (X)' (ibid.: A8) which brings them together. For empirical judgements, this X will be an experience which synthesises subject and predicate, e.g. an experience of a running vixen produces the synthesis appropriate to the judgement expressed by saying 'some vixens can run'. Such judgements thus extend our knowledge.

It would be natural to suppose that only contingent *a posteriori* judgements can be synthetic, because only experience can extend our knowledge, and that all necessary *a priori* judgements are analytic, because *a priori* reasoning is just a matter of drawing out definitions. If this were right, however, then metaphysical knowledge would be impossible, since contingent *a posteriori* judgements would not take us beyond immediate experience (beyond the veil of perception), and necessary *a priori* judgements would only tell us about our definitions, which we could not know to conform with the world itself (unless through the guarantee of God, as in Descartes). In order to show that metaphysical knowledge is indeed possible – that we can indeed establish through reason the legitimacy of our ordinary ways of understanding of the world – Kant argued that we must make room for synthetic *a priori* judgements, judgements which are necessary and knowable *a priori*, but which extend our knowledge rather than just draw out our definitions. He then further argued that the only metaphysical system which could accommodate these judgements is transcendental idealism, in which the empirical world is held to conform to the representational capacities of human cognition, and according to which metaphysical knowledge is understood as neither derived from experience, nor as a matter of definition, but rather as an elucidation of the general structural presuppositions of experience.

The reason that empiricism and rationalism were unable to recognise the possibility of synthetic *a priori* metaphysical judgements, was that they failed to fully grasp another important Kantian distinction, the distinction between sensibility, our passive cognitive capacity for objects to be *given* to us within intuitions, and understanding, our active cognitive capacity for objects to be *thought* about through our conceptualisation of them. Intuitions (given in sensibility) and concepts (applied in understanding) depend on each other: an intuition can only relate to an object when conceptualised, and concepts need a given object to be applied to. Hence the Kantian dictum: 'Thoughts without content are empty, intuitions without concepts are blind' (ibid.: B75). For Kant, rationalism's mistake had been to try to make do with concepts alone (i.e. innate ideas), and empiricism had '*sensualised* all concepts of the understanding' (ibid.: B327), the opposite mistake embodied in Locke's atomistic thesis that simple ideas were the building blocks for all others. Within the system of transcendental idealism, however, it is the combination of both intuitions and concepts which facilitates the synthetic *a priori* judgements of metaphysics.

After Kant, whose *Critique of Pure Reason* was first published in 1781, there is a peculiarly sparse period in the story of the Mirror of Nature idea, and things only really get going again with the 'linguistic turn' in the early twentieth century. This reflects the way in which the originators of analytic philosophy sought to downplay this period, something which fuels Rorty's suspicions about the unity of the subject. The main reason is that the next great philosopher after Kant was Hegel, and it was Hegelianism that dominated systematic nineteenth-century metaphysics, reaching its apogee in the British Idealism of F.H. Bradley; analytic philosophers like Bertrand Russell began their careers in rebellion against Bradley and his followers.

Hegel was dissatisfied with the inclusion of unknowable things-in-themselves within Kant's transcendental idealism, since he thought that philosophy should find a way of thinking about the world according to which everything is comprehensible, and nothing is off-limits to reason. To ascertain how reason could become 'at home in the world' (Hegel 1991: 36; discussed by Stern 2002: 11–21), Hegel described it in action, analysing the manifestation of reason in the progress of world history. Whereas for Kant, the human mind imposed a fixed conceptual scheme upon experience, for Hegel, our conceptualisation of the world is a work in progress, something that has been continually developing over the course of human history, and which will eventually culminate in absolute knowledge. Rather than adopting the Kantian approach of trying to determine the structure of experience imposed by each individual mind, then, Hegel analysed the structures manifested by collective movements of thought, thereby finding a way to incorporate such seemingly diverse topics as Greek tragedy and the French Revolution into his metaphysics. It is the combination of eclecticism, historicism, and limitless ambition which Rorty likes most about Hegel.

From the perspective of the new analytic philosophy, however, Hegelianism was both unscientific and overambitious, challenging rather than complimenting scientific knowledge at a time when the study of reason and the mind was becoming increasingly naturalistic and physiological; many of the key figures in the transition to naturalism which took place in the second half of the nineteenth century were eventually written out of the history of philosophy and into the history of a new subject called 'psychology'. Thus the first analytic philosophers sought to distance themselves from their immediate predecessors, the British Idealists, with histories written by analytic philosophers such as Popper and Reichenbach arguing that Hegel should not even be considered as Kant's successor (Popper 1968; Reichenbach 1951). These strategies were influential, and no doubt go some way towards explaining why the nineteenth-century philosophers we tend to remember these days are either political and moral thinkers, or else iconoclasts like Kierkegaard and Nietzsche; the 'unprofessional heretics' at a time when professors of philosophy were 'out of touch with the most vigorous thought of the age' (Russell 1991: 693), as Russell saw it.

The new linguistic philosophy set out to place philosophy firmly back on the Kantian 'secure path of a science'. It made central use of the Kantian distinctions between analytic and synthetic propositions, and between concepts and intuitions, though its advocates thought of themselves more as continuing the lineage of empiricism which stretched back to Locke. Instead of approaching the question of how our minds relate to the external world by focusing on subjective ideas, however, the new linguistic empiricism turned its attention to an objective medium of representation, and hence something more easily studied: the language in which we express our thoughts. The guiding idea behind this approach was that the grammatical form of language might be a misleading guide to its underlying structural or logical form, and that philosophical problems could be shown to result from taking grammar at face value. Such problems could then be resolved, or rather dissolved, by an analysis of the sentences in question to reveal the actual logical form or 'syntax' in question.

The analysis of the logical form of language was a similar venture in many ways to Kant's attempts to discover the general, structural features of representation; in Rorty's terms, both were attempting to uncover the general principles of operation employed by the Mirror of Nature. However, the advocates of logical positivism, the first major movement in linguistic philosophy, had a less ambitious conception of philosophy than Kant, for rather than seeking to vindicate the legitimate claims of metaphysics, they sought to enforce a sharp demarcation between, on the one hand, analytic philosophy, which was concerned only with clarifying the underlying logic of language, and on the other hand, metaphysics, which was to be exposed as nonsense, and hence eliminated (Ayer 1971: 69). The main methodological tool for the latter task was the verificationist criterion of meaning, which was that 'a sentence says nothing unless it is empirically verifiable' (ibid.: 98) or unless it is analytic. This in turn was based on the old empiricist conviction that all knowledge could be traced back to experience, the logical positivists simply giving this idea the linguistic spin that all claims to synthetic knowledge must provide a link to some possible observation which would bear on the truth or falsity of the claim in question. In a typical application of this principle, Ayer selected a sentence 'at random' from Bradley, and wrote:

such a metaphysical pseudo-proposition as 'the Absolute enters into, but is itself incapable of, evolution and progress', is not even in principle verifiable. For one cannot conceive of an observation which would enable one to determine whether the Absolute did, or did not, enter into evolution and progress.[1]

(Ibid.: 49)

Metaphysicians, according to the logical positivists, had been fooled by the surface grammar of language into overstepping the constraints on significant language use.

Now what the logical positivists meant by experiential observation was – with one crucial difference – the same as what empiricists like Locke and Hume had meant, i.e. whatever is 'immediately given in sensation' (ibid.: 71). The difference, however, was that the logical positivists rejected the label 'idea', on the grounds that this presupposed mental rather than physical status. Instead, they employed the neutral terms 'sense-contents' or 'sense-data', arguing that the mental–physical distinction is a 'logical construction out of certain sense-contents' (Ayer 1971: 163), or that it signifies only 'different forms of order . . . of the basic elements' (Carnap 2003: 299). This meant that the veil of perception problem was a 'pseudo-problem', because the question of the relation between our mental representations and the world presupposes that 'the world' is something beyond immediate experience, making statements about it unverifiable in principle. The legitimate question to ask, once we are clear about the logic of language, is rather how the physical world is constructed from sense-contents, a question which itself reduces to the linguistic question of how sentences about physical objects and mental states relate to sentences about sense-contents. This presents a good example of the logical positivist metaphilosophy, according to which the aim of philosophy is to provide definitions which lay bare the connection between language and experience, or, in terms of the Kantian distinctions, to provide analytic statements revealing relations of equivalence between ordinary sentences and sentences relating explicitly to sensory intuition. Such analyses were meant to show how language structures experience, and as a consequence, how experience bears on what we say.

Now philosophy of language and analytic philosophy generally has moved on a long way since the heyday of logical positivism, when a very young Rorty found himself studying under Carnap, the movement's leading exponent (Ayer was heavily influenced by Carnap). We shall cover a number of the most important developments from the mid- to late twentieth century over course of this text. However, it is enough for now to see how the project of trying to determine how language relates to experience can be seen as a continuation of the epistemological project of trying to demarcate the basis and scope of human knowledge, and thus as a continuation of the 'Mirror of Nature' problematic. This is how Rorty sees it, and that is why he thinks linguistic approaches to philosophy are just as hopeless as any other.

PHILOSOPHY

The idea that our minds and the languages we speak 'mirror' reality, or map onto it, or represent it, or are isomorphic to it in some highly abstract way, is probably as firmly ingrained as any philosophical idea could be. Rorty thinks that the academic subject we call 'philosophy' has been built around this idea. His view can thus be summarised:

> Philosophy is the subject which studies the Mirror of Nature (mind), in order to ascertain the conditions under which it is able to accurately reflect nature (knowledge), by investigating the structure and capacities of the mirror (as expressed in language).

Many contemporary philosophers of mind would deny that they conceive of the mind as a 'Mirror of Nature', many contemporary epistemologists would deny that their work has anything to do with foundationalism, and many contemporary philosophers of language would deny that their work is continuous with the seventeenth-century problematic. Nevertheless, the idea that philosophy aims to systematically spell out the connections between thoughts, words, and the world is hard to deny, and that is all the target Rorty needs, since his critique is wide enough to undermine this whole endeavour if successful.

It does seem rather implausible, however, that Rorty alone would be able to take on nearly all philosophers, alive and dead, and win. He is driven on by Dewey's view that,

> intellectual progress usually occurs through sheer abandonment of questions ... an abandonment that results from their decreasing vitality and a change of urgent interest. We do not solve them: we get over them. Old questions are solved by disappearing, evaporating, while new questions corresponding to the changed attitude of endeavor and preference take their place.
>
> (Dewey 1910: 19)

But could philosophical questions really go the way of mediaeval questions about angels? The key factor there seems to have been that people stopped believing in angels, so maybe we need to stop believing in minds. But think back to our example: what would it even mean to be mistaken about that woman having a conscious point of view on the street panning out in front of her? Some things are a lot easier to say than to believe. Moreover, is it not entirely obvious that there are better and worse ways of acquiring knowledge? Meteorologists succeed in forecasting the weather, astrologers fail. But if we have minds, and some ways of acquiring knowledge are better than others, then why not theorise systematically about minds and knowledge? And even if Rorty could persuade us that this minor academic activity is somehow socially undesirable, philosophers would still be able to occupy themselves with the task of working out how the marks and noises we produce relate to the environment. The answers may not change the world, but who said they were supposed to? They might just be interesting, or at the very least something which people in the future might want to look up if they became curious.

3

THE ORIGINS OF THE MIRROR
(*PMN*, CHAPTER 1)

MARKS OF THE MENTAL

(§§1–2)

In Part One ('Our Glassy Essence'), which comprises the first two chapters, Rorty's target is the mind–body problem, which as we have just seen is the basis of the whole 'Mirror of Nature' conception of philosophy which he wants to undermine. The specific task of Chapter One ('The Invention of the Mind') is to persuade us that the mind–body problem is not a 'perennial problem', a matter of common-sense which would occur to anybody who reflected, irrespective of the age or circumstances in which they lived, but is rather a theoretical deliverance of our own particular intellectual past: an 'invention' of the seventeenth century.

We cannot seriously engage with the question of whether the mind is physical or non-physical if we do not know what we mean by 'the mind' in the first place, and Rorty does not think that this should be taken for granted. Relying on a common-sense grasp of the division between the mental and the physical as a starting point for philosophy of mind might perhaps be a reasonable approach if we thought that this way of dividing the world up preceded Descartes, and that Cartesian Dualism was simply a theory designed to make sense of ahistorical intuitions. But if our intuitions in fact derive from Descartes's theory, then such a starting point would allow dualism to set the terms of the debate, and would place physicalism at an immediate disadvantage, given that if physicalism is true and we do indeed live in an exclusively physical world, it is not obvious why we should have ever made a mental–physical distinction (17). By conceding the high ground of common-sense to dualism, physicalism multiplies obstacles for itself, for it must not only overcome the theory of dualism, but also explain dualistic intuitions. Moreover, if our common-sense idea of mind is as theoretically laden as Rorty thinks it is, then by accepting it, even philosophers of mind who think that dualism is a defunct theory may in fact be serving only to perpetuate its influence. Hence Rorty's starting point is to try to instil some scepticism about the idea of a theoretically neutral, common-sense conception of mind.

The most obvious criterion for a common-sense idea of mind, Rorty thinks, is non-spatiality. However, he also thinks that this idea is not easily detached from Descartes's substance dualism, which held that minds were non-spatial substances whose existence is independent of the physical world. P.F. Strawson, the main 'neo-dualist' Rorty has in mind in §1, argued that substance dualism was untenable on the grounds that it is committed to the possibility of individuating minds solely in terms of their mental predicates, but that this is in fact impossible: we can individuate the minds of people only by reference to their bodies. Without resort to physical predicates, and thereby the procedure of counting minds by counting bodies, Strawson argued, we would be at a loss to distinguish one mind from a million minds thinking the same thoughts (Strawson 1974). Consequently, the 'neo-dualist' abandons mental substances, and holds instead that the mental–physical distinction holds between irreducibly different properties of human beings, or between irreducibly different states of human beings. According to Rorty, however, this shift leaves non-spatiality an unsuitable criterion for the mental, since though we might be able to understand the mental–physical distinction as the distinction between 'bits of matter and bits of mind-stuff', there are complications in trying to understand it as the distinction between 'spatial and nonspatial states of spatial particulars', i.e. human bodies (21). The main complication is that there are states of human bodies other than

mental states which we might as easily classify as 'nonspatial' –
Rorty's examples are build, fame, and health – and so non-spatiality
cannot be a sufficient condition of mentality.

In a parallel discussion in his paper 'Incorrigibility as the Mark of
the Mental', Rorty makes a similar point by saying that thoughts
and sensations can indeed be located in space, but only vaguely –
they are wherever the person having the thought or sensation is –
and that the inappropriateness of making more precise spatial
specifications of shape and size is characteristic of states generally,
and not mental states in particular. Again, the point is that once the
dualist switches from talking about substances and parts of substances, to states and properties, then non-spatiality will not present
a sufficient condition of mentality. The more general suggestion,
however, is that the present day intuition that spatial notions are
uniquely inapplicable to the mind hark back to Descartes's original
theory, in terms of which it makes sense, but without which it
appears arbitrary. The reason non-spatiality came to be associated
with mentality, according to Rorty, was 'Descartes's preoccupation
with dreaming' and 'habit of treating objects dreamt of as "mental
objects"', since it was by treating 'images of physical objects had in
dreams or hallucinations as paradigmatic of the mental' that
Descartes 'confused the mental with the inexistent or the imaginary' (Rorty 1970: 410–11). According to Rorty, however, the only
reason that the physical objects which appear in dreams do not exist
in space is the trivial reason that there are no such objects, a fact
which has no tendency whatsoever to show that mental states of
dreaming about non-existent objects are themselves non-spatial.

In further bringing out the complications of trying to tie
mentality to non-spatiality, Rorty notes an interesting asymmetry
between the mental–physical and immaterial–material distinctions.
Assuming that 'physical' means the same as 'material', as we have
been doing, he points out that it is not so clear that 'mental' means
the same as 'immaterial'. But given that 'physical' is the opposite of
'mental', and 'material' is the opposite of 'immaterial', this raises
the question, 'How can two distinct concepts have synonymous
opposites?' (20). The simple answer, of course, is that they cannot,
but there are a number of options for alleviating the tension.
The most obvious option would be to contrast 'physical' with 'non-

physical' rather than 'mental', thereby creating a more straightforward parallel with the immaterial–material contrast. This move, however, only serves to underline Rorty's point, which is that our ordinary understanding of the mental cannot be glossed through a simple contrast with the physical or material, since the class of non-physical, immaterial, or non-spatial items generally, is wider than the class of mental items.

At this stage, all Rorty is trying to show is that the mental–physical distinction is not as obvious as we might have thought, and that it takes only a little scrutiny to open up technical and theoretical quandaries. This is not to say that he is in any doubt that we do have strong intuitions (or 'so-called intuitions'[1]) about the mind. Rather, what he doubts is that these intuitions reflect something integral to the human condition, rather than simply our familiarity with Cartesian ways of talking, or just the ease with which people in our society can be introduced to Cartesian ways of talking. Dualistic intuitions, for Rorty, are 'our readiness to fall in with a specifically philosophical language-game' (22), the concept of a 'language-game' being central to Wittgenstein's later philosophy, where it is used to emphasise, amongst other things, the vast multiplicity of functions which language can perform, in contrast to the logical positivist view that it is possible to isolate a uniform underlying structure to language. In saying that our grasp of the mental–physical distinction is our ability to play a certain language-game, Rorty is claiming that there is nothing more in common between the items we group together as mental than that the rules of the Cartesian language-game require such a grouping, and in saying that the language-game is 'specifically philosophical', he is claiming that it has no overlap with the rest of life, and hence could be abandoned without loss.

To go any way towards establishing these claims, Rorty must show that there is no common feature which unites all those items we intuitively classify as 'mental', i.e. that there is no unified 'mark of the mental'. There are two traditional candidates for this role: phenomenal consciousness and intentionality. The idea of phenomenal consciousness, as Rorty uses it, is the idea of there being 'something it is like' from a subjective point of view, according to which phenomenal properties are felt properties, such as what it feels like to be in pain, to taste liquorice, or to think of a number. The view that phenomenal character unites the mental derives from Descartes's claim that thought is the essence of mind, in the broad sense of 'thought' which he defined as follows:

> *Thought.* I use this term to include everything that is within us in such a way that we are immediately aware of it. Thus all the operations of the will, the intellect, the imagination and the senses are thoughts.
>
> (Descartes 1985: 113)

The idea of intentionality, on the other hand, is often described as the mind's directness upon the world, or the property mental states have of being 'about' something else. So, for example, if Tom believes the oven is hot, then his belief is directed upon/about the hotness of the oven, and the proposition *that the oven is hot* is the intentional content of his belief. The view that intentionality unites the mental derives from Franz Brentano, who claimed that intentionality is 'characteristic exclusively of mental phenomena. No physical phenomenon exhibits anything like it' (Brentano 1973: 88).

In Rorty's view, however, neither phenomenal consciousness nor intentionality can unite the mental, and his basic reason for thinking this is that some phenomenal states are not intentional, and some intentional states are not phenomenal. Bodily sensations are a standard example of mental states which are phenomenal but apparently not intentional, for though there is certainly something it is like to be in pain, it sounds at the very least odd to say that a pain is directed upon or about anything, rather than just a plain and simple feeling. And dispositional propositional attitudes provide the standard example of mental states that are intentional but apparently not phenomenal. Dispositional propositional attitudes are states such as beliefs, desires, intentions, etc. that are not currently being thought about. So, for example, there is nothing it is like to believe that Rorty is an American except when that belief is occurrent, i.e. when it is explicitly being thought about, but this of course does not mean you stop believing that Rorty is an American when the thought is not consciously occurring to you: the belief remains (and so is intentional), but is dispositional (and hence not phenomenal).

Attempting to overcome these apparent counter-examples to treating either phenomenal consciousness or intentionality as the mark of the mental has been a major preoccupation within recent philosophy of mind, but though there have been several developments since Rorty wrote *PMN*, they all conform to the basic strategies he anticipated (22–23).

The first option is to construe bodily sensations such as pains as perceptions of the state of one's own body, and thus as states with intentional content. This strategy is known as Intentionalism or Representationalism.[2] So, for example, Armstrong, who pioneered the approach, analyses the pain report 'I have a pain in my hand' as equivalent in meaning to 'It feels to me that a certain sort of disturbance is occurring in my hand, a perception that evokes in me the peremptory desire that perception should cease' (Armstrong 1968: 314). Armstrong then analyses perception in terms of the paradigmatically intentional state of belief. The objection Rorty anticipates to this form of Intentionalism is that any such analysis will seem to miss out the phenomenal aspect of pain, i.e. the subjective feeling which strikes us as something additional to simply registering that we have sustained bodily damage. However, contemporary intentionalist theories have been designed with the express purpose of overcoming this sort of objection. Such theories are distinctive in claiming that 'Phenomenal character (or what it is like) is one and the same as a certain sort of intentional content' (Tye 1995: 137), as one of contemporary intentionalism's principal exponents puts it.

The second option is to restrict attributions of mentality to states with phenomenal properties, thereby 'abandoning' (23) states without phenomenal properties, such as dispositional propositional attitudes. But again, there is now a more viable approach available, in the form of John Searle's 'Connection Principle', which provides a neat counterpart to the Intentionalist proposal. The principle claims that 'The notion of an unconscious mental state implies accessibility to consciousness' (Searle 1992: 152), and the idea behind it is that our concept of mind was only developed to cover conscious phenomenal states, but nevertheless extends naturally to 'neurophysiology capable of generating the conscious' (ibid.: 172), i.e. dispositional propositional attitudes which become occurrent when we think of them, though it does not apply where there is no possible connection to consciousness. The objection Rorty anticipates to proposals such as Searle's is that 'whatever the mind–body problem is, it is not the feeling-neuron problem' (23). This is very misleading, however, both historically and in terms of Rorty's own subsequent discussion, for the phenomenal-physical connection has indeed been central to the mind–body problem since at least Locke, and Rorty reaffirms this throughout the chapter.[3]

Both Intentionalism and the Connection Principle, then, seem to offer the 'mark of the mental' which Rorty thinks is required for us to take the mind–body problem seriously. And yet he quickly dismisses such approaches. We might regard this dismissal as highly suspect in light of these new theories, both of which claim to reveal a deep connection between intentionality and phenomenal consciousness, and which thereby offer an explanation of why apparently disparate types of state became associated. Rorty's objection to intentionalism is already out-dated, and his objection to proposals based on phenomenal consciousness, such as the Connection Principle, is inconsequential. However, in spite of all this, the reason for Rorty's dismissive attitude to these approaches is, in fact, very interesting indeed: it is that from his perspective, both approaches 'gerrymander', i.e. take an unfair advantage. Both Intentionalism and the Connection Principle work from the basis of our intuitive grasp of what counts as mental, and try to find a feature to unite all these items. Now if we assume that our intuitions reflect a real mental–physical distinction that exists within nature, then it will indeed seem worthwhile to search for an underlying unity to the apparently disparate categories of 'intentional' and 'phenomenal'. But this, of course, is exactly the assumption which Rorty is out to challenge. From his perspective, then, we first need to determine why we classify each of these apparently disparate categories as 'mental', whilst remaining neutral on the question of whether or not their apparent disparateness conceals an underlying unity (for a contrasting view, see Crane 2001: 1–3).

A third option for explaining the category of mind, and the one Rorty himself favours, is the 'family resemblance' approach, formulated in a table (24). On this view, occurrent thoughts and mental images – Descartes's model for the mind, according to the 'Incorrigibility' paper – are the paradigms of the mental, and are both intentional and phenomenal, with purely intentional and purely phenomenal states counting as mental in virtue of resembling these

paradigms. This has the consequence that phenomenal and intentional states need have nothing intrinsically in common with each,
and it was exactly in order to get across this idea of a loose grouping
with 'no one thing in common' that Wittgenstein originally introduced the terminology of 'family resemblances' (Wittgenstein 1953:
§§65–67). For this reason, the family resemblance approach could
hardly be said to be neutral on the question of whether or not there
is an underlying unity to the mental, and so if Rorty were to argue
for it by setting out to demonstrate an insurmountable gulf between
the intentional and phenomenal, then he too would be guilty of
gerrymandering. But he does not. Rather, he asks the two separate
questions of how the intentional came to be contrasted with the
physical, and how the phenomenal came to be contrasted with
the physical. This leaves all the options open: we may count both the
phenomenal and intentional as mental because of their intentionality, or because of their (connection to) phenomenal consciousness,
or simply because of a family resemblance.

Rorty's answer to the first question, of why the intentional came
to be contrasted with the physical, turns on the fact that intentionality is not an observable feature of physical things. So for instance,
once we understand a language, we can see ink marks as sentences,
and hear oscillations in the air as conversation, but these intentional
properties are not 'immediately evident to all who look' (26), since
we would fail to recognise them if we did not know the language in
question. The reason we can fail to recognise intentional properties
no matter how much observational scrutiny we engage in, is that
marks and oscillations do not mean anything in themselves: their
meaning is not intrinsic to them, as we naturally suppose their
physical properties to be. Rather, marks and oscillations mean something only as interpreted by us, and this fact encourages the view
that interpretation involves the superimposition of meaning by
mental states which do have intrinsic intentionality. Brain states, it
seems, are not qualified for the job of superimposing meaning, given
that they too are physical, and hence we have just as much reason to
consider them intrinsically devoid of meaning as marks and oscillations. Leibniz illustrated this with his influential example of walking
around a giant thinking machine, such as a brain, and failing to 'see
anything that would explain a perception' (Leibniz 1973: 181).

Brains, it seems, have as little claim to intrinsic intentionality as any other physical thing, and so the physicalist who wants to claim otherwise has an intuition to overcome.

However, according to the Wittgensteinian 'use theory' of meaning which Rorty endorses, to know what inscriptions and sounds mean is just to know about the various ways in which they are used in relation to other inscriptions and sounds. Consequently, when we are unable to read off intentional properties from physical inscriptions and sounds, this is only because we are unable to place the inscriptions and sounds within a wider context. So in the case of Leibniz's example, Rorty claims that if we were able to see the various brain states as parts of a larger system – as related to all sorts of other brain states, as well as to states of the outside world – then we would indeed be able to 'see thoughts' (26), in the sense that we would be able to see the neural states as intentional (as representing something or another), just as we are able to hear sounds as meaningful words when we can relate them to the larger system of a language. So the fact that meaning cannot be seen in isolation does not establish a significant contrast with the physical. Moreover, this feature of needing to be understood in context is not even specific to those items we intuitively classify as 'mental', according to Rorty, but applies generally to any functional state such as beauty, build, fame or health, examples which were used earlier to illustrate non-spatiality, since non-spatiality is itself just another consequence of being functional, i.e. of needing to be understood in relation to other things.

If we understand meaning correctly, then, we will see that there is no more reason to regard intentional states such as beliefs and desires as non-physical, than there is any other sort of functional state. But if, on the other hand, we think of meaning as intrinsic rather than relational, then we will expect to be able to see meaning in isolation. Now since physical things like marks, oscillations, or neurons are not intentional in isolation, the traditional misunderstanding of meaning encourages the assumption that they derive their intentionality from something which is intrinsically intentional, and hence from something which contrasts with the physical. Beliefs, desires and other mental states are then thought to fit the bill because of their connection to the phenomenal, since in the process of thinking, intentional content does indeed seem to be intrinsic. For example, during the time in which the belief that Rorty is an American is occurrent, and there is something it is like to be thinking that thought, there seems no room to question what the thought is about, let alone whether or not it is about anything at all. Unlike a mark, which can be interpreted one way or the other (as an English word, a French word, or just a mark), a thought that is currently being entertained seems to have an interpretation already built into it. So Rorty's explanation of why we intuitively classify intentional states as mental (and thus contrast them with physical states), is that such states can become phenomenal. Though this answer superficially looks compatible with either the Connection Principle or family resemblance options, it is in fact only compatible with the latter, since Rorty has argued that the association of the intentional and phenomenal is based on a misunderstanding of meaning, rather than on a unifying mark of the mental.

The second question, then, is why the phenomenal came to be contrasted with the physical, and here Rorty's answer is that phenomenal properties have been conceived as properties for which there is no appearance–reality distinction. The intuition is that if it appears that you are in pain, then you really are in pain (imagine the absurdity of someone saying 'it really seems to hurt, but it is not pain'), but if it appears that you are tall (in a fairground mirror, for instance), it does not follow that you really are tall. However, as Rorty points out, appearing is an epistemological notion – a way of being known – and so it is not obvious why our privileged access to phenomenal properties like pain should be thought to generate a metaphysical contrast with the physical. After all, phenomenal properties might just be a sub-set of physical properties that are known in a special way, i.e. known in such a way that we cannot be mistaken in ascribing them to ourselves, unlike other physical properties such as tallness. To generate the prerequisite metaphysical contrast between the phenomenal and the physical, then, the intuition that there is no appearance–reality distinction for phenomenal properties must be interpreted metaphysically as meaning that, 'Feelings just *are* appearances. Their reality is exhausted in how they seem' (29). This is the notion of appearance employed in setting up both the mind–body and veil of perception problems, the former problem arising when we try to relate the subjective appearances of consciousness to the objective reality of the physical world, and the latter when we try to understand how knowledge can reach beyond subjective appearances.

The resort to this move, however, seals Rorty's case for the disunity of mind, since he does not think this interpretation of the appearance–reality distinction can be detached from a commitment to non-physical particulars, as in Descartes's original theory of substance dualism. The reasoning is as follows. If we are thinking of sensations such as pains as having an essence, i.e. their appearance, then we must be thinking of them as particular things, rather than as properties or states of people. This is because only things have essences, and it makes no sense to describe a property or state of a person as exhausted by its appearance. Thus intuitions which are supposed to be about what is essential to mental states, turn out to really just be intuitions about mental particulars. This is a view which is shared by other philosophers – it is a theme in work of William Lycan, for instance (e.g. Lycan 1987: 16–18) – but Rorty goes on to make the further, distinctive claim that intuitions about mental particulars are themselves confused, and are really just intuitions about universals. Dualistic intuitions, he thinks, ultimately derive from 'hypostatising' universals, i.e. treating properties as if they were particulars, and so the intuition that the essence of a particular pain is the way it appears (i.e. feels), is simply the result of treating painfulness itself – what is in common between each and every instance of pain – as if it were a thing. The contrast between the phenomenal and the physical, then, is just the contrast between the universal and the particular, and the resistance we feel to identifying subjective sensations with objective physical states is really just our resistance to identifying universals such as painfulness with particular instances of pain. And of course, this is just a result of our having misconceived phenomenal states like pains in the first place.

And so concludes Rorty's 'fast dissolution' of the mind–body problem. It has the following outline:

> The intuition that the intentional is non-physical is explained by the confused assumption that intentionality must derive from the phenomenal, since it cannot be intrinsic to anything physical. The intuition that

the phenomenal is non-physical is explained by the even greater confu-sion of treating phenomenal states as hypostatised universals. So there is no good reason to group the intentional and phenomenal together as mental, thereby contrasting them with the physical. The only bond holding together the intentional and phenomenal is a family resem-blance: the fact that some states (those Descartes modelled the mind on) are both intentional and phenomenal. Consequently, since there is no good reason to contrast either the intentional or the phenomenal with the physical, and there is nothing which all the items we intuitively classify as 'mental' have in common, then there can be no special problem of understanding how minds fit into the physical world. So the mind–body problem is a sham.

By interrogating our reasons for ever contrasting the mental with the physical in the first place, Rorty approaches the mind–body problem at a different level than is usual. In doing so, he lays down a challenge to both Intentionalism, and to attempts to unify the mental on the basis of consciousness (e.g. the Connection Principle): the challenge to the former is to explain how intentionality alone was able to generate intuitions of a mental–physical contrast, and the challenge to the latter is to explain the mental–physical contrast without resorting to intuitions about phenomenal particulars.

MINDS AND UNIVERSALS

(§§3–4)

As things stand, there is a vital missing link in Rorty's attempt to dissolve the mind–body problem. For suppose we grant that there was never any good reason to contrast the intentional with the physical, and hence that there is nothing intrinsically puzzling about the existence of intentional states in a physical world. Furthermore, suppose we grant that the reason we have been unable to incorporate phenomenal states within the physical world is that they have been conceived of as hypostatised universals. Still, none of this bears on the problem of explaining why certain mental states are only subjec-tively accessible: the problem of privileged access. Rather, it makes a solution to this problem all the more pressing, since the conception of the phenomenal which Rorty criticises as hypostatising universals – the conception of consciousness as appearance – provides a metaphysical explanation of the epistemological fact of privileged access. The reason that phenomenal states are only known through their subjective appearances, according to philosophers like Descartes and Locke, is that subjective appearance is their nature. If we reject this explanation, as Rorty urges, then we need another one, and if the mind–body problem is to be dissolved, this explanation must not provide any reason for contrasting the phenomenal with the physical. To this effect, Rorty needs to argue that privileged access, and hence the phenomenal itself, is 'a matter of how we talk' (32), thereby denying that privileged access is even an epistemological fact, in favour of the view that what we think of as privileged access is nothing more than a social convention. This argument, which is needed to complete Rorty's case, is postponed until Chapter 2.

In the meantime, Rorty switches influences from Wittgenstein to Heidegger and Dewey – as promised in the preface – his aim no longer being to expose the conceptual confusions which the mind–body problem encapsulates, but rather to historically explain how those confusions arose. The transition is striking, as the compressed and cryptic exposition of the 'fast dissolution' is replaced by the full weight of Rorty's scholarship, the footnotes occasionally overwhelming the text. The question arises, however, of what function this history is supposed to perform. Rorty says, continuing his Wittgensteinian analogy between philosophy and therapy, that philosophy needs to 'relive its past' in order to understand how present day intuitions of a mind–body problem arose, rather as a neurotic is cured by reliving his or her past on the psychiatrist's couch. But putting aside the analogy – they can always be pushed too far – what is the point of understanding how the intuitions arose if Rorty has already 'dissolved' them anyway? If the dissolution worked, then uncovering further historical confusions would seem to be unnecessary, an attempt to overdetermine his conclusions, rather than an essential part of the argument (cf. Choy 1982).

This objection, however, does not give sufficient credit to Rorty's metaphilosophical agenda. Rorty is not just trying to undermine the intuitions which make us think the mind presents an obstacle to physicalism. Rather, he is trying to dissuade us from adopting any philosophical position about the mind at all: his target is not so much the mind, as philosophising about the mind. Without Rorty's history, it would be perfectly reasonable to respond to the 'fast dissolution' by looking for ways around it – it might be argued, for example, that the mind–body problem can be stated in such a way that the accusation of hypostatising universals simply cannot be levelled. But once the history is in place, any temptation to re-state or re-invigorate the problem is removed. This is because Rorty's history portrays the contemporary mind–body problem not as the most recent formulation of a 'perennial problem', but rather as a thoroughly contingent deliverance of history, a residue of anti-quated reasoning that no contemporary philosopher should want to associate with. According to that history, the confusions Rorty has identified in the contemporary problem result from historical confu-sions which generated the problem in the first place, and so there can be no prospect of detaching them from the problem: they are constitutive of what it is. Thus Rorty's fast dissolution and historical deconstruction of the mind–body problem are really two parts of one integrated argument: the former showing us what is wrong, the latter dissuading us from trying to do anything about it.

According to Rorty, the persistence of the mind–body problem, its ability to regenerate itself and outlive the generations of philoso-phers who have claimed to have solved or dissolved it, is due to the variety of issues to which an understanding of the mind would seem to hold the key. This has allowed for unending shifts of emphasis, so that theories of mind which appear to deal satisfactorily with one issue, may simply serve to deaden interest in that issue and focus it onto another. The reason for this tendency of philosophers to be dissatisfied with any solution that is put forward, according to Rorty, is that reason and personhood are amongst the cluster of issues which the mind–body problem bears upon. These issues have a direct link to the philosophical 'cravings' (34) which produced the problem in the first place, and which have perpetuated it ever since. These cravings are to do with asserting human uniqueness and moral worth, and it is because of their influence, woven into a long process of historical serendipity, that we have found ourselves preoccupied with 'rather dusty little questions' (33) concerning the relation between physical and phenomenal states. Rorty's automatic and unargued assumption of an ulterior motive for interest in technical philosophical questions is highly contentious – presumably there need be no similar motives for interest in technical scientific and mathematical questions – but is nevertheless entirely typical of his approach, and something he inherits from Dewey and Heidegger; whether it is justified ultimately depends on the results it achieves.[4]

The connections Rorty points out between consciousness, reason, and personhood are plain enough. Consciousness, we are inclined to think, sets human beings and animals apart from the rest of the world, and engenders a moral worth unconscious objects lack. We have to worry how we treat other people and animals, but we can kick chairs and eat plants without compunction. The additional factor which sets human beings apart from animals, granting them an even higher moral worth than consciousness alone can bestow, is rationality. People, but not animals, can reason with themselves and others in the present, can draw up plans for the future, and can understand themselves through their pasts. This idea that we distinguish people from animals on the basis of reason and not just species, is reinforced by the thought that though *Homo sapiens* are the only people on Earth, we can readily imagine classifying a species on another planet as people, in order to set them apart from alien animals, though none of these life-forms had anything more in common with us genetically than any other. Now though these connections between consciousness, rationality, and personhood are indeed plain enough, Rorty's plan is to break them down. Being 'plain', 'obvious', 'intuitive', or 'plausible', is never anything more than familiarity with a certain way of talking, according to Rorty, and we are always free to change how we talk. Moreover, since Rorty thinks that these inherited ways of talking generate an insoluble mind–body problem, and delude us into making misguided attempts to prove human uniqueness, he has a strong motivation for attempting to break their hold through historical deconstruction.

The present day connections between consciousness, reason, and personhood were forged, according to Rorty, when the Greeks decided upon knowledge of universals as the distinguishing characteristic which raises us above the level of the animals, and when they modelled this superior form of knowledge on vision. The Greek philosopher Rorty particularly has in mind is Plato, the usual suspect for historical deconstructers ever since Nietzsche (Nietzsche 1990: 50–51). There are a number of reasons why Plato considered knowledge of universals to be the highest form of knowledge. One of the most important was that knowledge of particular states of affairs was considered problematic because of the transitory and changing nature of the world, a world in which everything is always becoming something else – a seed becomes a sapling, becomes a tree, etc. – and then going out of existence. This idea that change stands in the way of knowledge was central to ancient Greek philosophy. A related obstacle to knowledge was presented by the so-called admixture or compresence of opposites. The idea here was that properties are only ever found together with their opposites, and never in a pure form, raising questions about how we are able to know, or even talk about, things of which we have had no direct acquaintance. So, for example, Helen of Troy may be the most beautiful woman in the world, but she is not beautiful compared to the goddess Aphrodite – her beauty (compared to other women) is mitigated by her lack of beauty (compared to the goddess) – and just as there are no examples of complete or perfect beauty in the world, so there are no examples of complete virtue, complete courage, perfect circularity, absolute straightness, etc., despite the fact that we talk about and claim to know about these and countless other properties.

Plato's account of knowledge of universals provided a solution to these problems, by imposing a dualism between the ordinary and changing world of becoming where we live, and the transcendent and changeless world of being where universals reside. Knowledge was then explained as the soul's contact with the changeless universals – pure beauty, pure circularity, etc. – with mundane examples of beauty and circularity, such as beautiful people and circles drawn in the sand, said to partake of the perfect forms to a greater of lesser degree. These forms were the original hypostatised universals: they were universals conceived of as things, though things on a higher plane of existence than the one we occupy. The words Plato used for a form were *idéā* and *eîdos*, which in old translations were both rendered in English as 'idea'; that is why it was once standard practise to refer to the 'Platonic Ideas'. According to conventional wisdom, however, this was a bad translation, since Plato meant something very different from what is now meant by 'idea', i.e. he did not mean a subjective mental phenomenon, as per Locke's definition. That is why the word 'form' is used instead (from the Latin 'forma'). However, according to Rorty, the etymological link is actually of great significance, because seventeenth-century philosophers such as Locke gave 'idea' its modern sense by effectively just modifying Plato's forms to make them internal to individual thinkers, thereby reconceiving the objective contents of Plato's transcendent world as the subjective contents of our newly invented conscious minds. Hence our predilection to conceive phenomenal states as hypostatised universals results from the fact that our modern ideas are simply a rehash of the ancient ones.

This view is supported by striking parallels between Plato's conception of the forms and the contemporary mind–body problem. Most striking is the invocation of transcendence: Plato's forms occupy a transcendent world because the ordinary, physical world contains only individual, particular things. The subjectivity of consciousness, on the other hand, seems to present us with a 'fact of transcendence' (see chapter 2 above) because we conceive of the ordinary, physical world in exclusively objective terms. The suggestion, then, is that intuitions of subjectivity, which seem to force the mind out of the ordinary world, do so because these intuitions are inextricably mixed up with Plato's theory of forms: hypostatised universals, whether conceived of as the original Platonic forms or their distant ancestors phenomenal properties, simply have no place in the physical world.

Another striking parallel is that ideas in the modern, psychological sense, play similar explanatory roles to those which Plato designed his forms to play. Though the ancient problem of knowledge of the changing is not addressed as such in the modern era, the constancy of our ideas, when combined and ordered in various ways, plays a similar unificatory role for philosophers such as Locke as did the changelessness of the forms for Plato. And if we consider the compresence of opposites problem, of how it is possible to know (e.g.) beauty itself when we never encounter it in unadulterated form, a natural modern response would be that beauty is 'just an idea'. Leaving aside our dismissive attitude, in contrast with the reverential, quasi-religious attitude with which the forms were to be regarded, this response is recognisably the same as Plato's.

By hypostatising universals and modelling our knowledge of them on vision, then, Rorty thinks that Plato set the mould for the whole Mirror of Nature problematic. The forms occupied a transcendent world, and since knowledge of them was conceived visually, the point from which the forms were 'seen' also needed to transcend the physical world. This made the mind doing the 'seeing' transcendent, and originated the mental–physical distinction; as Rorty makes the point, using the example of the form of parallelness, 'The more wispy the mind, the more fit to catch sight of such invisible entities as parallelness' (40). Now Rorty is certainly right that Plato thought there was an important analogy to be made between the soul's contact with the forms and vision; both *idéā* and *eîdos* have strong visual connotations, and Plato talks about the 'the eye of the soul' (Plato 1961: *Republic* 533d) and the need to turn the 'soul's gaze upwards . . . to that which deals with being and the invisible [i.e. invisible to the eye of the body]' (ibid.: 529d). Plato also says that vision is superior to the other senses, as does Aristotle (ibid.: 507c-508d; Aristotle 1984: *Metaphysics* 980a). According to Rorty, however, there was 'no particular reason' for privileging vision in this way:

> it is fruitless to ask whether the Greek language, or Greek economic conditions, or the idle fancy of some nameless pre-Socratic, is responsible for viewing this sort of knowledge as looking at something (rather than, say, rubbing up against it, or crushing it underfoot, of having sexual intercourse with it).
>
> (39)

But can it really have been anything like this arbitrary? Could our talk of getting 'clear', having a 'view', 'seeing' the point, etc., have just as easily been based on some other activity than looking?

For a start, there seems nothing arbitrary about modelling knowledge on sense experience, given that sense experience is the basis of most if not all of our knowledge of the world. And of the senses, vision would seem to provide the widest array of information: psychologists, at least, have no compunction about saying that vision is 'the dominant human sense' (Humphrey 1992: 31). Smell, for instance, would have made a very poor model for knowledge, since smell tells us very little about what something is, by contrast with vision, which tells us about size, shape, colour, texture, relative position, etc., not to mention all that can be inferred on the basis of vision, such as whether something is threatening, climbable, hot, slippery, etc. A different line of response is taken by Ian Hacking in an early reaction to *PMN*, who argues that the Greeks modelled knowledge on vision because geometry was their paradigm of knowledge, and there is a 'natural' analogy between looking at particular figures (drawn in sand, for instance), and reasoning to universal geometrical truths. According to Hacking, theorising on the basis of the best available knowledge at the time – geometry in ancient Greece, the New Science in seventeenth-century Europe – is 'typical of Western philosophy' (Hacking 1980: 585). A third response to the 'why vision?' question is provided by Dewey (Dewey 1930: Chapter 1). Dewey's explanation is that since the forms were required to be unchanging, and hence needed to be apprehended in a way that would leave them unaffected, vision thereby emerged as the natural model on the grounds that looking at an object does not change it. Though Dewey does not consider that the same could presumably have been said of hearing and smell, his explanation certainly accords well with Greek philosophical concerns, and Rorty's lightning dismissal of it – on the grounds that the visual metaphor for knowledge might rather have determined the idea that knowledge is of the changeless – is simply careless: it makes no sense given that we can see things changing.

There seem to be a number of good candidates for a 'particular reason' why knowledge was modelled on vision, then, and combining them would probably provide the best explanation of all; in any case, we certainly know enough not to have to go in for baseless speculation about 'the idle fancy of some nameless pre-Socratic'. Rorty, of course, is keen to assert the arbitrariness of modelling knowledge on vision because he wants to show that the Mirror of Nature problematic arose for no particular reason. He has, however, provided no reason to think the choice of a visual metaphor was in fact arbitrary, or even any reason to think that the choice of a different metaphor would have made any difference to the development of the Mirror of Nature problematic anyway. For instance, suppose the Greeks had modelled contact with the forms on listening; might not similar problems about representation have grown up around the 'Echo of Nature'? Now it is notable that Rorty deliberately avoids suggesting different sense modalities as alternatives to looking – he opts for 'rubbing up against' rather touching and feeling – and this is no doubt to side-step this sort of response. But even with the very physical alternatives he suggests, it is not hard to imagine a parallel but recognisably 'Mirror of Nature'-like problematic arising. For instance, we can dream of crushing things underfoot, and crush them to a greater or lesser degree, which might well be all that is required to generate questions about the conditions required for crushing (knowledge) to take place. Moreover, Rorty overlooks the fact that the direct physical contact involved in rubbing, etc., is actually irrelevant to his argument, given that the reason he gives for the 'eye of the mind' being immaterial would apply equally to any alternative model: whatever has contact with the forms would have to be 'wispy'.

Rorty's expositional problem, which makes his argument look weaker than it is, is that though he does have criticisms to make of the origins of the Mirror of Nature problematic, they have precious little to do with vision, though he continually implies that they do. He wants to follow Dewey, who blames visual metaphors for dislocating knowledge from action, and is also no doubt influenced by the discourse of 'anti-ocularcentrism' within continental philosophy, which blames a whole host of ills – sexism, class structure, etc. – on Western society's preoccupation with vision, the most distancing of the senses (cf. Jay 1993). And yet Rorty's critique is not really anything to do with distancing. It is to do with hypostatising universals, and having ideas forced upon us by a non-human agency, neither of which has any particular connection with vision. Moreover, even if the selection of a visual metaphor for knowledge was for some reason responsible for our coming to think of knowledge in representational terms, the only actual confusion Rorty has pointed out so far is 'Plato's muddled attempt to talk about adjectives as if they were nouns' (33). So even if Rorty is right that the metaphor of the mind as a mirror, our Shakespearean 'glassy essence' (*Measure for Measure*, Act II, Scene II), has captivated intellectuals throughout the ages, and perpetuated representationalist conceptions of knowledge better than any argument could ever have done, this has no tendency to show that some other poetic metaphor could not have done the same job, nor that the job was not worth doing.

What Rorty's case really depends on is showing that the mind–body problem is the consequence of an ancient confusion about universals. By pointing out strong parallels between the ancient and modern problems, he has certainly made this plausible. One line of response, however, would be to deny that Plato was confused at all, given that the debate about universals rages to this day, and there are still plenty of Platonists – called 'realists' in this context – who argue that properties cannot be reduced to particulars, by contrast with nominalists like Rorty who think there are only particulars. The contemporary debate about universals certainly enjoys a degree of autonomy from the mind–body debate which either belies Rorty's analysis, or else shows up the confusion (or simply lack of historical awareness) of the participants to those debates, for contrary to what Rorty's analysis would lead you to expect, a physicalist is not automatically thereby a nominalist, the most notable case in point being David Armstrong, who is as well known for his physicalism as his realism. Simply defending realism, however, would not explain the parallels Rorty has pointed out, and would leave us none the wiser about whether the problem of universals does or does not have anything to do with the mind–body problem. A better sort of response, one which properly engages with Rorty's historical deconstruction, would involve showing either that the parallels are lacking in any significance whatsoever, or else that they have a different significance from that which Rorty invests in them. The former option sounds like an uphill struggle, given the centrality of the problem of universals to Greek philosophy, and the enormous influence of the Greeks on the seventeenth-century originators of modern philosophy. The latter option, then, is the best route to critically engage Rorty on these matters.

One such alternative explanation of the connection between mind and universals, an explanation diametrically opposed to Rorty's, but which also connects ancient thinking about universals with the modern mind–body problem, is defended by Howard Robinson. Robinson's story has the following outline. Metaphysics originates in the Greek recognition that the world must contain 'the veins of generality' (Robinson 1991: 11) in order to be thinkable. The reason for this is that human thought is essentially expressed in language, and language contains both names and predicates, i.e. terms for particulars and terms for universals. Hence for a subject-predicate sentence such as 'John is tall', there must be both something answering to the name, and something answering to the general predicate, otherwise the thought expressed by the sentence would fail to connect up with anything in the world. So the generality of thought, as revealed by its linguistic expression, requires that the world itself must contain generality, or at least the potential for generality, in order to be thinkable by us. Greek preoccupation with conceptual thought or intellect, then, reflected opposition to nominalism, a view which seemed both naïve and pre-philosophical in its failure to recognise the preconditions of cognition meshing with the world. By the seventeenth century, however, nominalism had triumphed, and the world was thought to contain only particulars. Since generality was no longer believed to reside in the world, it was relegated to the mind, and to mark this shift away from the previous anti-nominalist preoccupation with intellect, the sensory or phenomenal aspect of mind came to the fore. Descartes's nominalism was limited to holding that 'universals were formed in the mind' (ibid.: 12), but later philosophers sought to remove generality not only from the world, but from the mind as well, a trend which led empiricists like Locke to construe general conceptual thought in terms of particular sensory images.

Robinson, then, presents a very different picture to Rorty, according to which the problem of universals is integral to the mind–body problem not because of the inheritance of an ancient confusion, but rather because of new approaches taken to problems recognised in ancient times, problems which, having persisted from the beginnings of Western thought, have as good a claim to perennial status as any. The different ramifications involved in accepting Rorty's picture over Robinson's, or *vice versa*, provides an excellent illustration of the importance of philosophy's history to its contemporary debates.

HOW OLD IS THE MIND–BODY PROBLEM?

(§§5–6)

How can it be, asks Wallace Matson in 'Why Isn't the Mind–body Problem Ancient?', that the Greeks – 'not the dullest people who ever lived' (Matson 1966: 95) – did not address the mind–body problem? If the problem really did not occur to them, as Matson contends, then this certainly would cry out for an explanation, given that from our perspective, it seems the most vivid and unmissable of philosophical problems, a problem '[a]ny teaching assistant can set up . . . so that any freshman will be genuinely worried about it' (ibid.: 92). So how could Plato and Aristotle have overlooked it? Matson's answer has two main parts. The first is that the Greeks drew the mental–physical distinction in a different place to us, so that sensations were physical, and only intellect was mental. Thus there is a sense in which 'mind–body identity was taken for granted' (ibid.: 93) by the Greeks, given that the contemporary mind–body identity theory is primarily concerned with identifying sensations (i.e. phenomenal states) with bodily states. The second is that the Greeks did not conceive of sensations as immediate objects of awareness through which we are mediately aware of the external world. In other words, they did not conceive of sensations as Lockean ideas. This conception of an idea, the main target of Matson's paper, is the 'sophism' which generates the mind–body and veil of perception problems, and we can 'congratulate the Greeks on never having thought of it' (ibid.: 100). Rorty sums up Matson's paper by saying that 'in Greek there is no way to divide . . . events in an inner life – from events in an "external world"' (47).

Matson's thesis lends clear support to Rorty's position that the mind–body problem is an invention of the seventeenth century, not a perennial problem. Both agree that the conflict between mental and physical arose when the concept of mind was extended to incorporate the phenomenal, but was not felt prior to this when sensations were regarded as physical. Nevertheless, Matson's claims are not as bold as Rorty makes them look. Matson does not say that there is no Greek equivalent to 'sensation', as Rorty implies. Rather he says that the translation of *aisthēsis* as 'sensation' (it is also standardly translated as 'consciousness') is 'seldom right' because 'an *aisthēsis* must have a cause, though it may turn out not to be what it was thought to be at first', and he goes on to concede that on some rare occasions in Aristotle's *On Dreams*, the related word *aisthēma* is used in such a way that it is 'perhaps inevitable to translate it by "sensation", "sense impression", or even "sense datum"' (a usage explained by the 'spooky context' (ibid.: 101)). It is not at all clear why Matson does not think these concessions compromise his thesis of 'no sensations, no mind–body problem' – Aristotle could presumably have raised the mind–body problem for dream sensations – but in any case, they clearly cast doubt on Rorty's stronger claim that the Greeks had no conception of the mind as 'events in an inner life'.

Greek philosophy is, in fact, filled with passages it would be very hard to make sense of without assuming that some conception of subjective conscious experience is being drawn upon. In the *Phaedo*, for instance, Plato says that,

> when the soul uses the instrumentality of the body for any inquiry, whether through sight or hearing or any other sense – because using the body implies using the senses – it is drawn away by the body into the realm of the variable [i.e. the realm of becoming].
>
> (Plato 1961: *Phaedo* 79c)

This would seem to imply that the soul has awareness of bodily experiences. Or, to take another example from Plato, death is said to be one of two things in the *Apology*:

> Either it is annihilation, and the dead have no consciousness [*aisthēsis*] of anything, or . . . [it is] a migration of the soul from this place to another. Now if there is no consciousness, but only a dreamless sleep, death must be a marvellous gain.
>
> (Plato 1961: *Apology* 40c–d)

Without any conception of 'events in an inner life', it is hard to see why death would be conceived of as 'a dreamless sleep', rather than as 'permanent cessation of breath', or by means of some other outward criterion. And a third example, one which Rorty draws our attention to (50) without indicating why he thinks no reference to inner events is being made, is Plato's statement that 'thinking is . . . the inward dialogue carried on by the mind with itself without spoken sound' (Plato 1961: *Sophist* 263e).

Matson and Rorty both seem to rest their case on the Greeks not having considered the mind–body problem in exactly – or near enough exactly – our own terms. Rorty's footnotes are filled with apparent counterexamples to his claims, which he responds to by pointing out minor discrepancies between the ancient ideas in question and their post-seventeenth-century counterparts. He concedes, for instance, that ancient scepticism employed the 'notion of the veil of ideas', but only in an 'incidental' manner (46), and that the idea of 'inner space' may have been employed by the Stoics.[5] In fact, if we look to the other major strand of Hellenistic philosophy, Epicureanism, we find the Roman philosopher Lucretius discussing the view that the eyes are doorways through which the soul peers into the outer world, it being not the eyes that see (or the ears that hear, etc.) but rather the soul within (Lucretius 1951: 107; see also Epicurus 1993: 32–33). Lucretius was a materialist ('the substance of the mind . . . must consist of particles exceptionally small and smooth and round', he says (op. cit.: 102)), and hence rejected this clear division of the inner mind from the outer world, but the view was evidently extant. Now if Rorty were only trying to show that conceptions of mind changed radically in the seventeenth century, these exceptions need not be particularly significant. But he is trying to show that the mind–body problem is not a perennial problem, and also that there is not a real problem 'somewhere in the neighborhood' (34). For this, the evidence threshold needs to be set much lower, given that perennial problems can presumably be formulated in radically different ways by different cultures in different periods. What Rorty needs are not minor discrepancies, but reasons to believe the ancients had no conception of a distinction between subjective consciousness and the objective world. And even just scraping the surface, the evidence that they did have such a conception is overwhelming.

Nevertheless, Matson and Rorty are right that the relation between phenomenal consciousness and the physical world, a problem capable of inducing a 'vertiginous sense of ultimate mystery' (McGinn 1991: 7) in some contemporary philosophers, did not seem to have particularly worried the ancients. They may also be right that this is because sensations were generally regarded as bodily. However, this only serves to cast aspersions on the contemporary mind–body problem provided that we make the anachronistic assumption that the Greeks considered the physical to be philosophically unproblematic. Matson and Rorty tempt us into thinking of the Greeks as sharing an outlook with contemporary physicalists except for their lack of any troublesome Cartesian intuitions about the non-physical nature of phenomenal properties. But the Greeks thought the physical world was deeply problematic: it was the realm of becoming in which change was an obstacle to knowledge. Hence though Greek philosophers did not focus on sensations in particular, this is only because they found the whole physical world problematic. For Plato, the physical world was an imperfect appearance of the reality of transcendent forms. For Aristotle, the physical world was conceived hylomorphically – as a combination of form and matter – which most commentators agree is radically unlike any sort of contemporary physicalism; Myles Burnyeat, for instance, describes Aristotle's conception of matter as 'pregnant with consciousness' (Burnyeat 1992: 26). When this is taken into account, the fact that Greek philosophy was not preoccupied with consciousness can just as well be taken to show that an ancient problem concerning the entire physical world was eventually refined into a more localised problem about sensations, as that the contemporary problem has no provenance and is by implication spurious.

For the remainder of the chapter, Rorty turns his attention to the transition between the old mental–physical distinction which pitted intellect against the rest of the world, and the new mental–physical distinction which pitted phenomenal and intentional states against the rest of the world. The key figure in the transition is of course Descartes, and the question Rorty is most concerned to address is 'how Descartes was able to convince himself that his repackaging was "intuitive"' (56). This is not very different from the question Rorty already answered in the fast dissolution, namely of how the phenomenal and intentional became unified as the mental. The answer then was that through a misunderstanding of meaning – specifically Locke's misunderstanding of how words acquire meaning – phenomenal presence was invoked to account for the intrinsic intentionality of mental states. However Rorty now wants to go back a stage from this, in order to portray Descartes as the originator of a conceptual revolution which was based only on a 'badly argued hunch' (58), but which nevertheless caught the imagination of later philosophers like Locke, who were able to normalise the doctrine.

The feature Rorty thinks Descartes found to replace grasp of universal truth as the mark of the mental was indubitability, i.e. being beyond doubt. As Rorty points out, however, any attempt to argue directly for dualism on the grounds that mental states are indubitable but physical states are not would be fallacious (55). Suppose, for instance, that I tried to argue as follows: I can doubt my body exists (since I could be dreaming), but I cannot doubt my mind exists (since I am thinking whether I am awake or asleep), therefore my mind must be separate from my body. This is fallacious because in talking about what I can or cannot doubt, I am no longer just talking about my body and my mind, but rather about my body-as-thought-about-by-me and my mind-as-thought-about-by-me, i.e. my body and mind as intentional contents of my mental states. That this sort of argument does not work when intentional properties (as Rorty puts it) are involved is more easily seen if we switch examples: I can doubt Tully was a Roman (I have never heard of him), but I cannot doubt Cicero was a Roman (I know about Cicero), so Tully must be somebody other than Cicero. Here we reach a false conclusion simply because I did not know that Cicero and Tully are identical, and likewise the former argument may be generating a false conclusion simply because I do not know that the mind and brain are identical.

There is much disagreement to this day about how Descartes's argument for dualism is to be interpreted, but it is rare to find him accused of quite this blatant a fallacy (see Patterson 2000). Rorty, however, is less interested in determining the actual form of argument Descartes employed, than in working out the underlying 'hunch' which allowed him to see a way out of the Aristotelian tradition; the argument from doubt, or something like it, was just a case of 'finding bad reasons for what we believe on instinct' (56), as Bradley is often quoted as having said about metaphysics (despite the fact that he was joking[6]). The hunch Rorty thinks he has detected is that Descartes saw a similarity between not being able to doubt mathematical proofs, and not being able to doubt occurrent sensations: just as when you think about '$2 + 2 = 4$' you cannot seriously entertain the possibility that this is false, so when you have a headache you cannot seriously entertain the possibility that you do not have a headache. Now given Descartes's Aristotelian background, he would have considered thoughts (e.g. about mathematics) as the paradigms of mind, and so seeing a similarity between thoughts and sensations would have allowed him to employ that similarity as the new mark of the mental. His motivation for wanting to do so was that he was trying to provide foundations for the New Science, and one of the main changes it brought to our understanding of the physical world was the idea that colours, sounds, and other qualities naturally attributed to objects around us are in fact secondary qualities, dependent upon the more fundamental particles and forces described by mathematical physics. As Galileo put it,

> the tickling is all in us, and not in the feather. Of precisely a similar and not greater existence do I believe these various qualities to be possessed, which are attributed to natural bodies, such as tastes, odours, colours, and others.

> (Burtt 1932: 75–76)

By finding a similarity between thought and bodily sensations like pain, as well as sensations of colour and sound, Descartes was able to expel all of these qualities out of the physical world and into the mind, as seemed to be required by the New Science.

Rorty portrays Descartes as having 'one foot still implanted in the scholastic mud' (60), his views awkwardly positioned between the Aristotelian tradition he was trying to overcome, and the Cartesian tradition his work would inspire. This is seen from the fact that though he drew sensations into the mind, he nevertheless denied that sensations belong to the essence of mind: the mind could exist as a 'complete thing' with reason alone (Patterson 2000: 100). He was able to strike this balance, holding onto his deeply ingrained Aristotelian intuition that only thought was truly mental whilst removing sensation from the physical world on behalf of the New Science, only by dividing sensation into both a mental and a physical component, i.e. sensing as an act of mind or thought, and the concomitant mechanical process occurring in the body (ibid.: 90). This compromise had some unhappy consequences, not least that it turned animals into unconscious machines, for the reason that thought was now involved in sensation, and animals could not be attributed thought; Aristotelian philosophy had been able to deny that animals think whilst allowing that they feel, but this option was now closed to Descartes. The next generation of philosophers, however, were able to turn their backs on Aristotelian philosophy more completely, by taking Descartes' new criterion of indubitability as the mark of the mental as their starting point, and ironing out the inconsistencies they saw in Descartes himself. Thus Descartes's own emphasis on the clarity and distinctness of ideas as a criterion of truth, and his view that knowledge must be based on innate ideas, was supplanted by the notion of the indubitability of ideas, since this was the revolutionary aspect of Descartes's thinking which struck his successors most forcefully.

Once Cartesianism took hold, so Rorty's story continues, philosophy was never the same again. As Rorty puts it, 'Science rather than living, became philosophy's subject, and epistemology its center' (61). And there does seem to be something to this: Greek philosophy was preoccupied with wisdom and living well, Roman philosophy with how to live without fear of death, and Medieval philosophy tried to make sense of the Christian world-view. None of this, however, seems to have much to do with the mainstream of philosophy ever since Descartes. As Rorty sees it, the end product of this transformation of philosophy was that philosophy became preoccupied with issues of no relevance 'to any human interest or concern' (68), by which Rorty means social and moral concerns. In fact, Rorty thinks that today's mind–body problem is not just useless but positively ridiculous, for the following reason. Sensations like pain are now the main focus of anti-physicalist intuitions, but philosophers who propagate these 'neo-dualist' intuitions reject Descartes's idea of mental substance, despite the fact that it was only by attributing sensations to a mental substance that Descartes was able to expel them from the body in the first place. Consequently they find themselves in the situation of thinking that sensation rather than thought provides the main mental–physical contrast, when the whole reason the contrast was originally set up by the Greeks was to assert the dignity of thought.

4

THE ANTIPODEANS
(*PMN*, CHAPTER 2)

FROM HISTORY TO SCIENCE FICTION

(§1)

The value of the history of ideas, for Rorty, is to 'recognize that there have been different forms of intellectual life than ours', and thereby see our problems as 'historical products' which were 'invisible to our ancestors' (Rorty 1998: 249, 267). By reflecting on the history of the mind–body problem, and thereby acquiring some grasp of how the world reached the point at which we were each of us able to discover and then engage with a ready-made problem, Rorty thinks our attitudes should be transformed. Such reflection reveals the contingency of the problem – that history might have delivered us a quite different mind–body problem, or even none at all – and thereby dissuades us from taking it for granted. Convinced of this, we must then decide for ourselves whether the problem is worth engaging with, disregarding its intuitive appeal as simply the ease with which we are able to fall in with an inherited pattern of talking. Rorty, as we have seen, thinks the mind–body problem carries various historical mix-ups in its trail, and hence is not worth bothering with. But the deeper, metaphilosophical reason for this negative assessment is his adherence to Dewey's view that problems should be evaluated according to their relevance to contemporary life. For Dewey, all problems originate in some sort of social need, but they tend to outlive their usefulness; this is what he thought had happened with all the traditional problems of philosophy. And this is what Rorty thinks has happened with the mind–body problem: ancient Greek philosophers felt the need to connect personhood and rationality, seventeenth-century philosophers felt the need to support the New Science, and the remainder in our hands is a problem with no relevance to twenty-first-century life whatsoever.

Now another way of reflecting on contingency, apart from looking at history, is through the use of imagination. That is why, in a move of no small audacity, Rorty takes us from ancient Greece to outer space, where we are introduced to the Antipodeans, an alien race whose history unfolded in such a way that they never came up with the concept of mind. Having no notion of mind whatsoever, the Antipodeans just talk about their brain states. Instead of saying 'I love you', an Antipodean says something like 'You give me brain state X-835'. One moral of this story is, of course, that we could have been just like the Antipodeans: they get on just fine without the concept of mind, and so could we. As Rorty puts it towards the end of the chapter, 'No predictive or explanatory or descriptive power would be lost if we had spoken Antipodean all our lives' (120). So thinking about the Antipodeans makes us realise that we could easily have lacked a mind–body problem, that if we had no mind–body problem it would make no difference to our lives, and that consequently we are safe to forget about it. That much is clear.

However, at this stage of the text, a much more pressing issue than bolstering the case for the dispensability of the mind–body problem, which the historical deconstruction is supposed to have already shown, is for Rorty to provide his 'anti-Cartesian' account of privileged access (69) which allows us to see 'the phenomenal as a matter of how we talk' (32). This is the vital missing link in the fast dissolution of the mind–body problem, and combined with the claim that this manner of talking would be obsolete if we knew as much brain science as the Antipodeans do, Rorty now looks poised to invoke the eliminative materialism of his 1965 paper 'Mind–body Identity, Privacy and Categories' in the company of the Antipodeans, the people without minds.

But it never happens. It seems inevitable until Section 5, and then the whole discussion of the Antipodeans is thrown into a new light. We remember Rorty's real agenda: undermining systematic philosophy and objective truth. We remember, in particular, that Rorty's motivation is metaphilosophical doubt rather than philosophical perplexity, and that he is somebody who refuses to 'bow down' to an 'authority called Reality' (Rorty 2000b: 376). What actually happens, then, is that he rejects eliminative materialism, advises that the best attitude to adopt towards the mind–body problem is boredom, and ultimately refuses to endorse any positive position on the mind whatsoever. He does, however, say that he is a physicalist, but by this point in the text it has become clear that this is a tactical, deeply qualified, pragmatist sort of physicalism, a position which anybody apart from Rorty or a Rortian would probably not want to call 'physicalism' at all.

Proceedings begin with Rorty describing his science fiction scenario. We Earthlings (the 'Terrans') discover a distant planet inhabited by humanoid life-forms who are like us in almost every way; they are physically similar to us, live similar lives, etc. The only significant differences are their lack of a concept of mind, and the highly advanced state of Antipodean neuroscience which has allowed reference to neural states to filter into everyday speech. This difference is a product of their history: the key stages in the development of the Terran concept of mind are lacking from the history of the Antipodeans. First, even though the Antipodeans use the person/non-person distinction in the same way we do, i.e. to include members of their own species (and presumably similar beings like us Terrans) whilst excluding animals and machines, it is not a distinction they think of as requiring any sort of explanation. So though the Greeks of ancient Terran history felt the need to explain personhood in terms of reason, their equivalents in ancient Antipodea cannot have experienced any similar social pressures. Second, the Antipodean's first technological breakthroughs were in neurology and biochemistry, so that at the point we discover them, they know vastly more about their brains than we know about ours. Again, a key point in the development of the Terran concept of mind has no parallel for the Antipodeans: Terran seventeenth-century philosophers inherited the concept of mind-as-reason, and reconceived it in support of the newly emerging physics, but their

Antipodean equivalents had nothing similar to inherit in the age of their newly emerging brain sciences.

According to the story, amongst the academics sent out to study and learn from the aliens are a team of philosophers, and it is the philosophers who dub them the 'Antipodeans'. This is a reference to the 'Australian Materialism' (the Antipodes is Australasia) which originated in the University of Adelaide in the 1950s, and resulted in physicalism becoming the dominant philosophy of mind in the latter half of the twentieth century. The theory which brought about this change was U.T. Place's 'Identity Theory', which was adopted and modified by J.J.C. Smart in his 'Sensations and Brain Processes', the classic paper of the idiom.[1] Since the ideas behind Australian Materialism are presupposed throughout Rorty's discussion of the Antipodeans, we need to backtrack at this point in order to properly understand what is going on.

In the 1940s, Gilbert Ryle had launched a powerful attack on dualism – 'the dogma of the Ghost in the Machine', he called it (Ryle 1963: 17) – arguing instead for a behaviourist understanding of the mind according to which concepts of mental states are concepts of patterns of behaviour. According to behaviourism, when we ascribe to somebody a mental state such as the belief that Rorty is an American, we are simply talking about that person's dispositions to behave, i.e. that when asked about Rorty's nationality, the person with this belief says or writes 'American', or points to a certain position on a map, or does something else appropriate to the situation. Now Ryle's behaviourism was given a mixed reception when it was first proposed because it was considered much more plausible for intentional states than phenomenal states. The reason was that having a phenomenal state, such as a sensation of pain, seems to involve a subjective reality in addition to any associated objective behaviour: we may wince and writhe in pain, but it is hard to believe that pain is only wincing and writhing. Thus a consensus emerged that phenomenal states – the mental states which eluded Ryle's analyses – were the crux of the mind–body problem. Rorty has already endorsed this consensus in the fast dissolution.

After Ryle, then, anti-dualists needed something physical to take the place of the apparently subjective reality which exists when we have a sensation like pain. The obvious candidates were brain states (or processes), but there was thought to be a 'logical' obstacle to making this move. This was that we do not mean the same by the words 'sensation' and 'brain process', and so even if it were true that when we talk about sensations we are in fact referring to brain processes, we could only be doing so by invoking the phenomenal properties which give sensation-terms their meaning. In other words, though we may be referring to brain states when we talk about pains, this could only be because they are painful states to be in, and so painfulness still has to be accounted for (Broad 1925: 612–24). Place short-circuited this objection by arguing that statements of mind-brain identity were to be construed as statements of scientific reduction, of which the most familiar example is 'water is H_2O'. Clearly 'water' does not mean the same as 'H_2O' – you can talk about water without knowing any science – but when it was discovered that water is in fact H_2O, no residual property of 'wateriness' was thought to remain, eluding our scientific understanding. Place's innovation, then, was to apply this model to the mind.

If in talking about phenomenal states we do not mean anything which compromises physicalism, the question arises of what exactly we do mean. This is where Smart's 'topic-neutral analysis' comes in. The aim of topic-neutral analysis was to give the sense of sensation terms without mentioning anything subjective, which was approached by using the circumstances in which sensations typically occur. The classic example is Smart's analysis of after-images (the spots you see after staring at a light-bulb, for instance):

> When a person says, 'I see a yellowish-orange after-image,' he is saying something like this: '*There is something going on which is like what is going on when* I have my eyes open, am awake, and there is an orange illuminated in good light in front of me, that is, when I really see an orange.'
>
> (Smart 1959: 149)

This leaves it open for the 'something going on' to turn out to be a brain state, and according to Smart, explains how 'the ancient Greek peasant's reports about his sensations can be neutral between dualistic metaphysics or my materialistic metaphysics' (ibid.: 150).

It was against this backdrop that Rorty wrote his 1965 paper, in which 'eliminative materialism' (as it was later dubbed) is presented as a new version of the identity theory, a 'disappearance' form of the theory in contrast to Place and Smart's 'translation' form (Rorty 1965: 189). Rorty argued that the 'magisterial neutrality' aimed at by topic-neutral analysis was a pipe dream, since the sort of discoveries about the brain envisaged by identity theorists might change the ways people talk to such an extent that the whole vocabulary of minds and mental states would become theoretically obsolete. Just as it would be better to say 'what people used to call "demoniacal possession" is a form of hallucinatory psychosis' than 'demoniacal possession is a form of hallucinatory psychosis', so it would be better to say 'what people now call "sensations" are identical with certain brain processes' than 'sensations are identical with brain processes' (ibid.: 190). The reason is that we cannot expect strict identities to hold between the entities referred to by contemporary or future science, and those referred to by super-stitious belief systems (e.g. demons) or outdated science (e.g. the replacement of the science of caloric fluid with that of kinetic energy). Insisting on retaining the old terminology simply opens up awkward objections: a witch doctor could justifiably object that the facts about demons (that they come from hell, have forked tongues, etc.) have not been preserved, just as a dualist could object that the facts about sensations have not been preserved.

Now water did not 'disappear' when it was discovered to be H_2O, nor tables when they were discovered to be 'clouds of molecules' (ibid.: 195), and yet demons and caloric fluid did. So what is the difference? Rorty's answer is: just convenience. It would be 'monstrously inconvenient' to stop talking about tables – 'although we could *in principle*' – whereas it is not only convenient but posi-tively desirable to stop talking about demons, since we now have better explanations of what was once explained supernaturally. Rorty, however, doubts it will ever be convenient to stop referring to sensations; only a 'fanatical materialist' would insist we should, and any predication that we one day will is 'almost certainly wrong' (ibid.: 198). His claim in this paper is simply that there is no princi-pled reason why we could not stop talking about sensations and just talk about brain states instead, just as there is no principled reason why we could not stop talking about tables and just talk about clouds of molecules instead. This means the identity theorist is free to take the theoretical advantages of the disappearance over the translation formulation. Confounding the image of eliminative materialism as an extreme view, then, it was – in Rorty's original formulation, at least – saying only that there is no good reason to think that sensations (or tables, or demons) will be explanatorily indispensable for all time. Rather than a bold and paradoxical statement of the non-existence of mind, it was actually just an instinctive Rortian trivialisation of a philosophical problem.

Returning to the Antipodeans, then, we can see that they are (apparently, at least) walking, talking proof that Rorty was right, not just that we could in the future learn to stop talking about sensations – we could learn the Antipodean language – but also that topic-neutral translation of sensation-talk presents physicalism with an unnecessary burden, given that the Antipodeans never talked about sensations to start with.[2]

Now the first thing Rorty does with his Terran team of philosophers is divide them into tough and tender-minded types (73). This distinction comes from William James, who thought the persistence of philosophical disputes was in large part due to a clash of temperaments (James 1995: 3). As Rorty makes the division, the tenders are continental philosophers – Hegelians and Heideggarians, specifically – and the toughs are analytic philosophers, though since he has no serious points to make with the continental philosophers, it is not long before a more significant division is made within the analytic camp. As we shall see, this business of dividing of philosophers into opposing camps is integral to Rorty's final conclusion – in a manner not far removed from what James had in mind – but for the time being we need only note that Rorty is using it as a distancing device, allowing him to talk about what 'the philosophers' would say without committing to being one of them himself. The more significant division occurs when the analytic philosophers decide (in line with the post-Rylean consensus) that the crux of the issue is whether or not the Antipodeans have sensations (or raw feels, or phenomenal properties, or qualia – all synonyms for Rorty). They then divide into those philosophers who think they do, and those who think they do not.

Rorty quickly dismisses any prospect of resolving the matter scientifically (74–75), saying later that any empirical result would 'weigh equally on both sides' (88). This is because the Antipodeans have been stipulated to have the same physiology and behaviour as the Terrans, and so no experiment would be able to turn up any difference. The result of using a 'brain switching' machine is just that the Antipodean ends up talking about sensations, and the Terran ends up talking about their brain, thereby resolving nothing. This is not altogether convincing, in actual fact, since we could just ask the Terran whether or not they fell unconscious during the period in which they were receiving input from the Antipodean's brain. If they did, and we trust the machine (as *ex hypothesis* we are supposed to), then presumably the Antipodeans do not have sensations. However we should leave this, because Rorty evidently wants to make his points elsewhere; it is what happens next that is of real interest.[3]

What happens next (76–77) is that the Terran philosophers start to question the Antipodeans to find out if they say the same things about their brain states as we say about our sensations. Now as we have already seen, Rorty thinks that the key to the mind–body problem is the metaphysical account of privileged access provided by the Cartesian conception of phenomenal states as subjective appearances. One of the main consequences of this conception is that you cannot be mistaken about whether you are having a sensation: it cannot seem to you that you are in pain (e.g.) when you are not, if pain itself is just a way that things can seem, i.e. the subjective appearance of hurting. Now according to the example, whenever we Terrans feel pain, we have stimulated C-fibres (a brain state), and whenever the Antipodeans are in the same circumstances in which Terrans feel pain – i.e. whenever they stub their toes, etc. – then they have stimulated C-fibres too. The difference is that Terrans report pain and Antipodeans report stimulated C-fibres. We already know that Terrans cannot be wrong about when they are in pain: it makes no sense to say 'it really hurts but isn't pain'. But can the Antipodeans be wrong about C-fibre stimulation?

They say they can. However, they also say that they cannot imagine being mistaken about their C-fibres seeming to be stimulated. Now one of the ground-rules about the Antipodeans is that they can detect the brain state correlated with any significant sentence in their language. In this case, it is brain state T-435, i.e. the brain state they are in when they are inclined to say (or actually say, or understand) 'my C-fibres seem to be stimulated'. Antipodeans can get T-435 – i.e. they can seem to have their C-fibres stimulated without actually having their C-fibres stimulated – in circumstances where they are tricked into expecting C-fibre stimulation: Rorty's example is that they are strapped to a fake torture machine, the switch is flicked, and they cry out 'my C-fibres seem to be stimulated!', just as a Terran in similar circumstances might cry out 'pain!'

This idea, that Antipodeans can imagine being mistaken about having C-fibre stimulation but cannot imagine being mistaken about seeming to have C-fibre stimulation, is not nearly as simple as it looks. It means that they can imagine seeming to have C-fibre stimulation but not really having C-fibre stimulation, but they cannot imagine seeming to seem to have C-fibre stimulation but not really seeming to have C-fibre stimulation. Even though they cannot imagine it, however, we are also told that there could in actual fact be a situation in which an Antipodean was seeming to seem to have C-fibre stimulation but not really seeming to have C-fibre stimulation. This is because they could seem to have T-435 (i.e. be inclined to say 'I seem to have C-fibre stimulation') without really having T-435. Antipodean brain science, however, has not yet reached the point where it can explain these 'weird illusions', and so nobody knows which brain state goes with only seeming to have T-435. And that is why Antipodeans cannot imagine being wrong about T-435: they do not know which other brain state to imagine.

What Rorty is trying to demonstrate here, is that the idea of a sensation as a phenomenal appearance – as something you cannot in principle be wrong about – is a dispensable fiction. For Antipodeans, how things seem is not a matter of what sensations they have, but rather what they are inclined to say. Like us, the only thing they cannot imagine being wrong about is how things seem to them, but whereas for us this is due to a logical barrier imposed by the nature of consciousness, for them it is due to an empirical barrier imposed by the current state of their science. For us, there is no distinction between pain, seeming pain, seeming seeming pain, etc., and this linguistic fact is supposed to reflect the nature of the phenomenal.

For them, by contrast, adding another 'seems' is just adding another physical state, but without resorting to what Rorty regards as the metaphysical excesses of the phenomenal, they are still able to stop short at 'seeming pain' without progressing to 'seeming to seem' and beyond. Now since Rorty thinks we could never tell whether the Antipodeans have sensations or not, and that we could not even persuade them we ourselves do, he also thinks there is no reason to consider the Terran or the Antipodean language better suited to one species rather than the other. So given that the Antipodeans can say everything we can without embroiling themselves in our unanswerable metaphysical questions, Rorty concludes that the only appearance–reality distinction we need is their non-metaphysical one, 'the distinction between getting things right and getting things wrong' (84), and that the only notion of 'how things seem' we need is their notion of what we are inclined to say.[4]

Rorty's argument is both intricate and intriguing. That something is not quite right, however, becomes apparent when we reflect on the fake torture machine example, and realise that at the end of the experiment, an Antipodean would say they seemed to have C-fibre stimulation (i.e. they did sincerely utter the sentence), whereas a Terran would deny they seemed to feel pain. The Terran expected pain, just as the Antipodean expected C-fibre stimulation, but it never seemed to the Terran that they were in pain (it seemed only that they were going to be in pain), whereas it did seem to the Antipodean that they had C-fibre stimulation (they were inclined to utter 'C-fibre stimulation!') This is a significant difference between how Antipodeans and Terrans talk about seeming. It means that the Antipodeans are certainly not using 'my C-fibres seem to be stimulated' to refer to pain (a suggestion Rorty makes on p. 79), since the Antipodean's C-fibres did seem to be stimulated despite the fact that the machine was a fake. Nevertheless, 'C-fibre stimulation' might still refer to pain, given that at the end of the torture machine experiment, the Antipodean will say 'my C-fibres were not stimulated' just as the Terran will say 'I felt no pain'.

However, whether or not the Antipodeans are using 'C-fibre stimulation' to refer to pain, the fact that they can be more sure about a situation which is neutral between whether or not they are being tortured, than they can about a situation in which they are being tortured, shows that the notion of 'being inclined to say' plays a role in the life of the Antipodean that has no parallel for the Terran. We see this from the fact that after the experiment, the Antipodean is sure about having been inclined to report C-fibre stimulation, but is not so sure about whether or not they were ever tortured. Any certainty a Terran had, however, would concern the torture itself. If the Terran remembered being tortured, they could infer (trivially) their inclination to say 'I am in pain'. If they remembered a hoax, on the other hand, they might not be so sure what their speech inclinations were when the switch was flicked. Nevertheless, it would in either case be the torture they were most sure about.

Not so for an Antipodean. Even in the midst of torture, the Antipodean is more sure about what they are inclined to say: they are more sure about a factor of the situation which leaves open the possibility that the torture is not real (their speech inclination), than they are about the factor of the situation which makes it real (their own C-fibre stimulation, whether or not this is pain). So since the Antipodean attitude to their speech inclinations has no parallel for human beings, we must conclude that Rorty has inadvertently imagined aliens who are so different from human beings that we cannot draw any firm conclusions from them. To meet this objection, Rorty could stipulate that Antipodean brain science breaks down over seeming C-fibre stimulation, rather than over seeming T-435. But apart from the contrivance, it would mean Antipodeans being unable to imagine error concerning their own C-fibre stimulation, though they could imagine error concerning other physical states (including the C-fibres of other Antipodeans). If this were true, however, then their C-fibre stimulation would be same as our pain in all but name. So the argument would fail in any case.

INCORRIGIBILITY AND PRINCIPLE P

(§§2–3)

Rorty must be on the right track about how Terran philosophers would react to the Antipodeans, because John Searle's real-life reaction to the example was that:

> Either they have pains as we do or they do not. If they do, then the fact
> that they refuse to call them pains is of no interest. (. . .) If, on the
> other hand, they really do not have any pains, then they are quite
> different from us and their situation is of no relevance . . .
>
> (Searle 1992: 250)

The problem with Searle's pithy response, however, is that Rorty
gives the Antipodeans their own philosophers saying 'either they
have pains or they do not' about us. So, as Rorty sets things up,
there are actually four options:

Terran Sceptic: the Antipodeans do not have sensations
Terran Other: the Antipodeans have sensations but do not
    know it
Antipodean Materialist: the Terrans do not have sensations
Antipodean Epiphenomenalist: the Terrans have
    epiphenomenal sensations

The second Terran position ('Terran Other') is the only one Rorty
does not name. He formulates it consistently throughout the chapter
in terms of 'not knowing about your own sensations', which has the
effect of making it sound absurd ('how could you feel pain without
knowing about it?') However, if the same position is put in Searle's
way – that the Antipodeans have pains but refuse to call them 'pains'
– then it is the example itself which sounds absurd ('how could they
not have a name for pain?') A more neutral formulation is readily
available, however, which is to describe it as the view that the
Antipodeans are sometimes talking about sensations when they talk
about their brain states.

We can hone down Rorty's discussion by dismissing the Terran
Sceptic and Antipodean Epiphenomenalist positions straight away.
Given that the Antipodeans are physiologically and behaviourally
just like us – they do not have hollow heads, or show indifference to
bodily damage, or anything like that – nobody who met them would
take seriously the Terran Sceptic view that they were unconscious
organic noise-making machines, in radical contrast to conscious
human beings. Likewise, given that the Antipodeans have no tradition of dualism, they are hardly going to take seriously an

Epiphenomenalist view according to which Terran sensations exist, but have no causal influence within the physical world. So the real choice is between the Antipodean Materialist position and a materialist version of the Terran Other position: as Rorty himself puts it, either 'they [the Terrans] think they have feelings but they don't' or 'they [the Antipodeans] have feelings but don't know it' (88).

There is much less to this choice than meets the eye. The Antipodeans think that our terms for sensations are simply 'placeholders' (83), which we only employ because of our ignorance of the brain states we are actually referring to. The Terrans, on the other hand, think that the Antipodeans are referring to sensations when they talk about brain states. Now on a perfectly natural reading, these are both the same view, i.e. they are both the Identity Theory. However, the fact that Rorty makes the Antipodeans deny the existence of sensations must mean that – ironically enough – he is thinking of them as holding the 1965 Rortian view, rather than the genuinely Antipodean view. So the choice is really just between the Identity Theory and Eliminative Materialism, i.e. whether to say that sensations are brain states, or that what Terrans call 'sensations' are brain states.

The real crux of the issue, however, lies in the background of this mock debate, and concerns Rorty's contention that the Antipodeans would not be able to understand the mind–body problem. As Rorty imagines it, the Antipodean reaction to the problem exactly parallels how we might react to superstitious people who believe in demoniacal possession. All we could do with such people would be to explain hallucinatory psychosis, and if they insisted on a residual 'demon-hallucination problem', we would have to put this down to their specific cultural history: we could not expect to understand their problem ourselves. Likewise, according to Rorty, the Antipodeans would feel that though they could explain their brain science to us, they could not really engage with our mind–body problem. Now if this parallel is right, then the difference between Antipodean Eliminative Materialism and Terran Identity Theory is as trivial as the difference between superstitious people coming to accept that demoniacal possession is hallucinatory psychosis, and us insisting that there never was any demoniacal possession. However, if the Antipodeans can indeed understand the problem, then the situation is altogether different: they must either think they know the solution, or else think that Terran philosophy has alerted them to a new issue. Either way, the mind–body problem survives unscathed.

Notwithstanding Rorty's many assertions to the contrary, however, it seems as if it would be easy to explain the mind–body problem to the Antipodeans; we just say to them something like the following:

> Note the difference between cases where you 'just know' that you are having C-fibre stimulation, and cases where you are observing C-fibre stimulation, either your own or somebody else's. What you know in the former case, the having of C-fibre stimulation, is what we call 'pain'. Why do we have a special name for that, given that the having of C-fibre stimulation is just one's own C-fibre stimulation? Because uniquely with brain states, the having of the state is a way of knowing about it; having a hair-cut, for instance, doesn't provide you with any extra way of knowing about the hair-cut itself beyond looking, feeling, being told, etc. It is because there are these two ways of knowing about brain states that we never realised they were the same thing: we were still in the process of naming brain states on the basis of observation. And come to think of it, didn't *your* brain science start like that, requiring you to later 'correlate' (as you so often say) the brain states you knew through observation with the brain states you knew through having had them?

Much the same point – basically that for the Antipodeans to make sense to us, they would have to understand the mind–body problem – was made by Kenneth Gallagher in his 1985 paper 'Rorty's Antipodeans: An Impossible Illustration?' Gallagher pointed out that an Antipodean child first learning to say 'C-fibre stimulation' would obviously not be observing their own brain. Rather, they would be observing their stomach, or knee, etc., just like an Earth child, and would then have to pick up a second meaning of 'C-fibre stimulation' when they learnt some brain science in later years. So since Antipodeans have these two senses of 'C-fibre stimulation' which they learnt to connect up at some point, they could hardly fail to understand our mind–body problem.

Contrary to the title of Gallagher's paper, however, the Antipodeans are not impossible in the sense of 'possible' Rorty is using, for there is presumably no physical obstacle to the universe containing humanoids who say the sorts of things Rorty wants them to. The problem is rather that given their inexplicable inability to understand the mind–body problem, Rorty must have inadvertently imagined aliens who are so different from human beings that we cannot draw any firm conclusions from them; this is the problem we encountered before. And that is always the danger with thought-experiments: you can imagine what you like, but there is no point unless the scenario can be made sense of. We could also, if we wished, imagine a race of aliens who tell us that they often relax by reclining on the sofa and imagining square circles. These aliens are just as possible as Rorty's Antipodeans, and they could just as easily confound all our attempts to make sense of their more puzzling utterances. But we would not learn anything from them either.

We have now seen the two main problems with Rorty's Antipodeans. The first is that Rorty makes the Antipodeans as capable of misidentifying their own brain states as any other physical state, despite the fact that these are the states they report in the circumstances we report our sensations. The second is that he makes the Antipodeans incapable of understanding the mind–body problem, despite the fact that unlike any other physical state, they know their own brain states by having them. Both of these radical disanalogies with the human situation undermine any conclusions we might have initially been inclined to draw from the Antipodeans; there are other problems in addition, but they are less germane to the plot of the chapter.[5]

Moving on now, we soon find the discussion of the Antipodeans taking on a new and more definite structure when Rorty introduces what he calls Principle P. This is the following:

> (P) Whenever we make an incorrigible report on a state of ourselves, there must be a property which we are presented with which induces us to make the report.

> (84)[6]

Of course, this is just another way of putting the ongoing theme that the reason we cannot be wrong about being in pain (e.g.), is that we are acquainted with a special property which we cannot be wrong about, i.e. a phenomenal property. In other words, Principle P formulates what Rorty calls the 'Cartesian account' of privileged access. As Rorty rightly says, this conception of phenomenal properties is the key premise in all the main objections to physicalism within the philosophy of mind; he singles out as prime examples both Saul Kripke's famous argument against the identity theory and what he calls the 'Brandt–Campbell objection'.[7] Rorty's plan now, then, is to undermine (P) by showing that it inevitably leads to one of three distinct dead-ends, in contrast with his own 'anti-Cartesian' alternative to (P).

So what is Rorty's much-promised 'anti-Cartesian' alternative, which allows us to see 'the phenomenal as a matter of how we talk' (32)? Well the reader would look in vain for anything like an explanation in *PMN*. Nevertheless Rorty was more forthcoming in 'Incorrigibility as the Mark of the Mental', and the basic idea is very simple. It is that all there is to privileged access – the idea that we can each of us know our own phenomenal states in a way that nobody else can – is the fact that we talk in such a way as to allow first-person reports of phenomenal states to trump third-person judgements about them. As Rorty put it,

> We have no criteria for setting aside as mistaken first-person contemporaneous reports of thoughts and sensations, whereas we do have criteria for setting aside all reports about everything else.
>
> (Rorty 1970: 413)

This linguistic practice arose because of the predictive advantages of taking people's sincere first-person reports of their phenomenal states for granted. The reason we cannot be wrong about when we are in pain, then, is not that we are acquainted with a special sort of subjective property that you cannot be wrong about (as per Principle P), but rather just because it is a rule of our language that if we sincerely say we are in pain, we automatically count as right: nobody can legitimately argue with us.[8]

Rorty sets up the choice between Principle P and his social practice account as the choice between two different accounts of incorrigibility, but it must be remembered that he has deliberately and consistently been running together incorrigibility, indubitability, and privileged access.[9] As traditionally understood, however, these are three different concepts. Privileged access is the way in which subjective phenomena are known to their subject, indubitability is the property of being beyond doubt, and incorrigibility is the property of immunity to being set right. Thus incorrigibility, unlike privileged access and indubitability, is applicable only to reports of phenomenal states: I may have privileged access to my headache and not be able to doubt it, but it is my report of having a headache and not the headache itself that cannot be set right by a third party. Thus by putting the focus on incorrigibility, Rorty's linguistic account obviously gets an unfair boost. Nevertheless, the choice is clear enough: on the one hand there is Rorty saying that the social practice of treating some reports as incorrigible explains our beliefs about privileged access and indubitably known phenomenal properties, and on the other hand there is the defender of Principle P saying that we have privileged access to indubitably known phenomenal properties, and are thus able to make incorrigible reports about them.

Next (91–96) Rorty sets out the three options available to the defender of Principle P, which are Behaviourism, Scepticism about Other Minds, and Materialism. Unfortunately, this section of the text is both unnecessarily complicated and riddled with off-putting expositionary inconsistencies: there is no need to struggle with it once the following few points have been registered.[10]

What Rorty means when he says that 'a species of behaviourism is entailed' by Principle P (94), is that if we accept that behaving in a certain way – i.e. making incorrigible reports – is sufficient for having sensations, then the Antipodeans must have sensations. Thus (P) rules out scepticism about the Antipodeans having sensations so long as we accept that when they talk about how things seem to them, they are in fact making incorrigible reports (in the sense intended by (P)). None of Rorty's three options ultimately involve accepting this, however. Behaviourism denies that there are any incorrigible reports or sensations at all. Scepticism about Other Minds is based on scepticism about whether the Antipodeans make incorrigible reports, though it presupposes that we Terrans do. And Materialism denies that first-person reports about how things seem are incorrigible reports about sensations, adopting instead the Anti-podean conception of seeming as being inclined to say.

So the options are:

1   *Behaviourism.* The Behaviourist accepts (P), but denies that reports of how things seem are incorrigible reports.
2   *Scepticism about Other Minds.* The Sceptic accepts (P), but thinks there is no way to determine whether the Antipodeans mean anything by the noises they make, thus concluding there is no way to know whether they have sensations.
3   *Materialism.* The Materialist accepts (P), denies that reports of how things seem are logically incorrigible reports of sensations, and holds instead that they are empirically incorrigible reports of physical states (see below for this distinction).

THE THREE OPTIONS

(§§4–6)

In discussing each of these three options, Rorty first tells us what he likes about it, and then tells us where it goes wrong. In each case, the option fails because it has been proposed against the backdrop of the imagery and conceptual paraphernalia of the Mirror of Nature, and the moral to be drawn is always the same: you cannot take on the Mirror of Nature problematic and win.

What Rorty thinks is good about the first option – behaviourism – is that it makes behaviour the only criterion for the attribution of mental states, and hence undermines traditional epistemological concerns about knowing other minds. For the behaviourist, there is no sensible question to be raised about whether an Antipodean who steps on a nail and screams is actually feeling anything, since exhib-iting pain-behaviour is all there is to feeling pain. Consequently, the problem of understanding the connection between knowing behav-iour and knowing mental states is cut off at its source. Now Rorty is of course right that in any normal circumstances it would be ridicu-lous to seriously entertain sceptical questions about other minds; confronted with the appropriate behaviour, such artificial doubts would fade away. Nevertheless, this only shows that behaviour is the only factor we need consider when ascribing mental states in normal circumstances, not that it is the only factor *simpliciter*, which is the stronger claim of the behaviourist. If we knew – for instance – that the Antipodeans had hollow heads, or were being radio-operated, or had been pre-programmed, then the situation would be quite different. So since it seems that physical constitution, environment, and history could also be relevant to the ascription of mental states, Rorty's view that an exclusive reliance on behaviour is to the credit of behaviourism is a questionable one.

The main thing Rorty dislikes about behaviourism is its claim to provide an analysis of the meaning of discourse about mental states, i.e. that all we really mean by 'pain' is a certain type of behaviour. As we shall see in Chapter 6, Rorty does not think there are any facts of the matter about meaning to be uncovered by the sort of painstaking philosophical analysis which Ryle specialised in. Rorty's more specific criticism, however, is not far removed from the standard criticism of behaviourism, namely that it denies the subjective reality of sensations. As Rorty sees it, Ryle was forced into 'paradoxically and fruitlessly' (101) trying to deny that we have privileged access to sensations, because he thought that in order to stop the sceptic inserting a wedge between behaviour and sensations, it was necessary to deny the existence of sensations altogether. Ryle thought this because he took Principle P for granted, and was thereby led to assume that his anti-sceptical claim that behaviour is our only criterion for sensation ascription, would still leave dualism as a live option. So since Ryle assumed that incorrigible reports about inner states must result from acquaintance with phenomenal properties, and because he also assumed that phenomenal properties were inseparable from dualism (Place's physicalist alternative was not yet extant), Ryle ended up arguing in vain that we do not make incorrigible reports at all, thereby sealing behaviourism's reputation as an implausible theory.[11]

According to Rorty, the anti-sceptical force of behaviourism can be preserved without denying the existence of sensations, by adopting his social practice account of incorrigibility. With such an account, we could agree that people have privileged access, but take this as nothing more than a reflection of the usefulness of the social practice of taking people's word for it when they report their own sensations. Such reports are empirically incorrigible but not logically incorrigible. That is, they are incorrigible in the sense that the best empirical evidence you can get for thinking that somebody has a headache, for example, is that the person in question has told you that they have a headache. This does not mean that the report is logically incorrigible, however, i.e. that it could never in principle be overridden. This is indeed how Principle P portrays the situation, for if phenomenal properties are subjective appearances, there is no possible way in which anybody could know those properties better than the subject his or herself. But with Rorty's social practice account, by contrast, there is no logical incorrigibility, only empirical incorrigibility, since though it may be current practice to take a person's word for it about their sensations, this could all change in the future; 'cerebroscopes' (brain-reading devices) might reach Antipodean levels of sophistication and go into mass-production, for instance.

Rorty finds just this sort of view, one which avoids the pitfalls of both the implausibility of behaviourism and the sceptical potential of dualism, in an interpretation of Wittgenstein by Alan Donagan (103–4). According to Donagan's Wittgenstein, sensations are private, inseparable accompaniments of behaviour, but they are not states or processes in their own right. This position provides a necessary connection between behaviour and sensations to rule out scepticism, but does not thereby raise the spectre of dualism, since if sensations are not states or processes, they cannot be non-physical states or processes (or physical ones, for that matter). So what are they, then? Wittgenstein's view on this matter was rather arcane – he said that a sensation 'is not a *something*, but not a *nothing* either!' (Wittgenstein 1953: §304) – and Rorty is rather dismissive of it. Rorty's own view, by contrast, is straightforward enough, but his first concern is with the metaphilosophy behind the scenes.

Rorty thinks that questions about sensations only seem important because of two principles integral to the Mirror of Nature problematic. The first is the epistemological principle that some things are 'naturally knowable directly and others not' (105). This principle has divided philosophers into two opposing camps, those who think mental states are known directly (e.g. dualists), and those who think physical objects are known directly (e.g. behaviourists). The second principle is the metaphysical 'Platonic Principle': that what is most knowable is most real. Due to the influence of this second principle, philosophers who think the mental is known directly have devised metaphysical systems based on mind, and philosophers who think the physical is known directly have devised metaphysical systems based on matter. In this way, then, the Mirror of Nature has subserved the classic stand-off between idealism and materialism, and it is against this backdrop that an understanding of sensations and other mental states has seemed to hold the key to determining the fundamental building blocks of reality.

In Rorty's opinion, however, the choice between whether mind or matter is more directly known and hence more real, has less to do with argument than temperament. The real divide, he thinks, is between two sorts of people, those who become philosophers to defend the uniqueness of existence against what they see as the levelling-down effects of intersubjective agreement, and those who become philosophers to defend the rationality of science against what they see as the empty gesturing of mysticism. The Mirror of Nature itself, Rorty thinks, is entirely indifferent to this divide, but it nevertheless provides both sides with an endless source of arguments to facilitate their interminable debates.

Rorty now turns to the second option – scepticism about other minds – the central commitment of which is that sensations have their own independent reality distinct from the behaviour that typically accompanies them. This is a misleading name for a position which somebody could easily hold without being a sceptic at all, but Rorty is simply making the point that it paves the way to sceptical problems. So what does Rorty like about this option? Surprisingly enough, he likes the sceptic's commitment to sensations as private entities, to the mind as a Glassy Essence, and to knowledge as a Mirror of Nature (107). How can Rorty – of all people – possibly approve of any of this?

The reason is that he does not believe in the Platonic Principle, or in any other way of ranking ontological status, since he does not believe in objective truth. Consequently, since he denies that there are any 'ontological facts' for philosophers to respect with their 'ontological commitments', Rorty has no qualms about saying that, 'raw feels are as good particulars as tables or archangels or electrons

– as good inhabitants of the world, as good candidates for ontological status' (107). Archangels are on a par with tables for Rorty, simply because they are both things we talk about. There are conventions for talking about archangels and conventions for talking about electrons, but electrons do not force us to talk about them any more or less than archangels do: there is no significant distinction between things we discover and things we make up within Rorty's pragmatism. What we talk about – what we grant ontological status – is just a matter of what it is useful for us to talk about. Hence he also has no qualms about saying that, 'The seventeenth century did not "misunderstand" the Mirror of Nature or the Inner Eye any more than Aristotle misunderstood motion or Newton gravity. They hardly *could* misunderstand it, since they invented it' (113). This ultra-relaxed attitude to ontology provides Rorty with his straightforward answer to the question of what sensations are: they are things like anything else.

What Rorty likes about the sceptic's position, then, is that it does not try to alter or adjust the seventeenth-century conception of mind, but simply accepts it undiluted; trying to improve on it would presuppose that minds existed before theories of minds. What he dislikes about scepticism, however, is that it accepts the epistemological principle that knowledge must have a foundation in what is most directly known, thereby transforming the social practice of talking about minds and sensations into a set of problems which subsequently seemed to require solutions. Thus, instead of being content to just tell the traditional and socially useful story according to which each of us knows our own mind best, the sceptic tries to base all knowledge on self-knowledge. Once this move is made, however, sceptical problems about other minds become inevitable, since we obviously cannot have self-knowledge of others. Subjective certainties suddenly seem to be the solitary thread connecting us to what we have now come to think of as an 'external' world, and we are led to believe that, 'everything . . . which is not a fragment of our own Inner Mirror – a part of our own Glassy Essence – is just a "posit", "an inference", "a construction", or something equally dubious which requires metaphysical system-building . . . for its defense' (112). Thus once we decide that the Mirror of Nature is what is most knowable and try to base all other knowledge on this, philosophy as it has been traditionally practised emerges as an inevitable and valuable pursuit.

In Rorty's view, however, the attempts of philosophers to secure the reality of knowledge against the threat of scepticism have been as futile as the doubts which initiated them, since we can doubt whatever we like and there is no way to prove otherwise. Without Cartesian epistemology such doubts would never have seemed particularly interesting, but the combination was a potent one: the idea of the solitary subject trapped behind a veil of ideas managed to inspire both a new literary genre and a cultural tradition of professional activities. People had found something new and apparently important to do. On Rorty's view, then, modern philosophy did not originate in response to the sceptical difficulties inherent within our ordinary or scientific world-views, but originated rather in the creation of those difficulties. As he puts it, 'Skepticism and the principal genre of modern philosophy have a symbiotic relationship. They live one another's death, and die one another's life' (114). In other words, scepticism is not the bane of philosophy, but rather its life-blood, in the same way in which the evil villain in a play is not a problem for the play, but rather an essential part of proceedings.

This whole drama could have been undercut, according to Rorty, through the realisation that just as there is no reason to think anything is more real than anything else, so there is no reason to think anything is more knowable than anything else. The latter conviction results from overdramatising the simple fact that we are more familiar with some things than others. If we are very familiar with something, then we can learn to report it non-inferentially, i.e. without going through any conscious inferences. It does not follow from this, however, that what is being reported is somehow especially suited to being known. When we see this, Rorty thinks, we should also see that there is nothing suspect about the privacy of sensation; privacy is just a trivial consequence of sensations being entities which we take each other's word about. Only when privacy is combined with the assumption that some things are more knowable than others does it start to seem problematic.

Once the epistemological principle is firmly in place, however, then if the public, intersubjective world is taken to be the foundation of other sorts of knowledge, knowledge of private sensations will seem problematic (as it does to the behaviourist), and if the private contents of the mind are taken to be the foundation of other sorts of knowledge, then knowledge of the public world will seem problematic (as it does to the sceptic). Nevertheless, so long as the epistemological principle is rejected, Rorty has no problem with privacy whatsoever, and that is why he makes the Antipodean's criticism of our belief in the existence of private entities so muted. The Antipodeans just regard our sensations as a little over the top, a little '*de trop*' (112), on account of the fact that they themselves never saw any reason to back up their incorrigible reports with special entities.

The third option – materialism – is to deny the existence of non-physical sensations. What Rorty likes about this option is the eliminative materialist's claim that there is no principled reason we should not one day talk only of neural states, just as Antipodeans do. What he dislikes is the metaphysics of materialism: its attempt to say what the mind really is. This leads the identity theorist to argue that the nature of mind has been misunderstood, and that it actually presents no challenge to materialism. Of course, Rorty does not think the mind has been misunderstood at all; its challenge to materialism is just a straightforward consequence of the particular mental–physical distinction which was invented in the seventeenth century. Consequently, he thinks topic-neutral analysis was bound to fail. His specific criticism of this approach, however, is that it fails to maintain the contrast between mental and physical, and hence fails to explain why there was ever thought to be a mind–body problem in the first place. In order to capture the full import of reports of mental states, the analyses would have to specify that it is the phenomenal rather than the physical 'something going on' which is intended, thereby undermining the whole exercise. The materialist might try splitting the concept of mind into a part which can be captured by topic-neutral analysis and a part which cannot, but this would just be another way of 'gerrymandering' (116).[12]

Rorty next sets about distancing himself from the 'cheap version of the identity of minds and brains' (118) he once proposed, namely eliminative materialism. He now thinks it is blighted by a similar problem to the identity theory: just as the topic-neutral approach cannot show that we never really meant anything compromising to materialism, so the eliminative approach cannot show that we never really referred to anything compromising to materialism. The reason is that by claiming that what people called 'sensations' are identical with brain states, the eliminativist invites the objection that since the word 'sensations' refers to sensations, and sensations do not exist, then people cannot have been referring to anything at all. To respond to this, the eliminativist would have to claim that a term for a mental (and hence non-physical) state can be used to refer to a physical state. Whether or not this is the case, however, is a question Rorty does not think can be resolved, since just as he does not think there are any facts about meaning to underwrite or debunk behaviourist and topic-neutral analyses, he similarly does not think there are any facts about reference to underwrite or debunk eliminative materialism. As a consequence of this, he no longer wants to say that since (logical) incorrigibility is the 'mark of the mental', and we could stop making incorrigible reports if we knew enough neuroscience, then the mind could one day cease to exist. Rather, he will now say only that logical incorrigibility is 'all that is at issue' (121) between Terrans and Antipodeans, and that our logical incorrigibility could fade into their empirical incorrigibility if we learnt enough neuroscience.

Rorty's stronger, metaphilosophical motivation for rejecting eliminative materialism is that he thinks of it as a response to the mind–body problem, and he does not want to get caught on the treadmill of the Mirror of Nature problematic, thereby perpetuating a jaded literary genre. The position he now wants to adopt is a 'materialism without mind–body identity', a non-metaphysical materialism which is not a position on the mind–body problem. Commentators have been surprisingly unruffled by this suggestion, apparently seeing no problem with Rorty's view that 'the materialist should stop . . . saying metaphysical things' (120) and 'realize how innocuous and how unphilosophical "materialism" really is' (Bernstein 1980: 755), thereby rejecting 'the sort of philosophical materialism that has been fashioned in opposition to Cartesian dualism' (Hornsby 1990: 41). Nevertheless, it is not at all clear what a non-metaphysical, non-philosophical materialism is supposed to be. Materialism is only ever talked about in philosophy, after all, and so long as the claim is that everything is physical *in some sense* (otherwise why call it 'materialism'?), it is hard to see how it could be entirely lacking in metaphysical import. So what does 'materialism' mean to someone who rejects ontology and objective truth?

Rorty hinted at an answer early in *PMN* when he said, 'Physicalism . . . is probably true (but uninteresting) if construed as predicting every event in every space-time region under some description or other, but obviously false if construed as the claim to say everything true' (28). However, it is only towards the end of the book that the shallowness of Rorty's commitment really emerges. What he says is that 'physics gives us a good background against which to tell our stories of historical change', and that although physical science provides no 'deep insight into the nature of reality', it has nevertheless provided the West with a useful 'genre of world-story', one which has proved malleable enough to survive all the changes in our understanding since the time of the Greeks (345). All he thinks, then, is that the presupposition that science can predict everything in space and time 'under some description or other' will continue to be useful. In particular, Rorty thinks that so long as physicalism is not problematised by the Mirror of Nature, and remains little more than scientific optimism, then it should prove useful for his own metaphilosophical purposes by dampening down interest in philosophical problems like the mind–body problem. The more we rely on science as 'the measure of all things' (124; Sellars 1997: 83), as Wilfrid Sellars put it, the less we should be tempted by a traditional philosophical standpoint which purports to pass judgement on science.

Rorty's physicalism, then, amounts to an historical acknowledgement of the crucial part science has played in our understanding of the world, combined with the tactical, metaphilosophically driven suggestion that scientific descriptions should continue to be privileged, in the hope that this closes off socially useless philosophical disputes. In later years, Rorty has renounced even this position as the 'overly fervent physicalism' (Rorty 1998: 47) of *PMN*, but it must surely have been the mildest, least fervent physicalism ever proposed.

Now the key to being a physicalist without thereby taking a stance on the Mirror of Nature problematic, according to Rorty, is not to think of the physical as having 'triumphed' over the mental (122). This is because the debate was driven by a clash of personalities rather than the unanswerable issues on the surface, and so all that could ever really count as a 'triumph of the physical' would be for the public rationality valued by the one type of philosopher to suppress the individuality valued by the other. But Rorty thinks there was never any threat of this anyway:

> The secret in the poet's heart remains unknown to the secret police, despite their ability to predict his every thought ... Our inviolable uniqueness lies in our poetic ability to say unique and obscure things, not in our ability to say obvious things to ourselves alone.
>
> (123)

Consequently, since physicalism and dualism were always irrelevant to the issues that motivated their advocates, Rorty thinks that we would all be well advised to ignore the mind–body problem and get on with something else.

CONCLUSION TO PART ONE

(§7)

There were three main parts to Rorty's treatment of the mind–body problem. First there was the fast dissolution, then the historical deconstruction, and then the thought experiment of the Antipodeans. Whilst discussing the three unsatisfactory conclusions that could be drawn from the Antipodeans, the final component of the fast dissolution was put into place, and Rorty is now prepared to claim – or at least strongly imply – that he has 'dissolved' the problem of consciousness (127). The final position which has emerged can be summarised as follows:

> The fast dissolution showed that the ontological divide between mental and physical turns on an epistemic conception of phenomenal properties as appearances. This is the conception of phenomenal properties enshrined by Principle P. To dissolve the problem, then, we must reject Principle P: our ability to make incorrigible reports is not based on the special nature of phenomenal properties, but is rather just a social practice. Once we make this move the whole idea of ontological status

is undermined, along with both the materialist's question of how the mind fits into the physical world, and the idealist's parallel question of how the physical world is constructed by the mind. Of course, people will continue to talk about minds – this is an unfortunate cultural inheritance we can do nothing about – and in doing so they will be talking about something ontologically incompatible with the physical. Nevertheless, now that we have seen through the mental–physical distinction, this will not concern us: we will refuse to comment on ontological issues. Moreover, now we see that privileged access is just a consequence of talking about private entities, we will no longer think the privacy of mind creates sceptical problems. This is because the mind is not the epistemically special basis of other sorts of knowledge, and so given that the social practice of ascribing mental states is based on behaviour rather than private acquaintance, behaviour is 'quite enough evidence' (102) for the ascription of mental states. Finally, we should pay science a compliment by endorsing a minimal sort of physicalism, since there is no reason people should not eventually just talk about physical states (though this will probably never happen), and widespread acceptance of physicalism would help to suppress interest in philosophy.

Now think back to the example of the woman walking past with which we began Chapter 2 above. Has Rorty explained why her subjective experience did not seem to fit into the objective street scene?

If we reject the assumption that the objective street scene is all that really exists, then we will not think that the woman's mind needs to be fitted into that scene, but it nevertheless still seems reasonable to ask how they are connected. Rorty would say that they are both just things we talk about, and that the only reason this particular connection strikes us as problematic is that we have intuitions based on the idea of an ontological divide. For this response to be plausible, however, it needs to be backed up by the claim that the mind is an invention of the seventeenth century, otherwise the idea of an ontological divide might just as easily be a response – an unfortunate one, perhaps – to the disjointed ways of talking which people with subjective access to some states of the world would inevitably develop. So the question to ask is: would the ancient Greeks really not have not been able to understand Descartes's *Meditations*? I find it very hard to believe that they would not, especially when reading their literature, looking at their art and architecture, etc. Moreover, even with the complete *carte blanche* of science-fiction, it does seem that Rorty has proved unable to imagine people who are just like us except for their lack of a mind–body problem. Maybe this just goes to show that you cannot 'escape from history'; maybe it just shows that Rorty is wrong about the mind.

5

THE ORIGINS OF PHILOSOPHY

(*PMN*, CHAPTER 3)

LOCKE'S MISTAKE

(§§1–2)

In Part Two, Rorty turns from mind to knowledge: from the Mirror of Nature itself to the mirroring it is supposed to be capable of. This is the part of the book where Rorty makes his main case against philosophy, a case for which Part One paved the way, and of which Part Three will draw out the ramifications. It divides into four chapters. In Chapter 3, Rorty argues that Descartes's invention of the mind, supplemented by two fundamental confusions – due to Locke and Kant respectively – paved the way to the invention of a new academic subject called 'philosophy'. In Chapter 4, Rorty argues that crucial developments within twentieth-century philosophy – due to Quine and Sellars – have completely undermined the viability of that subject. And in Chapters 5 and 6, Rorty argues that attempts to revive the fortunes of philosophy – either as philosophy of psychology or as philosophy of language – are ill-advised and hence should be discontinued.

Philosophy is supposed to be one of the oldest academic disciplines, possessing its own distinctive subject-matter which has been theorised about almost continually for 2,500 years. This is the standard view of the matter, the one 'built into the structure of academic institutions, and into the pat, unreflective self-descriptions of philosophy professors' (132). It is also a view which has been rigorously defended, receiving perhaps its definitive statement in Bertrand Russell's *History of Western Philosophy*.[1] Rorty, however, thinks that it is completely wrong: philosophy is actually no older than epistemology, and epistemology was an invention of the seventeenth century. According to the standard view, philosophy took an 'epistemological turn' in the seventeenth century, with knowledge becoming the pivotal issue of modern philosophy, rather than the tangential concern it had been within medieval and ancient philosophy. According to Rorty, however, this was not a change of emphasis but rather a new beginning; it was not 'to make epistemology the foundation of philosophy so much as to invent something new – epistemology – to bear the name "philosophy"' (262–63). The idea of philosophy as an independent subject studied continuously since antiquity is a post-Kantian concoction of the nineteenth century, developed by projecting Kant's concerns back in time. This is not to deny that there have been 'philosophers' throughout history, of course, but this is only because prior to its Kantian appropriation, the word 'philosophy' was general enough to incorporate serious learning of all types, an archaic usage which is still preserved in the multidisciplinary qualification 'Doctor of Philosophy' (PhD). So according to Rorty, then, philosophy is not particularly old after all: even the idea that it is old is not old.

As Rorty sees it, Kant made the crucial move in establishing philosophy as a specialism by isolating a core epistemological problematic in the work of key thinkers of the seventeenth and eighteenth century, and then presenting his Copernican Revolution as the culmination of a tradition. This provided a neat way of systematising an intricate, transitional period of intellectual history, despite the fact that the figures who thereby came to be credited as the originators of modern philosophy would not have recognised themselves in this role: they would have seen their work as contributing to science in its struggle for independence from religion, rather than as contributing to a third thing – philosophy – capable of passing judgement on religion, science, or anything else. Once science had effectively won this struggle, however, and the secularisation of intellectual life was unstoppable, then the epistemological theorising which Descartes and Locke had originated no longer served any clear purpose. At this point, it might easily have faded away had not Kant stepped in to transform it into a new autonomous subject, thereby clearly demarcating philosophy from science for the first time. By drawing on the representationalism inherent in Descartes's new conception of mind, Kant was able to fix the subject-matter of philosophy, professionalise it, and provide it with a history. Without Kant, 'Greek thought and seventeenth-century thought might have seemed as distinct both from each other and from our present concerns as, say, Hindu theology and Mayan numerology' (149). After Kant, however, aspiring philosophers had both a tradition to join and a highly technical *Fach* (speciality) to build a professional way of life around, and it was not long before the subject was filled with 'bald-headed PhD's, boring each other at seminars' (136), as William James put it to Rorty's evident approval.

So epistemology was invented in the seventeenth century, turned into a subject called 'philosophy' in the eighteenth, and projected back in time in the nineteenth. These are bold and revisionary claims, but it is hard to avoid the impression that Rorty is exaggerating. For a start, there was never any question of the Hindu theology/Mayan numerology analogy being apposite, since the intellectual life of the seventeenth century was directly influenced by the Greeks, just as its architecture, art, drama and literature was. And the influence was equally overt: though thinkers of this period did not describe themselves as 'Rationalists' or 'Empiricists' – these categorisations were indeed post-Kantian – they did describe themselves as 'Aristotelians' and 'Platonists', and they made frequent references to these and other ancient as well as medieval thinkers (see Woolhouse 1988: introduction). In fact, many key proposals of this period were explicitly set up as revivals, modifications or rejections of much older doctrines, and so the fact that we naturally read ancient texts like *Theaetetus* and *De Anima* as dealing with familiar post-seventeenth-century issues cannot be entirely due to projection.[2] Moreover, it is misleading to say that epistemology was invented in the seventeenth century, since the ancient world had theories of knowledge, its own tradition of scepticism – Pyrrhonian scepticism, named after Pyrrho of Elis (*ca.* 360–270 BC) – and even, as Michael Williams has pointed out, the notion of epistemology as a starting point of inquiry, analogous to Descartes's 'first philosophy' (Williams 2000: 201–7). The writings of Pyrrhonian sceptic Sextus Empiricus, who argued that we can never be certain of anything, may even have directly provoked Descartes's theory that mind is the source of certainty (ibid.: 202–3).[3]

This is not to deny that modern epistemology marked a departure from what had come before – as Williams also points out, the ancients had no notion of epistemology determining metaphysics, rather than simply preceding it – and neither is it to deny that the grand narrative Kant suggested in the *Critique of Pure Reason* was the decisive event in determining subsequent conceptions of philosophy. Nevertheless, this is all compatible with the considerably less dramatic claim that Kant spotted a continuity of concerns in intellectual history which had not been usurped by the New Science, and reconceived them as the subject-matter of an independent discipline.

Be that as it may, Rorty's leading idea remains the same: that philosophy was only able to carve itself out an autonomous niche in the age of modern science by drawing on the idea of a theory of knowledge, and that this idea only suggested itself because of the prevalent representationalism which the Mirror of Nature metaphor had inspired. Now for an historicist like Rorty, the very idea of a theory of knowledge is patently absurd, for the simple reason that the parameters of knowledge vary over time and between fields of inquiry. We might be able to profitably theorise about knowledge of biology in Europe in the eighteenth century, perhaps, but the idea of a theory of knowledge applicable to all human beings forever is simply beyond the pale. Nevertheless, philosophers were able to take this idea very seriously indeed, he thinks, because they were captivated by the image of the mind as a self-contained and private repository of representations which sometimes succeeded and sometimes failed to reflect the state of the outside world. This made it seem as if there must be rules of representation which our minds follow, and that these could be worked out. Moreover, the new sceptical challenges representationalism had spawned made the task seem important; responding to scepticism could never again be the 'languid academic exercise of composing a reply to Sextus Empiricus' (223) once the dramatic imagery of imprisonment behind a veil of ideas had caught on. And so because of the availability of a subject-matter safely isolated from the rest of the world, thus avoiding any potential for conflict with science, it was not long before the pointless and quibbling Scholasticism which modern science should have ended for good began to re-emerge in a new form.

The Mirror of Nature may have suggested this new pursuit, but for theory of knowledge to become a systematic and professional endeavour required two original confusions, the first and most 'basic' (161) of which Rorty attributes to Locke. The confusion, as Rorty sees it, was essentially a mix-up between causal explanation and justification. Locke thought that by providing a mechanistic account of the way in which ideas are built up from the raw materials provided by sensation, he would thereby be able to show which of our claims to knowledge were justified and which were not. So for instance, if I claim to know that the chair is white, then Locke assumes that in order to justify this claim, reference must ultimately be made to a sensation of white, given the empiricist assumption that all knowledge derives from experience. However – and this is the basis of Rorty's criticism – it is one thing to say that the sensation of white has a part to play within a causal explanation of how I came to know that the chair is white, and quite another to say that the sensation of white is what justifies my claim, and thus is what makes it count as an instance of knowledge. After all, I would not have come to know about the colour of the chair without oxygen to breathe, and so oxygen is also a relevant factor in causally explaining this particular instance of knowledge, though oxygen obviously does not justify my claim in any way whatsoever. Consequently, we should not assume that just because a conscious experience is a part of the causal explanation of a knowledge claim, that it must therefore contribute to the justification of that claim.

Rorty credits this criticism to T.H. Green, one of the originators of British Idealism, who spearheaded this movement in the nineteenth century with his influential Kantian criticisms of empiricism. As Green saw it, Lockean sensations were entirely unsuited to playing the justificatory roles required of them by empiricism, since they were 'dumb', that is, not cognitively structured in any way (Green 1874: 16; see also Blackburn 2005: 142). Sensations could contribute to the justification of beliefs only once they had been thought about, and hence related to innumerable other things which are thought about. Lockean sensations, however, were supposed to exist prior to thought – they were supposed to be the building blocks of thought – and this requirement rendered them, 'fleeting, momentary, unnameable (because while we name it, it has become another) and for the same reason unknowable, the very negation of knowability' (ibid.: 16).

So, for example, a white chair might cause certain sensations within us, but unless we recognise this as *the having of sensations of a white chair* – unless we think about what is happening in a certain way, and thereby relate it to all sorts of other things – then this would be 'less even than a dream', as Kant put it (Kant 1933: A112), with no prospect whatsoever of justifying the belief that the chair is white. According to Green, then, the empiricist project of building up thoughts from sensations is fundamentally misconceived, since human experience begins in thought.

Locke went wrong, Rorty thinks, because he was encouraged by the Mirror of Nature metaphor to think of knowledge as a confrontation with an object (as 'knowledge of' an object), instead of as a cognitive relation to a proposition (as 'knowledge that' such and such is the case). The former fits the imagery of bringing a mirror face to face with an object to reflect it, but the latter does not: how, for instance, do you come face to face with a proposition about philosophy (as opposed to sound-waves or ink)? Locke showed his adherence to the former model by comparing the mind to 'white Paper, void of all Characters' (Locke 1979: II.1.§2), the thought being that the mind starts out as a blank slate or '*tabula rasa*' (143) and is subsequently 'imprinted' by experience. However according to Rorty, Green, and ultimately Kant, it is not the mind's causal relations which are relevant to knowledge, but rather its cognitive relations: it is one thing for the world to have an effect on us, and another for us to recognise that effect and make something of it. Locke collapsed this distinction by treating imprinting as tantamount to understanding, because the Cartesian conception of mind he had inherited made him think it was, 'near a Contradiction, to say, that there are Truths imprinted on the Soul, which it perceives or understands not' (ibid.: I.2.§5). Nevertheless, even if sensory experiences are automatically understood, so that the causal impact of a white object on our eyes is automatically grasped as a sensation of white, for example, the fact remains that as far as knowledge is concerned 'the imprinting is of less interest than the observation of the imprint' (143). And once this concession is made, Locke's project is immediately undermined: all the epistemologically relevant action happens at the level of an observer one step removed from the mechanistic receiving and combining of ideas which Locke sought to describe.

KANT'S MISTAKE

(§§3–4)

Kant clearly saw this shortcoming in Lockean empiricism, and sought to rectify it with a model of experience essentially involving both passive receptivity and active thought. Locke himself had recognised the need for the mind to play an active role in combining and comparing ideas, but given his entirely sensory conception of ideas, there was no way to introduce the logical structure required for thought. We may, for example, be able to receive ideas of orange, black, a purring sound, etc., and we may also be able to group these ideas together, but it is entirely unclear how we are supposed to get from a group of sensory ideas to a predicative judgement such as 'the cat is on the mat'; in Rorty's terms, there is no way to get from 'knowledge of' sensations to 'knowledge that' a proposition holds true. Now as Kant sees it, this problem arises because empiricism overlooks a level of mental activity which must take place prior to the empirical ordering of ideas which Locke described. There must be such a level, Kant thought, because some concepts are presupposed for experience: they are the *a priori* conceptual conditions which allow us to recognise an object *as* an object, or even an idea *as* an idea. One such concept of vital importance to Kant's system is that of unity, for even to experience so much as a purr, we must recognise it as a unified purr. Consequently, as Kant sees it, the empiricist project of building up concepts from sensory ideas was doomed right from the start, since the ideas it starts with must already been conceptualised, given that we have empirical awareness of them.

Kant's own account of cognition involves two irreducibly different sorts of representation, intuitions and concepts (see Chapter 2 above). Passively received intuitions are particular-representations relating to single objects, and actively applied concepts are universal-representations relating to any number of objects. These two sorts of representation are brought together in an act of unification which Kant called 'synthesis', and it is the act of synthesising intuitions and concepts into a unity which constitutes a judgement. Thus, for example, a predicative judgement such as 'the cat is on the mat' involves synthesising intuitions of the cat and the mat with the concept 'is on'. Our ability to make an empirical judgement such as this, however, presupposes a prior level of synthesis in which the raw impact of the environment upon us – what Kant calls the 'manifold' – is first organised into space and time, and then organised into distinct unities through the application of the most basic concepts of all, those pertaining to objects in general. Since this original synthesising must take place prior to all experience, including experience of our own selves, Kant attributed it to the transcendental ego, by which he meant something which could not in principle be experienced, but which was nevertheless presupposed by the unity of experience, i.e. by the fact that synthesis unites representations within one consciousness. So for Kant, then, conscious experience is not in the least 'dumb', but rather permeated through and through with logical structure that has been built in *a priori,* and it is this structure which makes it capable of justifying our claims to knowledge.

Rorty's main objection to Kant's account could hardly be much simpler or more typically Rortian, and he wryly sums it up as follows:

> For a person to form a predicative judgement is for him to come to believe a sentence to be true. For a Kantian transcendental ego to come to believe a sentence to be true is for it to relate representations (*Vorstellungen*) to one another.

(148)

In other words, there is no point in saying anything more about predicative judgements than that we come to believe sentences to be true, and hence no point in embarking on the Kantian project of trying to explain them in terms of representations and transcendental egos. There seems to be a point only because of the Mirror of Nature idea, which makes us think of judgements as expressions of inner representations, and hence as something we must analyse in order to demarcate the scope of human knowledge and defeat scepticism. It is only against this backdrop that the Kantian idea of a synthesis of representations makes sense. For Rorty, however, predication occurs not through some mysterious transcendental activity, but rather through the humdrum activity of 'emitting sentences' (152), some of which we come to believe are true, i.e. some of which change our behaviour. Once representationalism is abandoned, then, Rorty thinks there is no longer any problem for the Kantian account of synthesis to address, that is, no problem of explaining how knowledge is possible; to the extent that there is any genuine problem in the vicinity whatsoever, it is the engineering problem of how to build sentence-emitters like us. So the 'confusion of predication with synthesis' which Rorty attributes to Kant is really just the mistake of trying to provide any representational account of predication at all.

As Rorty sees it, then, Kant only made it 'half way' (161) to a propositional conception of knowledge, because he was still operating within the framework of the Mirror of Nature: he realised that knowledge must be understood as a relation to something with the logical structure of a proposition, but he thought of a proposition as something which needed to be built up by the mind imposing a structure upon an unstructured manifold. Thus Kant is also guilty of confusing causal explanation with justification, albeit in a more sophisticated way than Locke, since although he does not think that the causal impact of the world justifies our beliefs directly, he does think that the world can justify our beliefs only on the assumption that it has been shaped and synthesised by the mind, and as Rorty points out, shaping and synthesising are 'causal metaphors' (161).

So according to Rorty, the whole Kantian story about receiving and shaping the manifold was ultimately just another causal account of how the mind reflects nature, though it was an account which was to play the definitive role in setting philosophy up as a separate subject.[4] It did this in two ways. First, it provided philosophy with a unifying theme: the distinction between universals and particulars. This distinction was central to Greek and Medieval thought, and so by reinventing it as the distinction between concepts and intuitions, and then polemically characterising his immediate predecessors as either Rationalists trying to make do with concepts alone, or else Empiricists trying to make do with intuitions alone, Kant supplied his 'new subject' with a history. Second, Kant's reinvention of the particular-universal distinction generated two more specific distinctions, namely the intuition-concept distinction and the analytic–synthetic distinction, and these were to become a mainstay of subsequent philosophical theorising: the 'twin pillars' (Skinner 1981: 47) supporting the Kantian edifice of systematic philosophy. These distinctions suggested and facilitated a systematic study of how the mind orders experience, one which would sift out what is given in experience from the interpretation we put on it, and would analyse the most basic conceptual presuppositions of experience. Since experience was supposed to be ordered inside the mind, thereby generating necessary truths, this needed to be an *a priori* study, one conducted through introspection, reasoning, thought experiments, and the like, and consequently a quite separate venture from empirical science. And so with the Kantian distinctions presupposed, and all the intricacy and ambition of the *Critique of Pure Reason* serving as a model of how far such *a priori* reasoning could take you, aspiring 'bald-headed PhD's' had their work cut out for them. Kant had made it plausible that one man's introspective diligence really could unlock the secrets of the universe, or at the very least make a distinctive contribution to knowledge.

Now following up on the historicist line he took with the mind–body problem, Rorty is very insistent that there is nothing obvious or inevitable about the intuition-concept distinction. Kant was not elucidating an undeniable feature of the human condition, namely that we passively receive data from the environment and conceptually work it over, but was rather engaged in a theoretical innovation, one which involved taking Locke's notion of experience – already a 'term of philosophical art' (150) – and splitting it into the two components needed for the Copernican transfer of Cartesian certainty from ideas to the world. Thus Rorty thinks it would be absurd to assume that, 'the man in the street, untutored in philosophy, could simply be asked to turn his mental eye inward and notice the distinction' (150). But is that right? Suppose that – to illustrate the distinction in a standard sort of a way – a game of chess is being played, and it is being observed by two people, a Westerner who knows chess, and a tribesman who has never heard of a board-game. The Westerner sees the movements of the players as movements within a game, as castling, checking, etc., but the tribesman does not see them as anything in particular. So what they are seeing is the same, but they are conceptualising it differently. Of course the tribesman is still conceptualising what he sees as people moving things around, but once we have got this far, it is easy to imagine an incremental stripping away of concepts until only the most basic effect of the environment is left. Whatever the merits of this way of thinking about experience, it is hard to see the man on the street having much trouble with it.

This may just be because the Cartesian conception of mind primes us for an intuition–concept distinction, however, and Rorty has already argued at length that there is nothing obvious or inevitable about that conception. But an alternative suggestion is that the distinction was already recognised by Plato in 'the dramatic difference between mathematical truth and more humdrum truths' (156), that is, between necessary truths known by means of the intellect, and contingent truths known by means of the senses. Kant's distinction could then just be seen as a development of this Greek discovery.

According to Rorty, however, this was not a discovery, but rather a consequence of the 'Platonic Principle' (Chapter 4 above) that how things are known determines what they are, which was in turn a consequence of choosing perception as a metaphor for knowledge. In short, Plato assumed knowledge was like seeing, recognised that we can be more certain of mathematical judgements than perceptual ones, and concluded that mathematical truths are 'seen' by the intellect rather than the senses. Rorty attributes this original move – of which Kant's distinction was just one descendent – to the religious urge to be compelled in our beliefs: for the objective truth to force us to believe the things we do. And with the addition of the Heideggerian theme that Western thought has simply been drawing out the consequences of Plato's original equation of existence with perceptual presence, Rorty reaches the conclusion that we can, 'take from Heidegger the idea that the desire for an "epistemology" is simply the most recent product of the dialectical development of an originally chosen set of metaphors' (163). A conception of knowledge as a relation to a proposition would have undercut the whole drama, however, for then certainty could be understood as just a lack of decent arguments against the proposition. Basic logical and mathematical truths do not force themselves on the intellect; it is just that nobody ever found any good reason to develop ways of disputing them.

6

LINGUISTIC HOLISM
(*PMN*, CHAPTER 4)

SELLARS ON GIVENNESS AND QUINE ON ANALYTICITY
(§§1–2)

Rorty considers Chapter 4 of *PMN* to be the most important part of his book; he says this in the Introduction (10), and he has repeated it in interviews ever since. It sees Rorty playing the role in which he is most comfortable, that of the metaphilosopher surveying developments within the subject, and drawing the wide-scale conclusions overlooked by constructive philosophers preoccupied with details. In this case, the conclusion is that the twentieth-century analytic movement in philosophy developed in such a way as to completely undermine itself; as he later put it: 'I think that analytic philosophy culminates in Quine, the later Wittgenstein, Sellars, and Davidson – which is to say that it transcends and cancels itself' (Rorty 1982: xviii). In this chapter, the emphasis is on Wilfrid Sellars and W.V.O. Quine, two figures widely regarded – especially by Rorty's generation – as the greatest American philosophers of the last century. Rorty's idea is that the combination of Sellars's attack on the 'Myth of the Given' and Quine's attack on the analytic–synthetic distinction collapsed the two Kantian distinctions which analytic philosophy depended upon. Moreover, though they did not realise it, Sellars and Quine were using 'the same argument' (170), one which weighs equally against representationalism, objective truth, and any conception of philosophy as what Dewey called the 'quest for certainty' (166, 171). This common message drawn from Sellars and Quine is the lynch-pin of *PMN*'s destructive case, and Rorty has boiled down and reshaped it so much since then that it has effectively become his own. No wonder, then, that he sets great store by this chapter.

Rorty's use of Sellars and Quine to show 'how the notion of two sorts of representations – intuitions and concepts – fell into disrepute in the latter days of the analytic movement' (168), is supposed to have ramifications reaching far beyond analytic philosophy, because Rorty has already presented philosophy itself as an essentially Kantian enterprise dependent upon the distinctions which he thinks Sellars and Quine collapsed. So even though analytic philosophy is just another neo-Kantian movement for Rorty – just 'one more tempest in an academic teapot' (Rorty 1992: 371) – it allows him to illustrate the fundamental flaw with all attempts to turn philosophy into a systematic and constructive venture.

Rorty begins, then, by placing the movement in historical context, filling in the gap in his story between Kant's transcendental idealism at the end of the eighteenth century and Russell's linguistic turn at the beginning of the twentieth. Now as was noted in Chapter 2 above, there is something rather curious about the way the nineteenth century tends to get glossed over by the *status quo* history of philosophy: within English-speaking universities, the basic curriculum covers the Greeks and seventeenth, eighteenth, and twentieth-century philosophy, but leaving aside moral and political philosophy, the nineteenth century is largely omitted – except perhaps for figures at the source of twentieth-century movements (such as Brentano and Frege). This could just be because nobody made any real advance on Kant until Russell, of course, but it would be very strange if that were true: why would philosophy grind to a halt at a time when other fields of inquiry were making accelerating progress? Rorty has an explanation.

As he sees it, the nineteenth century was a time in which the study Kant had conceived – a 'metacriticism of the special disciplines' (166) based on a theory of knowledge – was gradually coming to seem both less relevant and less credible. Natural science was in the ascendancy, with evolutionary theory and physiology leaving *a priori* reflection standing when it came to uncovering novel truths about human nature, and experimental approaches to psychology seeming more in tune with the age than appeals to introspection and transcendental arguments. Physicalism was the dominant metaphysics – idealism was influential in Germany only in the first half of the century and in Britain only towards the end of it – and knowledge was rapidly expanding without any apparent need for epistemological backing. In short, philosophy was being edged aside by science, a process reinforced by Comte's influential metaphilosophical claim to the effect that philosophy is proto-science (Comte 1974: 19), the 'fissiparious mother of all the sciences' (as one commentator memorably put it (Urmson 1960: 11)) from which individual disciplines break off to become scientific, rather than Kant's 'queen of all the sciences' (Kant 1933: Aviii) passing judgement on individual disciplines. And apart from being sidelined, philosophy was being directly undermined by challenges to its Kantian presuppositions, the most important of which from Rorty's perspective was due to 'holism', an idea first encapsulated in Hegel's statement that 'The True is the whole' (Hegel 1977: 11). This general Hegelian line of thought eventually led contemporaries as diverse as Bradley in England, James in America, and Bergson in France, all to mount holistic arguments to the effect that any attempt to split conscious experience into atomistic elements – such as Kantian intuitions and concepts – was to make an artificial and falsifying abstraction from an essentially unified whole. Transposed to a linguistic context, this is basically the same message Rorty finds in Sellars and Quine.

So since we are heirs to an essentially Kantian understanding of the history of philosophy, according to Rorty, the reason the nineteenth century seems like a quiet patch is that the creative thinkers were either being drawn to science, which was getting on fine without Kant's new discipline, or else to holism, which was undermining it. At the start of the twentieth century, however, there was a major backlash in the shape of two independent attempts to place philosophy back on the 'secure path of a science'. Thus Russell founded the Analytic movement and Husserl founded the Phenomenological movement. This was the point at which continental and analytic philosophy shot off at tangents, remaining substantially apart ever since. If Rorty's interpretation is right, however, this schism belies the fact that Russell and Husserl were actually united in a common Kantian cause, that of finding an *a priori* niche where philosophy could peacefully co-exist with empirical science, and could be practised with similar 'seriousness, purity, and vigor' (167). So the split was not ideological, as is usually assumed; it was just that Russell and Husserl worked out different ways of getting the job done.

Now there is something slightly jarring about uniting Russell and Husserl as fellow neo-Kantian revolutionaries, given that Russell was actually rather hostile to Kant, whereas Husserl was an out and out transcendental idealist, and given also that the standard continental complaint against analytic philosophy is that it is not Kantian enough. Nevertheless, despite substantial differences, Rorty is surely right to point out a strong Kantian affinity in the fact that Russell and Husserl both claimed to have discovered a new and rigorous philosophical method for revealing structural truths, i.e. logical analysis of the structure of language in Russell's case, and phenomenological analysis of the structure of consciousness in Husserl's case. And a parallel of a different sort between Russell and Husserl, one which is even more striking, is that they each inspired a protégé who was ultimately to rebel against their constructive programme. These wayward protégés were of course Wittgenstein and Heidegger, philosophers who Rorty thinks of as having brought holism and historicism home to roost after a brief neo-Kantian interlude.

For the purposes of mounting a case against atomistic and ahistorical approaches to philosophy, however, it is not to the 'edifying' philosophy (see Chapter 10 below) of Heidegger and Wittgenstein that Rorty looks, but rather to the constructive efforts of two systematic philosophers who spent their lives working within the analytic framework, namely Sellars and Quine. Now both Sellars and Quine presented what Rorty thinks of as their key arguments in the 1950s, and this fact yields at once yet another revisionary consequence for our understanding of the history of philosophy: analytic philosophy turns out to be even more surprisingly short-lived than philosophy itself. This is because Rorty thinks that Sellars and Quine unwittingly undermined not only their own constructive efforts, but the whole analytic movement. And so analytic philosophy only lasted 'some forty years' (167), by which Rorty means that it should only have lasted forty years, but has trundled on regardless ever since. That analytic philosophy did nevertheless continue, and in one sense has thrived – there is more of it going on now than ever before – has been achieved through a studied 'lack of metaphilosophical reflection' facilitated by the 'sociological fact' (172) that its place within academic institutions is secure. So it falls on Rorty's shoulders, then, to alert analytic philosophy to its own demise, though since his only reason for targeting the analytic rather than phenomenological fork of the neo-Kantian revival is 'autobiographical', i.e. Rorty knows it better, this critique is clearly intended to apply across the board.

With the context now set out, then, we can turn to Sellars's and Quine's arguments themselves. Rorty combines them into an argument of the following form:

1   Sellars undermined the intuition–concept distinction.
2   Quine undermined the analytic–synthetic distinction.
3   Analytic philosophy requires at least one of these two distinctions.

Therefore, analytic philosophy has been undermined.

So we now need to look at each of the three premises in turn.

To begin with Sellars, we first need to clear up a potentially misleading aspect of Rorty's whole discussion which has up until now been deliberately glossed over. This is that Rorty continually suggests that Sellars and Quine attacked one each of the 'two great Kantian distinctions' (172), which is a neat way of setting things up, but not very accurate. Quine's critique of analyticity was indeed an attack on one of Kant's distinctions, but Sellars's critique of the 'Myth of the Given' was in large part a Kantian attack on epistemological foundationalism. After all, Sellars was – alongside Strawson – about the most distinctively and self-consciously Kantian of all the great analytic philosophers: he used the term 'transcendental' approvingly, and his overarching project of reconciling our 'manifest' and 'scientific' images of the world was something he conceived of in Kantian terms.[1] Add to this the fact that Sellars never says or even implies that the given–interpreted distinction he is attacking is the Kantian intuition–concept distinction, and that most of Sellars's examples of givens are pre-Kantian, and there is little else to say on the matter.[2] As Rorty himself put it in his introduction to the new edition of Sellars's *Empiricism and the Philosophy of Mind*, 'The fundamental thought which runs through this essay is Kant's: "intuitions without concepts are blind"' (Rorty 1997: 3). So Kant's distinction cannot have been Sellars's immediate target: he was using it. In the final analysis, however, Sellars's critique has wide enough implications to undermine Kant's whole approach to knowledge anyway – in the rather less direct and more complicated way we encountered earlier (see Chapter 5 above) – but it is as well to know about this potentially confusing expositionary conflation even if it does not ultimately effect Rorty's argument.

The bulk of Sellars's critique of the 'Myth of the Given' in *Empiricism and the Philosophy of Mind* is concerned with the empiricist notion – revived by the analytic movement – that conceptual knowledge must be built up from pre-conceptual experience. The leading idea of this critique is already familiar to us from Green's claim that empiricists like Locke confused causation with justification, a comparison Rorty endorses later in *PMN* by referring to 'Green's and Sellars's criticisms of the empiricist notion of "givenness"' (253). Thus Sellars once wrote, as if echoing Green's description of sensations as 'dumb', that 'Sense grasps no facts, not even such simple ones as something's being red and triangular' (quoted in DeVries 2005: 5). The point, just as with Green, is that it is one thing to have a sensation of a red triangle, but quite another to grasp it as such, and it is only the latter which has epistemic significance. Sellars's general diagnosis of this problem is that empiricism has conflated two distinct notions, namely the notion of sensations as natural inner processes, and the notion of sensations as instances of immediate, non-inferential knowledge. Empiricism needs both of these, but they are in conflict with each other. On the one hand, it needs the having of sensations to be an unacquired ability – an ability we can share with pre-linguistic children and non-linguistic animals – in order to anchor claims to knowledge on the raw impact of the environment. But on the other hand, it needs sensations to be grasped conceptually – which Sellars thinks of as an acquired linguistic ability – in order for them to provide a foundation for more complex knowledge. This is because you cannot infer anything from a red sensation, for example, but you might be able to infer something from the fact that you are having a red sensation. As Sellars sees it, then, empiricism needs sensing to be both an unacquired ability and a conceptual feat, despite the fact that these two requirements are irreconcilable. In attempting to reconcile them nonetheless, empiricists engaged in a 'crossbreeding' responsible for 'mongrel' concepts such as Locke's 'simple ideas' and logical positivism's 'sense-data' (Sellars 1997: 21).

Sellars may have brought new clarity to criticism of sensory 'givens', but he was only updating an extant line of thought, one which had in fact been commonplace amongst philosophers between Green and Russell; Dewey, for example, wrote that, 'The history of the theory of knowledge or epistemology would have been very different if instead of the word "data" or "givens", it had happened to start with calling the qualities in question "takens"' (Dewey 1930: 170–71).[3] Experiential ideas are not given as atomistic units, for Dewey, but are rather taken up from a unified whole, an activity which presupposes interests, projects, and pre-formed conceptual abilities – a 'whole battery of concepts', as Sellars was later to put it (Sellars 1997: 44). For Sellars, this meant having a language, but the underlying idea that sensory givenness must be rejected for holistic reasons remained the same. Where Sellars's critique really was unprecedented, however, was in its generality and also in the far-reaching conclusions he was prepared to draw from it. Sellars makes it clear from the outset that he is targeting 'the entire framework of givenness' (ibid.: 14), i.e. the general idea that, as a matter of principle, some things can be taken for granted, or treated as beyond dispute. Consequently, even though Sellars mainly discusses empiricist proposals, what he has to say is intended to have much wider application. And his conclusion, the consequences of which we are about to see, is that *nothing* can be treated as an epistemological given: the idea that there are unquestionable foundations upon which all more rarefied knowledge is built is, quite simply, a myth. Knowledge is not based on any 'givens' at all; not the innately known first principles of the rationalists, not the sensations of the empiricists, and not even the basic conceptual categories of Kant's system. Human knowledge has no foundations, but is rather a 'self-correcting enterprise which can put *any* claim in jeopardy, though not *all* at once' (quoted at 180–81; Sellars 1997: 79).

Once we give up on the idea that there is some base level at which knowledge is an unacquired ability – something that just happens to us when we have a sensation, or which we discover as soon as we reflect – then Sellars thinks that we should be able to see that 'all awareness . . . is a linguistic affair' (ibid.: 63). Language is not some abstract code super-added to pre-linguistic awareness, but is rather the medium through which we first become aware of things by relating them to each other within an intersubjective and holistic web of significance. Since awareness of our own mental states is as much a 'linguistic affair' as anything else, Sellars is led to a conception of knowledge diametrically opposed to that offered by the Mirror of Nature. According to the Mirror of Nature conception, knowledge begins in acquaintance with our own private mental states, a fact which generates the veil of perception problem. But for Sellars, by contrast, the concept of a mental state is 'as intersubjective as the concept of a positron' (ibid.: 107): it is something we can only pick up by joining a community of language-users. Now since the linguistic context for talking about knowledge is normative, for it involves evaluation and justification according to standards of evidence, Sellars thinks that to describe a mental state as an instance of knowledge is not to give an empirical description of it at all – as for instance we might give a description of something's size or shape – but is rather to place it within 'the logical space of reasons' (ibid.: 76), i.e. the linguistic context in which it is conceptually related to a multiplicity of facts and states of affairs which might justify it or rationally be inferred on its basis. So, for example, to say 'John knows it is raining' is to place John within a context in which we expect him to be able to justify his utterances of 'it's raining' with other appropriate utterances. And that, for Sellars, is all there is to knowledge: it is a node within a linguistic practice, not a natural state such practices were built around.

The moral Rorty draws from this – a moral which has come to define his career, and which he has since managed to extract from the writings of a dizzying array of philosophers in addition to Sellars

– is that, 'there is no way to get outside our beliefs and our language', and that we should therefore accept that 'the True and the Right are matters of social practice' (178). Rorty has originated two catchy and hence regularly quoted metaphors for this idea over the years. First of all he said that we cannot 'step outside our skins' (Rorty 1982: xix), i.e. we cannot escape from our linguistic practices to check the adequacy of those linguistic practices to the world itself. Then later he said that there is 'no skyhook' (Rorty 1991a: 13), i.e. nothing is going to lift us out of our social milieu so that we can compare what people say about the world with the way the world really is. Both nicely encapsulate the idea he took from Sellars that human knowledge cannot be based on anything outside of human conversation, since there are no 'givens' to transcend the ordinary to-ings and fro-ings of rational discussion. And of course, Rorty thinks that philosophy itself provides the locus of attempts to 'step outside our skins', or attach ourselves to a 'skyhook', with its aim of establishing a 'permanent neutral matrix'(179) – an epistemology – capable of determining the ahistorical conditions under which accurate representation of the world is possible. As Rorty sees it, 'The urge to say that assertions and actions must not only cohere with other assertions and actions but "correspond" to something apart from what people are saying and doing has some claim to be called *the* philosophical urge' (179). The antidote to this urge is to realise the 'ubiquity of language' (Rorty 1982: xx); that we cannot go beyond what is said about the world in order to make contact with the world itself, and that we cannot escape either from the history that formed our languages, or from the societies they subserve, factors which shape everything we say or even think.

So we must give up on the urge to secure our beliefs against the vicissitudes of the social domain by anchoring them to a given, then, and content ourselves with knowledge being determined by 'what society lets us say' (174). For Rorty, this means giving up on three things: first, objective truth, for there is nothing outside the conversation which can force us to talk one way rather than another; second, philosophy, since this is a subject whose *raison d'être* is to determine the requirements for accurately mirroring the objective truth; and, third, representation, which is the mirroring relation between what we say and the objective truth. As regards representation in particular, Rorty's reasoning has been given an illuminating gloss by Robert Brandom in the following passage:

> Normative relations are exclusively intravocabulary . . . Representation purports to be *both* a normative relation, supporting assessments of correctness and incorrectness, *and* a relation between representings within a vocabulary and representeds outside of that vocabulary. Therefore, the representational model of the relation of vocabularies to their environment should be rejected.
>
> (Brandom 2000: 160)

The idea here is that if we reject the Myth of the Given in favour of linguistic holism, then whether something counts as correct or incorrect (i.e. how we normatively evaluate it) is determined by 'what society lets us say': it is a linguistic or 'intravocabulary' affair. Representation, on the other hand, is an 'extravocabulary' affair – it is a relation between language and the world itself – and yet representations are also supposed to be evaluable as either correct (when they correspond to the world) or as incorrect (when they do not). Since this correctness could not be determined by 'what society lets us say' – to determine it would require us to 'step outside our skins' – it follows that representationalism is incompatible with linguistic holism. So representationalism should be rejected along with the Myth of the Given.

Quine's critique of analyticity provides Rorty with a second route to the conclusion that justification is social and holistic, rather than based upon foundational (or 'privileged') representations. The main source of this critique is the 1951 paper 'Two Dogmas of Empiricism', in which Quine endorsed a form of pragmatism, a position he was later to distance himself from in favour of a more thorough-going physicalism (see Hookway 1988: 50–54); not surprisingly, it is the earlier period of Quine's career which Rorty prefers. The 'two dogmas' of the title were, first, the analytic–synthetic distinction, and, second, what Quine called 'reductionism', the idea that all statements can in principle be recast in explicitly observational terms. These two commitments were doctrinally connected within logical positivism (see Chapter 2 above), which saw it as a central task of philosophy to uncover analytic statements of equivalence between ordinary or scientific sentences, and sensory reports. This was supposed to show how language structures experience, and hence which experiences would be required to confirm or disconfirm any particular statement. Quine, however, thinks that this whole picture of language as fundamentally divided between the analytic sentences that provide definitions to structure experience, and the synthetic statements which have strict observational consequences, is rendered untenable by linguistic holism. The logical positivists had assumed that the preservation of their basic empiricist convictions would require both an analytic–synthetic distinction, and the possibility of 'reducing' synthetic statements to their observational consequences, but this was to dogmatically presuppose a false account of the connection between language and experience.

Quine presents an alternative account of the connection between language and experience, according to which,

> The totality of our so-called knowledge or beliefs, from the most casual matters of geography and history to the profoundest laws of atomic physics or even pure mathematics and logic, is a man-made fabric, which impinges on experience only along the edges.
>
> (Quine 1953: 42)

Thus rather than language consisting in a combination of synthetic statements which are individually answerable to experience (e.g. 'that vixen has lost its tail' is confirmed by some experiences and disconfirmed by others), and analytic statements of definition which are not answerable to experience at all (e.g. 'a vixen is a female fox', which is true simply in virtue of what it means), Quine instead thinks of language as a unitary holistic system in which all statements are collectively answerable to experience, so that 'our statements about the external world face the tribunal of sense experience not individually but only as a corporate body' (ibid.: 41). Quine's reasoning to this conclusion is essentially negative, in that he sees no way to derive strict observational consequences from individual sentences, given that there is always a choice about which beliefs to adjust in light of experience; for example, if I believe the vixen has lost its tail, but then apparently see its tail flick up, I do not necessarily have to retract my original belief, since in the circumstances it may seem more likely that I am hallucinating. And if we cannot derive observational consequences from individual sentences, then we cannot determine which sentences are entirely lacking in observational consequences. So reductionism and the analytic–synthetic distinction fall together.

Quine's positive proposal was that holism requires the notion of analyticity to be replaced with the notion of centrality to a belief system. On this view, statements that have been traditionally classified as 'analytic' are not in fact immune from experience, but are rather simply those statements most central to the belief system, and hence those most insulated from experience, just as the central parts of an island are those most insulated from the sea. This means that there is no principled reason why such statements should not be retracted or revised in the face of experience, though there is nevertheless a practical obstacle in the fact that since they are so central, and hence implicated in so many other statements, then any attempt to revise them is liable to send reverberations throughout the whole system, thus requiring all sorts of other changes to restore overall coherence. Revising statements traditionally classified as 'synthetic', on the other hand, is much less likely to have such implications, and so may be undertaken comparatively lightly: if I say 'that vixen has lost its tail', and you point out that its tail is just tucked away, I can probably retract my statement without any further consequences for my beliefs. Thus behind the false metaphysical picture of a principled distinction between matters of meaning and matters of fact, a picture enshrined in the analytic–synthetic distinction, Quine finds only a practical difference blown out of all proportion.

Easily the most counterintuitive consequence of Quine's view is that supposedly analytic statements such as 'a vixen is a female fox' are susceptible to empirical falsification. However, given the right circumstances, we can perhaps imagine this coming about; I have borrowed the following illustrations from a paper by Marcus Giaquinto (Giaquinto 1996). First, suppose that a discovery is made about foxes, namely that a surprising number of them are actually hermaphrodites. Moreover, of these hermaphrodites, some behave like female foxes and some behave like male foxes. In these circumstances, we might decide to align 'vixen' with behavioural role rather than gender (we previously assumed they matched up), in which case experience would have taught us that some vixens are not female foxes. And, second, to take an even more venerable example of analyticity – 'a bachelor is an unmarried man' – suppose that following a loosening up of the marriage laws and a successful advertising campaign by the international charities, an institution develops according to which males in Western countries need only sign a certificate on their eighteenth birthday to marry a third-world worker, thereby overcoming legal obstacles to economic migration. Signing has no effect on the life-styles of these young men, who act just like unmarried men always did prior to settling down with a long-term partner. So in these circumstances, we might decide to align 'bachelor' with behavioural role rather than marital status (they previously matched up), in which case experience would have taught us that some bachelors are not unmarried men. Now many philosophers would dismiss these examples as just changes in meaning, so that rather than experience disproving 'a vixen is a female fox', it was just that the word 'vixen' came to be redefined. The Quinean challenge, however, is to motivate this insistence on a semantic difference between what happens when experience leads us to reject 'that vixen has lost its tail', and what happens when experience leads us to reject 'a vixen is a female fox'. Quine thinks the mechanism in both cases is the same – experience calls for adjustments within the holistic belief system – and that those who insist on a semantic difference are simply in the grip of a dogma.

Rorty draws the same principal conclusion from Quine as he does from Sellars, namely that there is no way to short-circuit the judgement of society by appealing directly to representations in the Mirror of Nature. Just as Sellars showed that sensory givens cannot do the job, so Quine showed that analytic truths cannot do the job: there are no sentences which have special epistemic authority just because of what they mean, and hence there is no chance of using meanings to provide a foundation for knowledge. However whereas with Sellars the emphasis was on sensory givens being unable to do the job – since they lack conceptual form – with Quine the emphasis is on the impossibility of isolating analytic truths. This line of reasoning counts equally against both the analytic–synthetic and the intuition-concept distinctions, since if there is no way to separate out the sentences concerned only with concepts (the analytic ones) from the sentences concerned with experience (the synthetic ones), then neither can there be any way of separating out what is given in experience (the intuitions) from the interpretation we put on it (the concepts). Thus Rorty sees Quine's critique of analyticity as another way of using 'the same argument' – linguistic holism – to put paid to Kant's conception of philosophy as a systematic study of how the mind orders experience, as well to its neo-Kantian descendent – analytic philosophy – which interprets that task in terms of analysing the conceptual structure imposed on experience by language.

Rorty's continual emphasis throughout his discussion of both Quine and Sellars is on how linguistic holism shows the *uselessness* of trying to back-up knowledge with metaphysics. The problem with trying to ground 'what society lets us say' on inner representations in the Mirror of Nature is not ontological – as the physicalist's distrust of dualism is ontological – but is rather just that it does not work: knowledge refuses to be taken out of the social domain. Attempts to find something more steady and more authoritative than agreement within society have turned out to be irrelevant and thus fallen by the wayside, and the lesson we should learn from this is that beliefs cannot be imposed on us from beyond, as images are imposed on a mirror. In short, we need to stop trying to abdicate responsibility for our beliefs to an external body called 'objective truth'. This is a moral Rorty draws from Quine's pragmatism, according to which an experiential conflict with our body of beliefs does not dictate which of our beliefs should be abandoned, but rather leaves us with a choice about how best to go about maximising our communicative and predictive abilities. Quine often made a comparison between adjusting our beliefs to experience and repairing a ship at sea, a comparison he borrowed from Otto Neurath, who said that, 'We are like sailors who must rebuild their ship on the open sea, never able to dismantle it in dry-dock and to reconstruct it there out of the best materials' (Neurath 1981: 162). Thus any of the planks of the ship (i.e. our beliefs) may be replaced, but we must always keep the ship afloat (i.e. maintain a coherent belief system for coping with the world), since we cannot rest up in dry-dock to make our repairs (i.e. there are no epistemological foundations). And of course, we cannot use a skyhook either.

Now Rorty, of course, thinks that the combination of Sellars's critique of givenness and Quine's critique of analyticity completely undermines analytic philosophy; he says that it leaves it 'hard to imagine what an "analysis" might be' (172). This is the third and final premise in the overall argument, and though Rorty offers no explicit arguments, he does nevertheless provide examples of major methodological research programmes he thinks were rendered untenable by linguistic holism, the clear suggestion being that all the promising options for constructive philosophical analysis have been exhausted. It is not hard to see why he should think this, for Sellars and Quine's critiques have direct application to what were perhaps the best known and most influential programmes of analytic philosophy. First, the task of analysing the logical form beneath the grammatical form of language – analytic philosophy's original project – loses its potential for rigour if logical form is just another set of planks in Neurath's ship, and hence less something to be discovered than to be decided upon in context. Second, the logical positivist project of showing how the physical world is constructed from sense-data cannot even begin without appeal to both sensory givens, as undermined by Sellars, and also analytic statements connecting those givens, as undermined by Quine. And, third, conceptual analysis, which was central to 'ordinary language philosophy', and involved trying to make explicit what is merely implicit about philosophically interesting concepts – by testing their use in a variety of imaginative scenarios – is immediately rendered untenable if there are no analytic truths concerning our concepts to get right, just decisions to be made within society.

So we have reached the end of Rorty's argument, then; this represents a major turning point in *PMN*, for it is the culmination of the metaphilosophical critique that has been building up from the outset. The standard reaction philosophers are often inclined to make at this point is some sort of plea for moderation. So, for instance, it might be said that all analytic philosophy cannot be tarred with the same brush – let alone all systematic philosophy whatsoever – and that though Rorty perhaps has a good case against logical positivism and conceptual analysis, these are dusty old approaches whose failings have little bearing on the contemporary scene; Soames's response to Rorty's review was along these lines (see Chapter 1 above). A related response would be to deny that philosophy has anything to do with the Mirror of Nature anymore, so that Rorty's criticisms of Cartesian approaches to mind and language lack the anti-philosophical force he assumes for them, and are rather simply contributions to a growing post-Cartesian consensus (Baldwin 2001: chapter 11). Yet another response would be to appeal to approaches to epistemology other than foundationalism, pointing out that criticism of the latter is not thereby criticism of the former (Haack 1993). Another would be to accuse Rorty of setting up a false dichotomy between either objective truth or pragmatism, when there are a whole range of middling conceptions in between (Prado 1987). And another would be to appeal to more moderate forms of holism than the all-out version Rorty presupposes (see Fodor and LePore 1992).

Any of these responses may have the potential to circumvent Rorty's argument, though developing them would take us far beyond the current remit. There is, however, a distinct danger of missing the point if we are too hasty in pursuing one of these pleas for moderation. The reason is that linguistic holism was introduced at the end of Rorty's long historical sketch of how philosophy originated, and so to see its full anti-philosophical force requires that we see it within that context. After all, if it is at all plausible that philosophy originated in the search for a firmer basis for knowledge than society can provide, and if we agree this search was hopeless, then we cannot simply assume that overcoming the challenge of linguistic holism is a worthwhile venture. Why look for moderate alternatives to foundationalism and objective truth if the reasons people had for theorising about topics like knowledge and truth were never any good in the first place? Moreover, if we agree that neither the mind nor language is a Mirror of Nature, then the question immediately arises of why philosophical modes of investigation should be expected to work. Why should the nature of reference, modality, or phenomenal concepts – to take some examples of contemporary interest – yield to individual reflection if there is no Mirror of Nature to facilitate *a priori* access? Would it not make more sense to go out with clipboard questionnaires to find out about how particular communities use concepts such as necessity or reference? And what is philosophy trying to find out anyway, if its current inquiries have nothing to do with its dubious foundationalist origins? These are the sort of large-scale questions Rorty's critique raises, and that is why properly engaging with it would require an alternative metaphilosophical vision, not just a loophole.

Finally, before we move on, mention must be made of the name Rorty gives to the moral he discerns in Sellars and Quine: 'epistemological behaviourism'. It certainly makes sense – questions about knowledge are determined by (linguistic) behaviour within society, not metaphysical entities – and it would have been unremarkable but for the fact that Rorty decides upon it in preference to 'pragmatism', which he dismisses as 'a bit overladen' (176). This was quite a tactical error on Rorty's behalf, but he seems to have got away with it by calling his next book *Consequences of Pragmatism*. In any case, there is certainly no turn towards pragmatism in Rorty's work post-*PMN*, as has sometimes been assumed; it is just that he decided it was alright to call himself a pragmatist after all.[4]

BABIES, ANIMALS, AND MEANINGS

(§§3–5)

The sounds animals make are not sentences in foreign languages, but are rather auditory signs akin to our own sighs, laughs, and screams. After all, if there were animal languages, then we would have translated them centuries ago, and all the highstreet bookshops would currently be packed full of Dog-English dictionaries. It is, however, one thing to make this rather obvious point – which in itself would be enough to outrage large swathes of society – and quite another to deny that animals are even conscious. Nevertheless, this latter claim seems to be a consequence of Sellars's view that 'all awareness is a linguistic affair'. And since babies cannot speak a language either, it seems they too must lack awareness. These conclusions are hard to stomach, and so Rorty sets about a damage limitation exercise in Section 3 to show that linguistic holism does not have unacceptable consequences for babies and animals after all. If anything, however, his continual practice of comparing babies to either record-changers or photoelectric cells generates exactly the opposite effect, and as a whole, the section tends to distract from, rather than build upon, the powerful argument just presented.

Rorty first points out that Sellars only meant 'all awareness' in an epistemological sense, and hence did not mean to include 'awareness-as-discriminative-behaviour', which is just 'reliable signaling' (182). This is not a lot of use in dampening down the counterintuitive implications of linguistic holism, though, for it still lumps babies and animals together with record-changers and photoelectric cells, only counting as 'unaware' things which do not systematically react to the environment at all, such as tables and chairs. Rorty was apparently quite happy to accept this earlier on, when he wrote that, 'the way in which the pre-linguistic infant knows that it has a pain is the way in which the record-changer knows the spindle is empty' (110). He now seems to have changed his mind, however, and thus makes a distinction between 'knowing what X is like' and 'knowing what sort of a thing an X is' (183). This distinction has potential to turn the trick, because it allows for babies and animals to know what pain is like (for example), without knowing what sort of thing a pain is, and in this way it allows them to be distinguished from record-changers and photoelectric cells, which cannot even know what pain is like. But the problem with it, however, is that it directly contradicts linguistic holism by attributing a kind of non-linguistic knowledge to animals and babies.

Rorty does not make his strategy for getting around this problem very clear, but the general idea seems to be that knowing what pain is like is 'just to *have* pain' (184), and this sense of 'knowledge' – one insisted upon by 'ordinary speech' – is quite distinct from 'knowledge' in Sellars's sense of 'knowing what sort of a thing an X is'. So why does it count as 'knowledge' at all, and – more to the point – why can babies have it when devices like record-changers or thermometers cannot? Thermometers do not have pain, of course, but if pain is just an internal state with no special epistemological significance – a view to which Rorty is irrevocably committed – then why not say thermometers know what heat is like when they have certain internal states? The reason Rorty gives is that only the baby has the potential to acquire linguistic knowledge: it knows what pain is like because it has a 'latent ability' (184) to talk about pain, and thus to know what sort of a thing a pain is. But this is not to be understood in terms of 'inner illumination' (184): the difference between the baby in pain and the hot thermometer is neither that the baby's potential to talk means that it must have conscious states, nor even that the baby will one day acquire conscious states by talking. Rather, Rorty thinks the baby's potential to know about pain when it learns a language is akin to its potential to acquire legal rights and responsibilities when it comes of age (187). In other words, the baby knows what pain is like – i.e. it feels pain – because society says it does, and the reason society says it does is that the baby is a potential member of society who may one day be treated as a person who knows what they are talking about. What about animals, then? Rorty's answer is that 'the more attractive sorts of animals' (189) feel pain because their faces look human enough for us to imagine them talking; this is a 'courtesy' we extend to them as 'imagined fellow-speakers of our language' (190).

The only difference between knowing what it is like and exhibiting awareness-as-discriminative-behaviour, then, is whether or not society grants you admission to its moral community: babies and attractive animals are welcome, photoelectric cells and ugly animals are not. This difference concerns sentiment, not internal constitution, and hence constitutes a radically revisionary conception of what it is to have a sensation, or to know what a sensation feels like. One consequence – which Rorty makes no attempt to shy away from, but on the contrary seems to relish[5] – is that a change in our sentiments would mean a change in whether or not something has sensations. So, for instance, suppose computer designers perfect a 'sad face' that pops up on the screen whenever you go to switch the power off, and it is so convincing that people start leaving their computers continually on. In these circumstances, Rorty would presumably have no objection to saying that turning a computer off hurts it, and would not condemn the new practice of leaving computers on as irrational, just as he does not condemn as irrational the unequal treatment of koalas and pigs (which 'don't writhe in quite the right humanoid way' (190)). The reason, from Rorty's perspective, is that koalas (or computers) have feelings because of society's sentiments, rather than society's sentiments being a response to their feelings.

But is discriminative behaviour that attracts sentiment really enough for knowledge? After all, if the Myth of the Given is to be avoided, then sensations cannot have anything to do with justification, and it cannot be possible to infer anything from them. They are isolated and 'dumb' physical states of no more epistemic significance than any other – so why would a linguistic holist like Rorty want to call them 'knowledge'? The answer, I think, is that he has been forced into a messy compromise through a conflict of interests. On the one hand, Rorty is a convinced linguistic holist who thinks that knowledge is a complex pattern of inter-personal behaviour that can only be entered into once we have learnt how to use lots of different words. This steers him toward his original line that babies are not really any different from record-changers: they 'know' in the same way, i.e. only in a loose, metaphorical sense of 'know' (hence the occasional scare quotes). But on the other hand, Rorty is a sceptical metaphilosopher, and as such, he does not want be caught defending a revisionary metaphysical position, one according to which a near universal opinion of humanity – that babies and animals know their sensations in a way that unconscious devices cannot – is disproved by a philosophical argument.[6] His instinct is rather to acquiesce when public opinion says babies know about pain, and to yawn when philosophers debate whether they 'really' do or not.

So Rorty compromises by distinguishing two types of knowledge. The compromise is unsatisfactory across the board, however: it jars with linguistic holism by attributing knowledge outside the logical space of reasons, and it fails to appease common-sense one iota by using our sentiment rather than the baby's consciousness to distinguish it from a record-changer. This unsatisfactory state of affairs is symptomatic of a general problem for Rorty, one which we shall return to. This is that he cannot resist exciting Hegelian conclusions such as that 'the individual apart from his society is just one more animal' (192) – that the spirit only arises *en masse* – and yet he is supposed to be undermining philosophy, not updating Hegel. Thus instead of being content to draw negative conclusions from linguistic holism, Rorty allows it to morph into a positive proposal with its own drawbacks – just as Cartesianism had drawbacks with scepticism – thereby compromising his metaphilosophical stance and making himself look like just another partisan philosopher.

Next up after the discussion of babies and animals is Section 4, which is Rorty's critique of the philosophy of Quine; following it properly would require a detailed background in that philosophy, but it is largely self-contained and makes little contribution to the plot of *PMN* anyway. Quine himself wrote a response entitled 'Let Me Accentuate the Positive' (Quine 1990) in which he disputed virtually everything Rorty had said – the 'positive' is reserved for the final sentence – but without getting into the details of Quine's theories, or why he rejected Rorty's interpretations, it is nevertheless easy enough to pick up on the gist of Rorty's misgivings.[7]

Rorty is unhappy with Quine's ontological distrust of meanings, and more generally, with the fact that he takes ontology seriously, an attitude Rorty regards as a result of failing to realise 'the Hegelian implications of his own behaviourism and holism' (195). Quine made his definitive ontological statement in *Word and Object* – written some years after 'Two Dogmas' – when he said that if we want to 'limn' (i.e. emboss in gold, as on a medieval manuscript) the 'true and ultimate structure of reality' (Quine 1960: 221), then we should rely only on the language of physical science, and that 'intentional idioms' concerning meanings and mental states are merely 'loose talk': practically useful, perhaps, but ontologically misleading (ibid.: 206 and ff.). This is obviously a far cry from Rorty's ontological indifference, and so Rorty wants to show that Quine's meaning scepticism – his distrust of all things intentional – is detachable from his rejection of the analytic–synthetic distinction.[8]

As Rorty sees it, Quine's insight that meanings cannot be invoked to provide an explanation of a special sort of truth – analytic truth – showed only their uselessness for epistemological purposes, not that there was anything intrinsically suspect about them. Moreover, Rorty thinks that the very reasons that led Quine to reject the analytic–synthetic distinction should have made him realise the futility of trying to impose a principled divide between ontologically respectable and disrespectable language, since it is a consequence of holism and pragmatism that any way of dividing up the holistic belief system can be revised in light of experience. We revise our ontological commitments on pragmatic grounds as we go along, according to Rorty, and not in advance on the basis of philosophical arguments. Hence as long as intentional states are useful for explaining behaviour – which they currently are – then there is nothing wrong with them; we may one day want to give them up (if we meet the Antipodeans, for example), but we may also want to give up on entities talked about in current physics. So Rorty's view, in stark contrast to Quine's, is that 'ideas in the mind are no more or less disreputable than neurons in the brain' (209).

Quine mixed up epistemological impotency with ontological dubiousness, according to Rorty, because he was in the grip of his own dogma, an inherited distrust of non-extensionality. This is a logical feature of language, a key indicator of which is that terms referring to the same thing cannot be freely swapped in a non-extensional sentence without risk of changing the truth-value.[9] So, for instance, even though 'Venus' and 'Hesperus' are two names for the same thing, it can be true that 'Tom believes Venus is a planet' and false that 'Tom believes Hesperus is a planet', simply because Tom does not know they are the same – maybe he thinks Hesperus is a metal, for instance. If, however, the extensional sentence 'Venus is a planet' is true, then 'Hesperus is a planet' is guaranteed to be true. Many philosophers (e.g. Carnap) have considered this feature of sentences about mental states (such as Tom's belief) to be a sign of imprecision, and Rorty thinks that Quine inherits this attitude: non-extensionality is 'the real bugbear' (204) for Quine, and thus the real reason he thinks 'intentional idioms' are unsuitable for ontological 'limning'. As Rorty sees it, however, there is no reason extensional and non-extensional descriptions should not just peacefully co-exist. Even if the universe can be completely described in exclusively extensional language ('completely' in the sense that everything in time and space is covered), this does not discredit non-extensional language in any way, because 'the distinction between the universal and the specific is not the distinction between the factual and the "empty"' (207). Hence so long as non-extensional language remains even occasionally useful, there is nothing wrong with it, and whether or not we could in principle use an extensional alternative is neither here nor there. Only a lingering attachment to the idea of philosophy as an adjudicator between alternative descriptions of reality makes it seem as if there is a choice to be made.

7

NATURALISED EPISTEMOLOGY: PSYCHOLOGY

(*PMN*, CHAPTER 5)

QUINE'S NATURALISED EPISTEMOLOGY

(§§1–2)

Chapters 5 and 6 are about 'two attempts to preserve something from the Cartesian tradition' (210). According to the first, empirical psychology offers a new approach to the old Mirror of Nature problematic, and according to the second, the philosophy of language does. Rorty regards both of these attempts to reinvent epistemology for the latter half of the twentieth century as thoroughly misguided, because the moral he wants to draw from linguistic holism is not that a new, post-Cartesian approach to epistemological problems is required, but rather that there is no point in trying to solve these problems. As Rorty sees it, the twentieth century no more needed a new approach to epistemology than the seventeenth century needed a new approach to understanding angels; what was required for progress in both periods was the abandonment of old problems, not their reformulation. Epistemology might have been worthy of update had its concerns been perennial, but Rorty thinks they were rather just a specific, historical response to an intellectual need felt in the seventeenth century, when the transition from a religious to a secular culture left a vacuum of authority which objective truth seemed capable of filling. As it turned out, however, epistemology did not produce any useful results, and the cultural relevance it once possessed has long since evaporated. To modernise epistemology now would serve only to breathe new life into the idea of a non-human constraint on our beliefs, thereby holding back the secularisation process begun in the enlightenment. So Rorty's aim in these chapters is to disrupt and discourage, in order to try to prevent a new lease of life being granted to what he regards as a counterproductive and tedious literary genre.

The way he sets about this follows a standard pattern in the case of both empirical (or scientific) psychology and philosophy of language. First, he distinguishes a good and a bad interpretation of the proposal. The good interpretation has nothing to do with the Mirror of Nature problematic, and hence presents a perfectly legitimate intellectual pursuit. The bad one does, however, and hence falls foul of the 'line of thought' (213) which Rorty called 'epistemological behaviourism' (but nearly called 'pragmatism'). So new approaches to psychology and language have something good going for them, but they must not be bestowed with any philosophical significance.

Chapter 5 targets two particular attempts to bestow philosophical significance on psychology. The first is Quine's idea that psychology holds out prospects for the development of what he called 'Naturalized Epistemology', an epistemology purged of Descartes's aprioricism and foundationalism; others later adopted Quine's label for their own related programmes. The second is the functionalist idea that analogies between mental states and software states of computers can provide an updated and scientific account of the traditional epistemological notion of mental states as inner representations of the world. Rorty wants to undermine both of these, but before setting about this, his first task is to defend psychology from philosophical attacks on its legitimacy. This is because he wants to defend psychology from both philosophical 'criticisms' and philosophical 'compliments' (211): philosophers are just as wrong to criticise psychology as they are to read philosophical significance into it. In short, Rorty wants to keep psychology and philosophy completely isolated from each other, both because he thinks psychology is culturally harmless and philosophy is not, and because he wants to deprive philosophy of resources for regenerating itself.

It is a cliché – and a rather outdated one these days – that philosophers tend to regard psychology with at best suspicion and at worst derision. The origins of this cliché are not hard to understand, since psychology only became independent from mainstream philosophy relatively recently – in the late nineteenth century – and the presuppositions required to set up this new 'science of the mind' were philosophically controversial. The founders of psychology, such as William James, were philosophers of mind who wanted to study the mind scientifically, and so were prepared to forget about the mind–body problem to look instead for the causal mechanisms governing the interaction of mental states, rather as natural sciences look for the causal mechanisms governing the interaction of physical states. Psychology was to study cognitive processes as natural science studies physical, chemical or biological processes. Those philosophers who questioned the appropriateness of characterising the mind in terms of inner states, causal relations, cognitive processes, and the like, however, suspected that this new approach to studying the mind was based on philosophical misunderstanding. Such suspicions reached a head in the philosophies of Wittgenstein and Ryle, both of whom harboured an 'hostility to privacy' (117) based on ontological distrust of private mental entities for which no public, linguistic criteria of identity could be provided. Ryle's behaviourism forcluded any scientific study of subjective mental entities simply because it denied that such entities exist, and this meant abandoning 'the dream of psychology as a counterpart to Newtonian science' (Ryle 1963: 305), as well as,

> the false notion that psychology is the sole empirical study of people's mental powers, propensities, and performances, together with its implied false corollary that 'the mind' is what is properly describable only in the technical terms proprietary to psychological research.
>
> (Ibid.: 308)

As Ryle saw it, we learn about people's behaviour – and hence their minds – in a variety of different walks of life and fields of study, not just in psychology.[1]

Rorty sums up this line of thought as the view that there is no 'middle ground' (214) for psychology to study between brain science and our everyday understanding of behaviour, and that the idea of mental entities and processes standing in-between what brains do and what people do is just a legacy of Cartesianism. Rorty's response to this is predictable enough given his complete lack of ontological scruples: psychologists should be allowed to 'dream up' (216) whatever entities they want. The only issue from his pragmatist perspective is whether or not it is useful to talk about mental entities, and since psychologists do find it useful to talk about mental entities in order to explain overt behaviour, just as natural scientists find it useful to talk about unobservable entities to explain the observable world, then as far as Rorty is concerned there is no problem. He is more interested in why philosophers have thought there was a problem.

One underlying motivation for suspicion of psychology, Rorty suggests, is the old worry that mechanistic explanations of human behaviour threaten to debase us, reducing love, art, and anything else we value into just another natural phenomenon to be measured and catalogued. But a greater motivation, he thinks, comes from the opposite direction, in that philosophers have thought that psychology is not mechanistic enough, and that human behaviour should instead be physically explained in terms of brain activity and other purely physiological happenings. Rorty is suitably disdainful of this suggestion, which he regards as a vague residue of the formative influence of seventeenth-century science on philosophy; philosophers were so impressed by the idea that 'everything could be explained by atoms and the void' (217) that they never managed to get over it, though physicalist convictions are now, 'softened by a dim awareness of quantum mechanics, so that an ontological respect for insensate matter has been replaced by a sociological respect for professors of physics' (217). Rorty of course thinks that the 'respect' involved in the contemporary physicalist view that – in effect – reality consists in whatever physicists say it consists in, is an inheritance of religion. It must be remembered, however, that Rorty is himself supposed to be a physicalist; this section is thus a good reminder of how unorthodox that 'physicalism' is. And it is also a good reminder of the distance between Rorty's pragmatism and the eliminative materialism he once espoused, since the desire to 'cut straight through the mental to the neurophysiological' (217) is a principal motivation for most contemporary eliminativists, and Rorty has no time for it at all.[2]

The most substantial motivation for philosophical distrust of psychology which Rorty detects, however, is the concern that if mental states can only be known through private introspection, then hypotheses about them cannot be publicly tested and verified in accordance with standard scientific methodology. Thus philosophers have been moved to deny the existence of mental states and to malign psychology in order to avoid compromising scientific rationality. Rorty thinks this is a mistake. His reason is that once the Myth of the Given is abandoned, then introspective reports can be seen to be just as intersubjective as any other report; the fact that we are accustomed to taking people's word for it when they report their own mental states is 'a sociological rather than a metaphysical concern' (219), as explained by Rorty's social practice account of incorrigibility. So as long as mental states are not thought to provide a special and private sort of knowledge, they present no threat to the integrity of science. Psychologists can use introspective reports along with all sorts of other evidence when forming their hypotheses, and need only avoid the trap of treating them as the final word. So Rorty's conclusion, then, is that if we embrace linguistic holism, forget about ontology, and realise that minds are just things we talk about, rather than the magical ingredient of moral dignity, then all qualms about psychology fade away.

Section 2 is about Quine's Naturalised Epistemology, the paradigm case of epistemological significance being read into psychology.[3] Quine's idea was that the traditional epistemological project of determining how we ought to arrive at our beliefs through *a priori* reflection needed to be replaced by the scientific project of describing how we actually do arrive at our beliefs. Epistemology would thereby become a 'chapter of psychology' (Quine 1969: 82) studying the relation between theories about the world and the evidence we have for those theories. Of course, relating theory to evidence was always an epistemological concern, which is why Quine wants to keep the name, but the difference is that Quine rejects the foundationalist attempt to derive our theories from a more basic source of knowledge, i.e. from 'privileged representations' such as sense-data. As Quine once said in summary of his basic philosophical outlook,

The world around us pelts our nerve endings with light rays and molecules, triggering sensations. Growing up in a garrulous society, we
learn to associate patterns of these sensations with words and patterns
of these words with further words until we reach the point somehow of
talking about objects in the world around us.

(Quine 1995)

The epistemological task he had in mind, then, was to describe the
causal mechanisms by which happenings at nerve endings issue in
theories about the world. Since talk of 'nerve endings', 'causal mechanisms' etc. is already theoretically loaded, however, Quine clearly
has no ambition to get behind all theory, as per traditional epistemology, for any such project is ruled out by his holism. Rather, the
suggestion is that we rely on some theories whilst describing the
cognitive processes involved in building up others. Thus even
though Quine would agree with Rorty that we cannot 'step outside
our skins', he still thinks that a credible epistemological project
remains which is untouched by this point.

The standard line of response to Quine's proposal has been to
deny that it counts as epistemology. So, for instance, Barry Stroud
has argued that Quine's psychological study cannot be epistemology
because it does not respond to scepticism: knowing how your theories causally relate to the external world is of little use if you are
entertaining doubts about the external world, and hence doubts
about all of the (apparently) causal relations within it (Stroud 1984:
209–54). And Jaegwon Kim has argued that Quine's study cannot be
epistemology because it does not account for justification: working
out the mechanisms by which we build up scientific theories does
not show we are right to build them up that way – maybe we should
be emulating the cognitive processes used by astrologers instead, for
instance (Kim 1988). Now Rorty's critique (which predates those of
both Stroud and Kim) also takes the general line that 'naturalized
epistemology' is not really epistemology. However, whereas Stroud
and Kim both think that Quine's mistake was to lose what was
valuable in the tradition, Rorty thinks that Quine's mistake was to
assume that the tradition had any value at all. Stroud and Kim think
Quine is too radical, but Rorty thinks he is too 'genial' (223, 229),
and the result of this geniality, according to Rorty, is that Quine's

proposal is unmotivated. Worse still, Rorty thinks that it is actually unstable as well.

Rorty thinks Quine was led astray by a lack of historical awareness, a criticism which has deep resonance for him, since disregard for history is at the heart of his misgivings about analytic philosophy in general, and Quine in particular had a reputation for treating the history of philosophy with disdain.[4] The problem, as Rorty sees it, is that Quine simply takes for granted the desirability of a systematic account of human knowledge. This is why he is not content to just renounce foundationalist epistemology, but instead wants to find a new approach to replace it. In Rorty's view, however, foundationalism is the only reason anybody ever took epistemology seriously in the first place. Epistemology seemed important in the seventeenth century because the Mirror of Nature idea promised to provide a foundation for knowledge which would uphold the claims of the New Science against Scholasticism. It would allow defenders of the New Science such as Descartes and Locke to make 'an invidious distinction between Galileo and the professors who refused to look through his telescope' (225).[5] Moreover, foundationalist epistemology was required to defeat scepticism, because this was an inevitable consequence of reprentationalism. Now Quine of course shares none of these concerns, as is evident from the fact that the psychological study he envisages can neither legitimise science nor respond to scepticism. But as far as Rorty can see, there never was any other reason to want a systematic account of the relation between theory and evidence. Consequently, rather than genially saving what was good in the tradition, Rorty thinks that Quine has simply invented a new and unmotivated study.

Rorty also thinks naturalised epistemology is unstable, on the grounds that there is no way for it to straddle the divide between causal and sociological conceptions of evidence and theory. Quine thought that once foundationalism is rejected, and we accept that anything regarded as evidence for our theories will be as theory-laden as anything else – for there are no pre-theoretical givens – then there is no longer any obstacle to using an ordinary physical criterion of evidence, such as neural input. However, as Rorty points out, 'As electricity, neural input is not new; as "information" it is problematic' (227). This is because from the point of causal mechanisms, there is no reason to bestow epistemological significance on one part of the causal chain (e.g. neural input) rather than another (e.g. impact on the retina). In Rorty's view, then, there is no stable resting point for naturalised epistemology to occupy between an ordinary conversational conception of theory and evidence on the one hand, and a scientific description of a physical thing causally interacting with its environment on the other. By calling one arbitrarily selected part of the causal chain 'evidence' or 'information', Quine made his idea for a purely causal study look as if it had more to do with epistemology than it actually did.[6] Moreover, the fact that he even wanted to link justification to the causal impact of the environment shows that Quine did not fully grasp the consequences of linguistic holism. If he had, Rorty thinks, then he would have abandoned the last vestiges of his commitment to empiricism, and realised that justification must be left entirely within the social domain; 'sociology and history of science' (225) are much more likely to provide insight into how evidence relates to theory than psychology is.

THE INFINITE REGRESS ARGUMENT

(§§3–4)

One of the main philosophical objections to psychological explanation in terms of mental entities is that such explanations generate infinite regresses. This is again an objection associated with Wittgenstein, Ryle, and their followers, but it has resurfaced in many forms and is still discussed today (e.g. Crane 2003: 154–56). The basic idea is that by appealing to mental entities and processes, psychology does not explain anything, but rather just pushes everything back a level, thereby replacing questions about how people perform cognitive tasks such as visual recognition, memory, imagination, etc., with parallel questions concerning mental entities. For example, according to this objection, trying to explain how a man can visually recognise dogs by appealing to his idea of dogs, simply replaces the question of how he can recognise dogs with the question of how he can recognise when something matches his idea of dogs. Of course, the matching might be conceived of as a mechanical process in the brain, with the experience of a dog somehow 'slotting' into a pre-formed neural template, but this kind of causal explanation cannot in itself account for knowledge; causation and justification must be kept apart, as Sellars argued. Consequently, in order for the man's idea of dogs to have epistemic relevance, he must be able to know when it matches up with what he is seeing. But how he knows this is no easier to understand than how he knows when he is seeing a dog, and if we try to explain it with yet another idea – the idea of matching, say – then all the same issues arise again, and so on *ad infinitum*.

Another way this argument is often put is in terms of the 'Homuncular Fallacy', according to which it is said that trying to explain cognitive tasks in terms of mental entities is like positing little men (homunculi) inside our heads to perform the cognitive tasks for us. The problem with this, of course, is that the homunculi themselves then require smaller homunculi inside their own heads, and these smaller homunculi require even smaller homunculi, etc., thus generating an infinite regress. And as with all such regresses, what this shows is that the required explanation has been put off indefinitely, thereby rendering psychological explanations as useless as infinite instructions for assembling flat-packed furniture.

Rorty's attitude to the infinite regress argument is equivocal: he defends its use in certain specific cases, namely those in which the psychological explanation has been loaded with philosophical signif-icance, but he considers all other uses of it to be 'incautious' though 'understandable' (242). Rorty mounts his limited defence of the argument in response to an objection that was made to it in an early paper by Jerry Fodor (Fodor 1966). Fodor – a psychologist before he became a philosopher – made his objection using the example of our ability to recognise 'Lillibulero', a seventeenth-century political song with a melody everyone knows.[7] Underlying Fodor's objection is the idea that we can recognise Lillibulero in a potentially infinite number of ways, which is obvious when you think about it, for you could start the melody at almost any pitch, use almost any sound or variety of sounds, play it at almost any tempo, harmonise it in any number of ways, mess around with the relative tuning and rhythmic relations, and combine all of these variations indefinitely. However, though Lillibulero could be recognisably performed in an unlimited number of ways, it is nevertheless true that every time that we hear it, we hear a particular set of sounds, such as somebody whistling it at a bus-stop, or an orchestrated version on a crackly radio, for instance. The moral Fodor draws from this is that our 'recipe' (231) for recognising Lillibulero must be highly abstract: it must abstract away from the particularities of concrete performances to pick up on an underlying pattern they all have in common. It is the need to account for this abstractness, then, which justifies psychological explanation, and so contrary to the claims of the infinite regress argument, positing a level of explanation between common-sense and physical description is not at all superfluous, but rather required to make scientific sense of our ability to detect abstract constancy across wide-ranging physical variation.

Fodor's defence of psychological explanation has the effect of linking it up with the history of philosophy, because within the empiricist tradition, the mind's ability to abstract away from particularity was always thought to be the key to understanding the connection between sensory experience and our complex linguistic descriptions of the world. Locke, for instance, thought that 'the power of *Abstracting* . . . [and hence] the having of general Ideas, is that which puts a perfect distinction betwixt Man and Brutes' (Locke 1979: II.11.§10), and Berkeley's alternative empiricist system was in large part a consequence of his differences with Locke over how to understand abstraction. Moreover, if we take seriously Rorty's claim in Chapter 1 that the empiricist conception of an idea is effectively of an internalised and hypostatised universal, then we have a link all the way back to Plato. As Rorty sees it, then, Fodor is defending psychology by portraying it as a new scientific approach to an old philosophical problem. This is exactly what Rorty is most opposed to.

Rorty's basic response is that Fodor's appeal to abstractness does not undermine the infinite regress argument because 'what holds of recognition should hold of acquisition' (232). The point is that if we grant that recognising Lillibulero requires that we have an abstract formula in mind – some very general pattern we are able to detect within widely divergent musical performances – then the question arises of how we learned this formula. If we learned it by listening to Lillibulero, then we must already have possessed an abstract formula which allowed us to recognise the pattern. This cannot have been the formula for Lillibulero, of course – that would make the account circular – but it could perhaps have been the abstract formula for melody recognition. And yet if we make this move, a regress will have been initiated, because now the question arises of how we acquired the formula for melody recognition. Consequently, if recognition requires an abstract ability, and if this means that learning to recognise requires an abstract ability as well, then a psychological account of the abstract mechanisms required for recognition will not be able to explain either recognition or abstraction, but will rather just generate another regress.

Rorty's more principled objection is to Fodor's use of the abstract–concrete distinction. What mainly concerns him is that this distinction might be used to reinvigorate the mental–physical distinction, with the distinctive feature of mind being thought of as its power to make abstractions from concrete physical reality. As Rorty sees it, however, the abstract–concrete distinction is entirely interest-relative, such that, for example, if the frame of reference is Lillibulero, then a particular recording is concrete and the concept of melody is abstract, but if melody is the frame of reference, then Lillibulero is concrete and the concept of sound is abstract. This means there is no reason to think of our ability to detect similarities among potentially infinite permutations as any different in principle from the ability of a thermometer to detect temperature while ignoring the other factors in the environment, or the ability of a photoelectric cell to detect light while ignoring the other factors in the environment. Only the idea that the abstract–concrete distinction marks a real and fixed distinction in nature makes us want to draw a significant contrast between, on the one hand, a thermometer and photoelectric cell simply reacting to a concrete factor in the environment, and on the other, an adult human being recognising the abstract pattern required for a set of sounds to count as Lillibulero. Once we see that nothing is intrinsically abstract, however, then Rorty thinks we should no longer regard our ability to recognise complex patterns as calling for some unique kind of explanation; the question of how abstraction in thought is possible should elicit nothing more than the 'pointless remark that nature has evolved suitable hardware to get the job done' (235).

The need for psychological explanation, in Rorty's view, is a practical rather than a principled matter. It is not that the unique nature of mind requires a unique form of explanation, but rather just that the complexity of human physiology makes a level of explanation between common-sense and physiology practically indispensable. Thus the justification for talking about mental entities and processes in psychology, according to Rorty, is just that the complexity of the brain requires its operations to be divided up into distinct subroutines. This means that, 'the notion of psychological states as inner representations is unobjectionable but fairly uninteresting' (242). It is 'unobjectionable', because the infinite regress argument has no force against the positing of mental entities as a practical device; the distinctive features of the Mirror of Nature will not be explained in this way, but no attempt should be made to explain them anyway. If psychologists can explain behaviour by talking about mental entities as if they were little men representing and abstracting inside our heads, that is fine with Rorty. It is 'uninteresting', however, because the usefulness of this level of explanation provides no philosophical insight into the nature of mind whatsoever. In particular, it does not show that the mind is software running on the hardware of the brain, as many functionalists believe, since for Rorty there is nothing more to the psychology/computer program analogy than the fact that functional descriptions are useful for talking about people, just as they are useful for talking about computers. This is just because people and computers are both types of complex physical system.

Rorty is so keen to emphasise his view that the only justification for explaining people in psychological terms is the complexity of human physiology, that he goes so far as to claim that, 'if the body had been easier to understand, nobody would have thought that we had a mind' (239). So if the correlations between human behaviour and physiology had been obvious enough, he thinks, then there would have been no use for psychology as an intermediate level of explanation between the two, just as there is no use for psychology in explaining 'one-celled animals' (237). This is a striking claim, and one which needs to be evaluated in light of Rorty's incorrigibility account of the concept of mind. If that account is accepted, then the claim is credible, for if physiology had been obvious enough – if you could just see whether or not somebody's C-fibres were firing, for instance – then perhaps there would never have been any need for the institution of talking about private sensations to develop. However if the incorrigibility account is rejected, then the claim is not credible, because even if human physiology had been entirely obvious, people would still have noticed the difference between feeling their own physiological changes, and observing physiological changes in others. So whether the claim is regarded as credible or incredible really depends on whether you think the concept of mind is based on incorrigibility or consciousness.

The main point Rorty is trying to get across in this chapter, however, is just that psychological explanations are nothing to do with justification, that '[n]o roads lead . . . from psychology to epistemology' (246). Psychology is perfectly legitimate, but it cannot short-circuit the judgement of society in determining questions of justification and rationality. This is just a straightforward application of Rorty's view that causal explanation and justification must be kept strictly apart, a view to which the particular form of causal explanation used by psychologists makes no difference: 'The gap between explaining ourselves and justifying ourselves is just as great whether a programming language or a hardware language is used in the explanations' (249). Thus it is no more relevant to issues of justification to mention the mental processes uncovered by psychological research, than it is to mention blood flow, glands, or the motion of molecules. Even if psychologists were to discover that different populations have entirely different mental processes, this would have no bearing on which populations should be trusted, according to Rorty, because justification is public and social, rather than internal and mechanical. Neither would it make any difference if it turned out that all of our mental processes have been 'hardwired' into us by evolution. A causal understanding of the brain and its interactions with the environment simply cannot tell us what we ought to think.

8

NATURALISED EPISTEMOLOGY: LANGUAGE
(*PMN*, CHAPTER 6)

DUMMETT AND DAVIDSON

(§1)

The moral of Chapter 5 was that a causal understanding of the brain and its interactions with the environment cannot tell us what we ought to think, and the parallel moral of Chapter 6 is that an understanding of the mechanics of how languages work cannot tell us what we ought to think either. This parallel reflects the fact that Rorty interprets much twentieth-century philosophy of language as simply an alternative approach to naturalising epistemology, and hence as just another misguided attempt to take justification out of the social domain in order to transform it into the ahistorical concern of the philosopher. This approach to developing a new epistemology is as ill-fated as the last, however, because just as 'no roads' (246) lead from psychology to epistemology, so it is the case that, 'No roads lead from the project of giving truth-conditions for the sentences of English . . . to the construction of a canonical notion which "limns the true and ultimate structure of reality"' (300). Rorty thinks that this moral has been fully absorbed by the 'pure' philosophy of language of Donald Davidson, which he considers to be perfectly legitimate, just as he considers psychology to be perfectly legitimate. However, there is also an 'impure' form of philosophy of language which tries to link up the workings of language with the traditional problems of philosophy. So once again, Rorty's aim is to prevent a legitimate project from becoming infected with epistemology.

In the midst of the parallel plot unfolding, however, something of far greater importance occurs, which is that Rorty reveals both the extent of his alliance with Davidson, and the significance he reads into Davidson's work. This adds an extra layer of depth to Rorty's thought, and it makes it possible to glimpse his full metaphilosophical vision for the first time. This is an essentially historical vision of a development of thought reaching from Hegel to Dewey to Quine and Sellars to Davidson, as well as from Hegel to the current era via thinkers within the continental tradition. It is a vision first adumbrated in 'The World Well Lost' (in which Rorty began drawing metaphilosophical conclusions from Davidson's work on conceptual schemes two years before it was even published), and which reached its culmination in *PMN*; Rorty has been elaborating and refining it ever since.

Before commencing with the plot, we need first to address a question which must have occurred to just about everybody who ever reached this point in the book: why is Rorty suddenly prepared to endorse a form of philosophy? Up until now, philosophy has been up in the dock and has been found wanting on all counts; Rorty has been asking 'why we have such a phenomenon as "philosophy" in our culture' (229), and he has found no good reasons whatsoever. Yet suddenly we are being introduced to a 'pure' form of philosophy, practised by Davidson and others, which he seems to think is perfectly acceptable, even admirable. The legitimate project in Chapter 5 was scientific psychology – not philosophy at all – but now Rorty has apparently found a legitimate project for philosophy itself. The strangeness of this development is accentuated by the fact that within this very section, Rorty reiterates his view that, in effect, Descartes invented epistemology and Kant used it to invent philosophy (262–63). But if philosophy is just epistemology and epistemology is a cultural disaster, how can Davidson's brand of philosophy be deemed acceptable? Moreover, just to add to the tension, Rorty blithely traces Davidson's concerns right back through Frege to Plato and even Parmenides (257), making it seem as if philosophy (the proper, 'pure' variety) must be an ancient, autonomous, and legitimate subject after all, just as the conventional histories of philosophy always said it was.

These issues are not fully resolved until Part Three ('Philosophy'), but we can see where things are going straight away just by noting that Rorty's pragmatism is more than just theoretical: he evidently wants his writings to have an effect. Now since contemporary philosophy is fully professional and institutionally secure – it is, as he once rather begrudgingly conceded, 'a respectable intellectual discipline' (Pettegrew 2000: 210) – Rorty would have been well aware when he wrote *PMN* that there was no chance of philosophy coming to an end in the foreseeable future. So given that philosophy would inevitably continue, it is perhaps not too hard to see why Rorty might be attracted to an approach to language which, 'makes it as difficult as possible to raise philosophically interesting questions about meaning and reference' (299). With Davidsonian semantics, then, Rorty thinks that philosophy has found an activity which will help it to lose sight of its traditional concerns and thereby gradually turn its back on its Kantian origins. The apparent metaphilosophical optimism of this suggestion, however, is dampened down by the fact that Rorty thinks of the step from epistemology to semantics as a 'relegation' (179), that is, as a transition from something 'deep and philosophical' (in Rorty's curiously pejorative sense) to something 'shallow and unphilosophical' (248–49), and thus 'bland' (260–61) enough to be culturally harmless.

The plot of the chapter begins, then, with Rorty placing his distinction between pure and impure philosophy of language in an historical context. Now as we have already seen, Rorty thinks that analytic philosophy began as a neo-Kantian backlash against the holism and historicism that were taking over philosophy in the late nineteenth century. As such, it began as an impure programme in the philosophy of language, since Russell and the logical positivists did not want linguistic analysis to become the central task of philosophy primarily because they considered a systematic account of language valuable in its own right, but rather because they thought it offered a new and improved approach to the traditional problems of philosophy. This approach caught on, in Rorty's view, because it united the empiricist tradition on the one hand, with the Kantian distinction between passively responding to experience and actively ordering it. The empiricist element made philosophy look scientific, and the Kantian element provided the source of *a priori* knowledge required by philosophical methodology. Moreover, linguistic analysis updated both elements. It updated traditional empiricism, because unlike private and ontologically dubious ideas, sentences were public, natural, and thus more easily studied according to collectively agreed upon criteria. And it updated Kantian philosophy, because the active imposition of structure upon experience could now be construed as simply the imposition of meaning onto words, allowing the philosopher's quest for *a priori* insight into the structure of experience to be reconceived as the more scientifically respectable task of systematically analysing the semantics and logical syntax of language. Thus philosophy of language seemed both in touch with tradition and in tune with the times.

By the 1960s, however, the original constructive programmes of analytic philosophy of language had largely been either abandoned or else substantially modified. Many philosophers had been persuaded by Wittgenstein and the ordinary language philosophy he inspired, that the aim of constructing a systematic theory of meaning to lay bare the logical structure of language was illusory. The anti-foundationalist arguments of Quine and Sellars were also instrumental in bringing about this disillusionment, as was Quine's meaning scepticism, and though these arguments may not have played quite the definitive role Rorty implies, they were certainly representative of a general move away from the reductionism and phenomenalism that had characterised early analytic philosophy. Nevertheless, though the idea of producing definitions in terms of sense-data was largely abandoned, constructive philosophy of language continued in more sophisticated forms, and many philosophers persisted in their adherence to the analytic ideal of constructing a systematic theory of meaning; what had primarily changed was opinion over how this was to be achieved.

The main spokesman for continuing in this constructive vein has been Michael Dummett, Ayer's successor at Oxford, who is unusual amongst analytic philosophers for his interest in metaphilosophy, a subject on which his views can generally be relied upon to diametrically oppose Rorty's.[1] Dummett is known, amongst other things, for advocating a return to the 'fountain-head of analytical philosophy', namely Frege, on the grounds that Frege's original idea of using quantificational logic to produce a formal semantic theory is entirely detachable from the epistemological purposes it was put to by Russell and the logical positivists. So even though Dummett thinks that analytic philosophy of language has much to learn from the critiques of Wittgenstein, Quine, and others, he also thinks that its central, Fregean project has survived these critiques unscathed. That project, as Dummett understands it, is to understand the nature of human thought by working out the fundamental logical principles which govern the functioning of our languages, and Frege's great achievement was to make this project the foundation of philosophy, reversing the priority Descartes had accorded to epistemology. Thus philosophy of language is to be counted as 'first philosophy' (264), in Dummett's view, for the reason that unless we understand the nature of thought, we cannot be sure that we are thinking about other philosophical topics such as mind or knowledge in the right way (see Dummett 1978: 88–89, 442–43).

Rorty has little sympathy with the dethroning of epistemology which Dummett proposes, because he thinks that a far more radical break with the Mirror of Nature tradition is required. This is also the reason why he was dissatisfied with Quine's naturalised epistemology, of course, but the situation is considerably more obvious here, since the purposes to which Dummett has put his linguistic approach to philosophy are squarely antithetical to Rorty's project. The best known instance of this approach is Dummett's claim that the traditional metaphysical dispute between realism and idealism – Dummett coined 'anti-realism' as a more general and 'colourless' alternative to 'idealism' – should be construed as a dispute within the theory of meaning, that is, as 'a conflict about the kind of meaning possessed by statements of the disputed class' (ibid.: 155). In Dummett's view, then, the real issue is bivalence, which is the principle that a statement must be either true or false. Thus realist interpretations of statements are committed to bivalence, so that we might, for instance, think that the meaning of the statement 'there are five apples on the table' requires it to be either true or false, whereas anti-realist interpretations lack this commitment, so that we might, for instance, think that the principle of bivalence is inapplicable to a statement such as 'Guernica was Picasso's best painting'.[2]

Rorty has summed up his view of Dummett's approach by saying that, 'Dummett takes the upshot of Frege's linguistification of philosophy to be that the only way to make sense of a metaphysical disagreement is by semantic ascent – jacking up the old metaphysical issue into a new semantical issue' (Rorty 1991a: 148). What Rorty principally objects to about this approach is Dummett's implicit assumption that philosophy deals with perennial problems. Without this assumption, there would be no reason to think of a Fregean theory of meaning as offering a more precise and scientific approach to problems that had previously been tackled with inferior methods. Thus Rorty's dispute with Dummett is essentially metaphilosophical: whereas 'Dummett sees himself as having rehabilitated these fine old problems by semanticizing them' (Rorty 1991a: 128), Rorty regards the 'fine old problems' as a specific cultural product relevant only to a certain period of European history, and hence not worthy of rehabilitation. This is why Rorty has suggested, in relation to Dummett's semantic analysis of realism and anti-realism, that pragmatists should aspire not to have any intuitions about bivalence at all, since such intuitions invoke a contrast between those statements which depend upon a matter of fact (i.e. an objective truth) and those which do not (Rorty 1982: xxvi–xxix). The pragmatist should, in short, walk away from philosophy in both its metaphysical and semantic guises, and should only ever engage with impure philosophy of language on metaphilosophical grounds. Thus the only objection which Rorty thinks is needed to Dummett's 'last nostalgic attempt to hook up a new kind of philosophical activity with an old problematic' (264) is that it is motivated by a misreading of the history of philosophy.

Rorty is not against this 'new kind of philosophical activity', only the uses to which it is put by philosophers like Dummett, since the project of producing a theory of meaning based upon Fregean logic is a common denominator between the pure philosophy of language Rorty favours and the impure version he opposes. Davidson, who as already noted belongs to the former category, made an important proposal about the form this project should take in his 1967 paper 'Truth and Meaning' (Davidson 1984: 17–36), which was an influence on Dummett and many other philosophers of language.[3] Davidson's leading idea was that a theory of truth of the type already developed by the philosopher Alfred Tarski could be used as the basis of a theory of meaning. Tarski's aim had been to show how truth could be defined for a particular language, and the most remarked upon feature of his work (which mainly consists in symbolic logic) is the claim that an adequate theory of truth for a language would entail equivalencies of the following form for all sentences of that language:

> The sentence 'snow is white' is true in English if and only if snow is white.

Thus if we had a definition of truth for English, for example, then it would imply equivalencies of the above form for each and every particular English sentence. Davidson's idea was to use the truth-conditions stated by these sorts of equivalencies to build up a theory of meaning.

Now even though the above example may look trivial, the case is clearly quite different if the object language (the one for which the theory is being provided) is not one you speak. So, for instance, 'The sentence "la neige est blanche" is true in French if and only if snow is white', tells an English speaker something substantive, namely the conditions required for this particular French sentence to count as true. Davidson's suggestion is that the more of these truth-conditions we compile and systematically relate to each other, the more substantive the theory will become, until it eventually captures the meaning of individual sentences. So, for instance, if we knew the conditions in which 'snow is white' is true, as well as how this sentence inferentially connects up with other sentences such as 'snow is cold', 'magnesium oxide is white', 'sunglasses are essential for skiers', and a vast number of other sentences, then the claim is that we would know all there is to know about the meaning of 'snow is white'. As Rorty has put it,

> no single T-sentence [i.e. Tarskian truth-condition] . . . will tell you what it is to understand any of the words occurring on the left-hand sides,

> but . . . the whole body of such sentences tells you all there is to know about this.
>
> (Rorty 1991a: 143–44)

Davidsonian semantics is thus essentially holistic, since it attempts to build up a theory of meaning by analysing the inferential connections between large numbers of sentences, rather than by directly analysing individual sentences or their component words. The actual task of systematising these inferential connections with symbolic logic is highly complex, since there are many types of sentence construction used within natural languages, and the reformulation required to interrelate them all means that much more than simple disquotation (i.e. removing the quotes marks, as in the 'snow is white' example) is often needed to produce satisfactory truth-conditions.[4]

Unlike Davidson and other pure philosophers of language such as Brandom, Rorty is of course not too interested in the actual task, only the general idea of it, and this is conducive to his metaphilosophical agenda on many different levels. For a start, Davidson's holist approach eschews any attempt to show how language 'hooks onto the world' (265, 301) by splitting sentences into individual components and then relating the meaning of those components to the world itself, as for instance a traditional empiricist would relate the meaning of 'white' in 'snow is white' to the idea of white which is caused by white objects. Since Davidson has no need to appeal to the causal impact of anything outside of the inferential connections which give sentences their meaning, then, his approach entirely avoids the confusion of causation with justification which Rorty thinks infects the epistemological tradition. Justification, for Rorty and Davidson alike, is a social affair, and Davidson once expressed this – in a phrase Rorty often quotes – by saying that, 'nothing can count as a reason for holding a belief except another belief' (Davidson 1986: 310). So Davidson's philosophy of language is not at all infected by the Myth of the Given; Davidson was just as keen to avoid this as Rorty would have been if he had ever tried to devise a constructive programme.

Davidson is also clearly not trying to divide up culture by saying that different sorts of sentences have different sorts of truth-makers, some more objective than others, since according to his approach, sentences are simply made true by the right-hand side of a Tarskian truth-condition. So just as 'Mars has two moons' is true if and only if Mars has two moons, so 'Guernica was Picasso's best painting' is true if and only if Guernica was Picasso's best painting. As Davidson makes the point,

> Nothing . . . no thing, makes sentences and theories true: not experience, not surface irritations, not the world, can make a sentence true. (. . . .) The sentence 'My skin is warm' is true if and only if my skin is warm. Here there is no reference to a fact, a world, an experience, or a piece of evidence.
>
> (Davidson 1984: 194)

Thus Davidson is not embroiled in the traditional epistemological pursuit of trying to get outside of our theories to see how they relate to evidence, since Tarskian truth-conditions simply relate language on the one hand, to the world as we understand it on the other, and as we shall see in the final sections of this chapter, Davidson has an argument to show that the qualification 'as we understand it' is redundant in any case. Moreover, Davidson is not trying to naturalise epistemology, as his mentor Quine had done, since Davidson does not privilege any particular part of the world to count as the evidence for our theories, in the way in which Quine privileged 'surface irritations'. For Davidson, what counts as evidence is just as mundane and variable as what counts as the truth-maker.

In short, according to Rorty's interpretation at least, Davidson's project has nothing to do with epistemology. Rather, it is the 'philosophy of language of the field linguist' (Rorty 1991a: 132; Davidson 1986: 315), a reference to the fact that Davidson (following Quine) thinks that the most objective standpoint that can be taken on a language is that of the field linguist confronting an alien tongue, given that there is 'no skyhook' to lift us out of the confines of language in order to check how well it meshes with reality itself. Even from this more modest standpoint, however, the field linguist faced with a sufficiently alien object language would at first hear nothing but noise, which is perhaps as much objectivity as could reasonably be hoped for. Davidson's idea, then, is that by systematically correlating noises with environmental conditions, the field linguist would be able to make gradual in-roads into the syntax and semantics of the language. Since this is how the Tarskian truth-conditions for a language are to be compiled, the project is in large part empirical, with the specifically philosophical work being to systematise this linguistic behaviour using the logical techniques developed by Frege, Tarski, and others. There is nothing in any of this for Rorty to disapprove of: *a priori* insight into the structure of experience is not being claimed, no attempt is being made to pass judgement on one type of discourse to the detriment of another, and there is no agenda to relate semantic distinctions to traditional philosophical concerns. The aim is solely to systematise semantic distinctions. Consequently, Rorty sees in Davidsonian semantics the possibility of a clean break with the Kantian tradition, and he thus certifies it as 'pure'.

On an alternative interpretation, however, Davidson's philosophy of language is entirely continuous with the tradition, and represents a swing back to idealism. The thought here is that Rorty and Davidson's rejection of objective truth, and consequent attempt to conceive of truth within the confines of language, is simply an update on the idealist view that truth is confined to ideas. Or, to put it another way, if the truth-value and meaning of sentences is not determined by a relation to the world, but rather only by relations between sentences, then the world as conceived by the realist, i.e. a world indifferent to what human beings say about it, seems to have entirely dropped out of the equation. According to this interpretation, then, far from being a 'new kind of philosophical activity' (264), Davidson's approach would actually just be the latest manifestation of the traditional idealist response to the veil of perception problem, namely that we only ever meant to talk about this side of the veil anyway. Given how Rorty has been presenting the history of philosophy, this interpretation makes considerably more sense than he seems to realise, for if philosophy is a literary genre that keeps recycling itself, if the British Idealists were holists who tried to avoid the Myth of the Given, and if Russell replaced British Idealism with a linguistic version of Kantian philosophy which was both atomistic and infected by the Myth of the Given, then it seems much more likely that Davidson's innovation represents simply one more swing of the pendulum than that it represents a radically new beginning.

If Davidson is interpreted as making a move in the traditional debate between realism and idealism, however, then his position is immediately open to the realist objection that without a notion of truth as a relation between our theory of the world and the world itself, we cannot make sense of the possibility that our theories are wrong, or at the very least inadequate. Thus, so the objection goes, merely saying 'snow is white' is true if and only if snow is white, leaves no room to register the possibility that what we mean by 'snow is white' misrepresents the actual state of affairs we are talking about. This point becomes clearer if we consider an obsolete theory, such as the Aristotelian theory that the reason objects fall when they are dropped is that they 'seek the ground'. If we now consider the sentence 'cannonballs seek the ground', the Davidsonian approach will tell us that this sentence is true if and only if cannonballs seek the ground. Given what was meant by this, however, it seems that we will then have to admit that cannonballs do indeed seek the ground – for they do not just float when released in mid-air – and yet describing this sentence as true looks to be at best incomplete and at worst misleading. The reason, according to the realist, is that even though the sentence is true within the conceptual scheme of medieval science, this is a scheme which seriously misrepresents what happens when cannonballs fall to the ground. Thus a notion of truth as a relation between our theories and the world itself is required, rather than just the intratheoretical conception Davidson provides. On the surface, then, this looks like a traditional deadlock between the realist insisting that we need objective truth to measure our theories against, and the idealist insisting that we cannot have it since there is 'no skyhook'.

If such an interpretation could be sustained, then it would be disastrous for Rorty, and so his stated aim is to show that the issue between pure and impure philosophy of language, 'is not a replay of the issues which separated realists from idealists in the days of philosophy-as-epistemology, and indeed is not really an issue about language at all' (265). Rather, it is a metaphilosophical issue, an issue about what philosophy has been and what it can become. In order to argue this, Rorty will discuss the problem of theory change, according to which the traditional realist position would be that progress in science is the increasingly accurate representation of theory-independent entities, whereas the traditional idealist approach would involve relativising truth and reference to the conceptual scheme employed. Rorty thinks that debates about the nature of reference have been motivated by the realist urge to ensure that our words hook onto theory-independent entities throughout changes in theory, and thus that they exemplify an impure approach to the philosophy of language. His aim, then, is to show that Davidson is not on the idealist side of this debate, but is rather not in the debate at all.

THEORY CHANGE AND REFERENCE

(§§2–4)

The problem of theory change, as Rorty sets it up, is to decide whether our ancestors meant to talk about the same things we talk about, even though they had lots of false beliefs about those things, or whether their outlook was so radically unlike our own that they were not even talking about the same things. In terms of the earlier example, then, the issue is whether Aristotelian talk about 'natural downward motion' (268) was really just very skewed talk about gravity, or whether on the contrary the Aristotelians were not talking about gravity at all, but rather something which does not exist. Rorty's reaction to this 'conundrum' (266) is typical: he wants to know why philosophers care about the question, and why they assume it has a definite answer. Thus the philosophical question itself is dismissed out of hand before the discussion is even underway, since as far as Rorty is concerned, it is just obvious that either way of talking could be more useful, depending on what we want to explain and why we want to explain it; context is everything to a pragmatist of Rorty's mind-set.

Rorty's answer to the metaphilosophical question is that the reason philosophers have considered it important to determine whether our ancestors were talking about the same things as us, is that they have taken science to be the area of culture which best makes contact with the ahistorical, objective truth about the world, and thus have wanted to show that this contact could be preserved through historical change. As Rorty satirises this attitude, there 'jolly well is something out there' (267), and so ancient and modern theories alike must be about the same 'something'. This attitude is buttressed by taking a 'Whiggish' approach to history, which means looking at the past as a more or less steady progression towards our current views.[5] So we assume that our current scientific understanding of the world is on the right track, and then describe our ancestors as trying to talk about the same things we can now describe properly. This allows us to say that the Aristotelians were in fact talking about gravity when they talked about natural downward motion, which is of course the common sense view of the matter, and although common sense falters when we consider discourse about things which have no obvious modern counterparts, such as black bile and the aether, philosophical theory requires only that our ancestors talked about some of the same things as us in order to ensure that the rest of their discourse is 'intertwined' (267) with the world.

Rorty thinks this simple empiricist view of scientific progress as 'finding out more and more about the same objects' (275) was undermined when linguistic holists like Quine and Sellars showed that we cannot appeal to a world outside of our past and present theories in order to explain and evaluate those theories. In particular, Rorty thinks that Quine's rejection of the first dogma of empiricism – reductionism – undermined any prospect of forging a link between old and new theories by reducing them to reports of something neutral between those theories, such as sense-data, and that his overthrow of the second dogma – the analytic–synthetic distinction – meant that there was no longer any prospect of isolating past and present meanings in order to relate them to each other. In short, Quine undermined the idea that our ancestors meant to talk about basically the same things we talk about, despite their having many false beliefs about those things, by showing that we cannot draw a principled distinction between what we mean and what we believe.

A more direct challenge to the empiricist approach to theory change, however, and one which had a more immediate effect on the 1960s debate, was that of Paul Feyerabend, who argued against the assumption of 'meaning invariance' (270): that meanings remain the same before and after the development of a new theory (Feyerabend 1962). According to this assumption, the meaning of 'boiling', for example, would have been unaffected by the development of the molecular theory of water, since this theory simply provided an explanation of boiling, but Feyerabend argued that the new theory would also change what was meant by 'boiling', thereby altering the facts it originally set out to explain. His conclusion, then, was that our ancestors did not mean the same as we do, since progress in science involves a continual series of meaning-changes.

Feyerabend's challenge provoked efforts to produce a theory of rational meaning-change, so that even if science could no longer be distinguished from the rest of culture by its ability to produce progressively more accurate descriptions of the same things we have always been meaning to describe, it could nevertheless be distinguished by its use of rational criteria to determine when theories – and hence meanings – should change. In Rorty's view, however, such efforts were doomed from the start, because they failed to address the underlying and more radical challenge of linguistic holism, according to which change in meaning is simply change to the more central parts of the belief system. Given that such changes are 'incited' (272) rather than dictated by experience – for we must choose on pragmatic grounds how the system is to be adjusted – there can be no prospect of unearthing a priori criteria for rational meaning-change, because any purported criteria would be simply additional and equally revisable parts of the belief system.

Consequently, philosophy was unable to set science above other forms of inquiry in virtue of either its continual contact with the objective truth via some strictly observational common denominator between what was meant by past and present scientific terminology, or even in virtue of scientists only ever deciding to mean something new according to rational criteria. So the Kantian self-image of philosophy as the adjudicator of claims to knowledge was under threat; linguistic holism had deprived it of the ahistorical, representational conception of knowledge which had made this adjudication possible. In Rorty's view, of course, this was a good thing, since he rejects the claim that contemporary science represents the world more accurately than medieval science did, in favour of the pragmatist alternative that contemporary science is simply more useful for our society. This alternative does not privilege science in any way, since almost any contemporary form of inquiry could be expected to be more useful to us than a medieval one.

Epistemological ambition is persistent, however, and so given Rorty's way of looking at the history of philosophy, it was perhaps inevitable that there would be a Kantian backlash against this threat to the judicial status of philosophy. It is within this context that Rorty understands the emergence of the causal theories of reference which came to the forefront of the philosophy of language in the 1970s, the best known versions being those of Putnam and Kripke. The deep down motivation for these theories, as Rorty sees it, was to get our words back in contact with ahistorical, objective truth, so that philosophy could get back to business as usual. What the causal theorists themselves thought they were doing, however, was responding to idealism. Rorty considers this their fundamental error, for rather than interpreting linguistic holism as making the anti-philosophical point that there are no fixed meanings to provide a subject-matter for *a priori* philosophical analysis, they instead interpreted it as an updated form of idealism. The importance they saw in the causal theory of reference, then, was that it would undermine the arguments for this new form of idealism, thereby re-establishing realism in a similarly updated form. As such, the development of the causal theory of reference was, for Rorty, the paradigmatic 'impure' programme in the philosophy of language, since instead of responding to linguistic holism by giving up on philosophy, or else looking around for a 'pure' programme free of epistemology, its advocates immediately saw everything in traditional terms, and then duly made the traditional response of answering idealism with realism.

The causal theory of reference promised to re-establish realism by showing that our words can bypass meaning and lock onto a theory-independent world directly, simply by making causal contact with it. In this way, the realist could concede to Quine and Feyerabend that there is no way to show that we are talking about the same objects as our ancestors via some persisting common core of meaning, but insist nonetheless that the causally determined referents of our words have remained the same despite changes in meaning. To show that there is no good motivation for this sort of theory, Rorty responds to three of Putnam's arguments, which is not as arbitrary as it sounds since they are representative of the standard realist case (Putnam 1978: lectures II and III). The common theme of Putnam's arguments is that by relativising truth and reference to a conceptual scheme, and thereby rejecting any extratheoretical (or 'extravocabulary') conception of truth and reference, his antirealist opponent will find it impossible to explain certain evident facts about theory change. Rorty's strategy, then, is to respond on behalf of the antirealist, with the proviso that he will later show that the position he is defending is not antirealism at all; to this effect, he uses lots of 'sneer quotes' and sometimes prefaces 'antirealism' with 'so-called'.

Putnam's first argument is a variation on G.E. Moore's 'Naturalistic Fallacy', which purported to show that any attempt to define 'good' in terms of natural properties would inevitably fail since goodness is basic and indefinable (Moore 1903: Chapter 1, esp. §§10–12). Putnam's parallel argument is that any attempt to define 'true' as an intratheoretical notion rather than as a relation between our words and a theory-independent world must also fail, simply because the theory-independent notion of truth is the notion we have. Thus if we try to define truth in terms of usefulness or justification within our society, as the original pragmatists did, then the fact that it will nevertheless make perfect sense to describe a statement as true but useless, or true but not justified within our society, will immediately show that the definition has failed. In fact, such definitions fail even by their own lights, since 'truth is whatever you are justified in saying within our society' is not something you are justified in saying within our society, and there is probably little use in saying 'truth is whatever it is useful to say' if nobody believes you.

Rorty entirely agrees with Putnam about this, which is why he is always careful to formulate pragmatism as a thesis about justification rather than truth. He does not dispute that our ordinary conception of truth is an absolute notion of a correspondence between words and reality: this is 'unquestionable' (281). What he does dispute, rather, is that this notion of truth has any explanatory value, and so since he is not proposing a revisionary analysis of this notion of truth, but rather its abandonment, Putnam's point is irrelevant. Rorty's own views on what to say about truth have undergone subtle changes throughout the years, but the core of his position is that pragmatists should never try to define 'true', that the 'difference between justification and truth makes no difference' (Rorty 1998: 41) because there is no criterion for truth except for justification, and that we only need a minimalist notion of truth of the sort essentially captured by disquotations such as '"snow is white" if and only if snow is white', but with provision made for a few special uses, notably the 'cautionary' use which qualifies currently justified beliefs as 'perhaps not true' on the grounds that future generations might not consider them justified. Truth in Putnam's sense, however, is Rorty's target, and though he is prepared to grant that there is an innocent notion of truth which pragmatists can countenance, he does not think it is particularly interesting.[6]

Putnam's second argument is that an extratheoretical conception of truth is required to explain the convergence of past scientific theories to present ones. The idea here is that theories from 100 years ago are more similar to our own than those of 200 years ago, which are in turn more similar to our own than those of 300 years ago, etc., and that since this progression cannot be explained in terms of justification alone – for all of the theories were justified in their own time – the explanation must be that we are getting closer to the objective truth. Rorty's simple response is that it is present rather than past justification that explains convergence. Progress throughout the history of science is simply progress 'by our lights' (298): it is progress towards the understanding of the world which we have now. Rorty adds that we are only tempted to think that making sense of scientific progress requires something fixed and external to our theories, if we think of theory change as something like a complete change to everything we believe, whereas in fact 'a "new theory" is simply a rather minor change in a vast network of beliefs' (284). Thus there is always lots of theoretical continuity to measure our progress against.

Putnam's third argument is that extratheoretical truth is needed in order to block the so-called 'Pessimistic Meta-Induction from Past Falsity'. A standard example used to illustrate this argument is the phlogiston theory of combustion (285), which explained burning in terms of the release of a substance called 'phlogiston'. This theory turned out to be false, as seventeenth-century science generally has, and so we now know that phlogiston does not exist. But given that scientific theories have continually turned out to be false throughout the history of science, it seems likely we are now in the same situation as regards electrons, gravity, and everything else which contemporary science talks about: no doubt they will all turn out not to exist as well. This argument is a 'meta-induction', then, because it starts from the inductive premise that past theories have turned out to be false, and then makes an inductive inference to the pessimistic conclusion that present theories will turn out to be false as well. If it is right, then it would seem to suggest a strongly antirealist metaphysic according to which we only ever refer to socially constructed theoretical entities which subsequent generations can be expected not to refer to anymore, since they will have constructed their own. A causal theory of reference, however, promises to block this argument on behalf of realism, by showing that our words can cut straight through our theories to the things they approximate. Thus even if it turns out that nothing really fits what we mean by 'electron', we will have still been referring to something, albeit something which future theories will describe more accurately.

Rorty does not think this argument either needs to be or can be blocked. It does not need to be blocked, because if our descendants decide that there are no electrons, then they will simply 'tell the same sort of story' (286) about us as we tell about our ancestors; they will say that although talk of 'electrons' was justified in our time, we were wrong because the only entities which exist are the ones they talk about. Whether they then relate our talk of 'electrons' to something they talk about, as we might perhaps relate 'natural downward motion' to gravity, or whether on the contrary they just dismiss talk of 'electrons' as completely wrong, as we might dismiss talk of 'phlogiston' as completely wrong, will depend on the standards of justification of the future society, the purposes the future historian of science has for talking about 'electrons', and most obviously of all, what future science says about the world. Whatever we imagine them saying, however, no appeal to an objective truth beyond justification is needed to assure ourselves that we are talking about the same world as them, for this can be done entirely in terms of what they will consider justified. Now there is an obvious sense in which this response fails to engage with the argument, of course, because the meta-induction could always be re-applied to the science of our descendants: maybe none of the entities they will talk about exist either. But this is exactly Rorty's intention, since he does not think that radical scepticism of the traditional type which inserts a wedge between truth and all possible justification can ever be answered; it is rather to be ignored.

It is the impossible dream of undermining scepticism, however, which Rorty thinks has generated interest in the causal theory of reference, but in one of his most striking and ingenious deflationary diagnoses, Rorty goes on to argue that the usual considerations adduced in favour of causal theories trade off an 'equivocity of "refer"' (289): they appeal to our intuitions about 'reference' in an ordinary sense that has nothing to do with scepticism, in order to motivate a theory of 'reference' in a philosophical sense that does have to do with scepticism. Thus one of the most important disputes in the philosophy of language – perhaps the most important of all – turns out to be one big confusion.[7]

The dispute in question is that between the descriptionist or 'intentionalist' (the term Rorty uses) accounts of reference which originate with Frege and Russell (Rorty refers to Strawson and Searle, who developed the approach), and the referentialist or causal approach of Kripke and Putnam. According to the intentionalist approach, reference proceeds via descriptions, so that the referent of a term is whatever best fits the descriptions associated with that term. The causal theory is standardly motivated by a certain type of apparent counter-example to this approach, originally developed by Keith Donnellan, which is supposed to show that what we intend to refer to may not always coincide with what best fits our associated descriptions. So, to use Donnellan's original example, it seems that I could successfully refer to somebody at a party as 'the man drinking a martini' even if they were actually drinking water, and would be in no danger of accidentally referring to another man – one I had not even noticed, perhaps – who just happened to be the only man at the party drinking martini (Donnellan 1966).

A well known variant on this example is Kripke's case of Gödel/Schmitt (Kripke 1972: 293–303), which is the blueprint for

Rorty's own examples (285, 290). Kripke takes it that the only description most people associate with the name 'Gödel' is 'the man who discovered the incompleteness of arithmetic'. He then asks us to imagine that unbeknownst to anyone except Gödel, it was actually Schmitt who made the discovery; Gödel stole Schmitt's work (and maybe even murdered him too). The question then is whether the 'ordinary man' refers to Gödel or Schmitt when he uses the name 'Gödel'. According to the intentionalist view, Schmitt is the referent, because he fits the description 'the man who discovered the incompleteness of arithmetic', but Kripke thinks it is obviously Gödel, and hence that this result counts strongly against the intentionalist view. This motivates Kripke's alternative to intentionalism, which is that reference is achieved through causal links within society; the name 'Gödel' refers to Gödel in virtue of causal connections between individual uses of the name and the man himself. Putnam made a similar point when he referred to a 'division of linguistic labor', the idea again being that reference is determined by causal links within society, rather than on the basis of the descriptions individuals associate with terms (Putnam 1975b). Thus Putnam argued that even if I cannot tell the difference between elm and beech trees, and associate exactly the same descriptions with each term, I can still use the term 'elm' to refer to elm trees only, simply in virtue of living in a society where there are people who can tell the difference; I lean on the competencies of others to bring my words into causal contact with their proper referents.

This seems like a straightforward dispute about reference, then, which is how it is generally regarded: the causal theorists motivate their approach with the above sorts of example, and then intentionalists respond by trying to accommodate the examples within their own approach (e.g. Searle 1983: Chapter 9). In Rorty's view, however, the examples concern only 'reference' in the ordinary sense of 'talking about', i.e. in the sense that what you are referring to is just what you are talking about. This notion has nothing to do with existence, for we can talk about fictions just as easily as we can talk about real things. But Rorty thinks that the causal theory of reference, by contrast, is concerned with a distinct, philosophical notion of reference as 'a factual relation which holds between an expression and some other portion of reality whether anybody knows it holds or not' (289). This notion of reference does presuppose that what is being referred to exists, because such a relation could not hold between a speaker and a nonentity. Since the above examples and the causal theory of reference are concerned with different notions of reference, then, the former do not motivate the latter.

Rather, all that the examples actually do, in Rorty's view, is illustrate an internal distinction within the ordinary 'talk about' sense of reference, namely the distinction between 'talking about' and 'really talking about'. This distinction comes in useful when we need to place the 'relative ignorance of the person being discussed in the context of the relatively greater knowledge claimed by the speaker' (292). So, for example, we might want to say 'you think you are talking about a man drinking martini, but you are really talking about a man drinking water', or 'you think you are talking about Gödel, but you are really talking about Schmitt'. Consequently, the examples show that intentionalism fails to provide the correct criteria for 'really talking about', because sometimes the object fitting our associated descriptions will not be what we are really talking about. However since the notion of 'really talking about' marks only an internal division within the ordinary notion of reference, and is nothing to do with the philosophical notion of reference, the failure of intentionalism to satisfactorily account for the former provides no motivation for a causal account of the latter. In short, the examples only seem to motivate the causal theory because the ordinary notion of 'really talking about' has been confused with reference in the philosophical sense.

This diagnosis immediately raises the question of what Rorty does think should be said about 'really talking about' and 'reference in the philosophical sense'. The answer is: not much. This is because he thinks determining what we are 'really talking about' is just a matter of 'historiographical convenience' (290), there being absolutely no reason to expect a unified account covering all cases to be possible, and no reason to want one anyway. On the other matter of 'reference in the philosophical sense', Rorty has sent out mixed messages. In *PMN*, he calls it a 'term of philosophical art' (289), suggesting that it may have its uses in formal semantics, but in a slightly later treatment, he is already calling it 'pointless, a philosopher's invention' (Rorty 1982: 127). The important point, however, is that reference in the philosophical sense is not something we have intuitions about, unlike reference in the ordinary sense, and that it is only by conflating these senses that causal theorists have been able to generate a debate, and make that debate seem relevant to scepticism. Thus Rorty concludes that,

> The quest for a theory of reference represents a confusion between the hopeless 'semantic' quest for a general theory of what people are 'really talking about', and the equally hopeless 'epistemological' quest for a way of refuting the sceptic.

(293)

The 'hopeless semantic quest' provided philosophers with plenty to talk about, by drawing on our inconclusive intuitions about reference (in the ordinary sense) in a wide range of imaginative scenarios. And there seemed to be some point to this, because the conflation made it seem as if these intuitions concerned the question of whether reference is an extratheoretical relation, a relation guaranteed to make contact with something real no matter how badly we describe it. Thus Rorty takes himself to have undermined the most powerful case which impure philosophy of language ever had for connecting semantics with epistemology.[8]

The fact that Putnam changed his mind on these issues in around 1977 allows Rorty to draw the discussion to a close with Putnam 'recanting' and his own view winning through by unanimous agreement. As an expositionary device, this could hardly appear much more contrived, which raises the suspicion that we have not been presented with a fair range of options; after all, Rorty, Putnam, and Davidson are all American neo-Wittgensteinians of the same generation, each with considerable debts to pragmatism.[9] On balance, however, the choice of Putnam to represent impure philosophy of language is vindicated by the fact that the approach Putnam and Kripke developed still dominates philosophy today; Rorty is just lucky that Putnam changed his mind. In any case, the later Putnam deepens Rorty's critique by arguing that causal theories could not in principle establish an extratheoretical link between words and theory-independent objects, because causation itself is as theory-laden as anything else we talk about. So, for example, positing a

NATURALISED EPISTEMOLOGY: LANGUAGE **169**

causal link between our term 'electron' and something theory-independent is no guarantee that our descendants will regard our talk about electrons as really talk about entities which they endorse, because they may well think we were wrong about causal links as well as electrons. The familiar moral to be drawn, then, is that there is no way to use one part of our holistic belief system, such as the theory of reference, to make contact with an objective truth outside of our belief system. All justification is social, and there can be no external guarantees that we are on the right track.

THE THIRD DOGMA OF EMPIRICISM

(§§5–6)

Rorty now generalises the criticisms he has been making of attempts of naturalise epistemology in Chapters 5 and 6, by saying that any naturalistic account of the relation between theory and evidence will necessarily be intratheoretical, and hence trivially self-justifying, since the 'evidence' and the 'relation between evidence and theory' will already have been understood according to 'our theory' anyway, as indeed will 'our theory'. Traditional epistemology made this sort of comparison non-trivial by distinguishing our theories from the world as it exists independently, the point being to show that our new theories are closer to the objective truth than our old ones were. In this way, metaphysics seemed to make sense of human progress. However, Rorty and (later) Putnam think that the extratheoretical conception of truth this required, according to which the objective truth is entirely independent of what humans may think, is incoherent. Such a conception would entail that even if in the distant future we devise an 'ideal' science, a 'theory of everything' so perfect that nobody ever finds anything wrong with it, it might still be the case that this theory fails to capture the objective truth. The problem, however, is that there is no perspective from which we could ever know this to be true; there is 'no skyhook' which would enable us to compare the ideal theory to the objective truth and see where it went wrong. This conception of truth is incoherent, then, because to assert it is to implicitly appeal to an impossible perspective.

This was the reasoning which led Charles Peirce, the founder of pragmatism, to propose the alternative that, 'The opinion which is fated to be ultimately agreed to by all who investigate is what we mean by truth and the object represented by this opinion is the real' (Peirce 1932: §407). For Rorty however, this was just an awkward concession to the tradition, a needless attempt to 'capture the realists' intuition that Truth is One' (Rorty 1982: xlv; for further discussion see Rorty 1991a: 129–32). Rorty thinks this intuition is rather to be abandoned, since there is no reason inquiry should converge on one point. Moreover, just like any revisionary account of truth, Peirce's approach falls foul of Putnam's Naturalistic Fallacy argument, thus providing the metaphysical realist with a natural comeback. So rather than trying to rework the idea of objective truth, then, we should just resign ourselves to the fact that progress in science has not brought us closer to 'Nature's own conventions of representation' (298), since nature 'has no preferred way of being represented' (300); all we are doing when we tell stories about scientific progress is 'complimenting ourselves' (298). The compliment, however, is just the empty one that our understanding of the world (as we understand it) is now better than it ever has been before, the triviality of which raises the question of whether we still need to bother with the qualification 'as we understand it' after objective truth has been abandoned.

This is where Davidson's argument against the scheme–content distinction comes in. This distinction, which Davidson describes as the 'third, and perhaps the last' dogma of empiricism (Davidson 1984: 189), is just an extension of Kant's distinction between concepts and intuitions, the original 'conceptual scheme' being the twelve concepts which Kant thought provided the fundamental conceptual structure of experience (the 'Categories'). The familiar Kantian idea is that we can distinguish the structure we impose from the data we receive, or more specifically, the conceptual scheme which organises experience from the experiential content being organised; Putnam memorably dubbed this the 'cookie-cutter metaphor' (Putnam 1987: 19), since we tend to imagine minds cutting malleable experience into objects, rather as cookie-cutters cut malleable dough into cookies. In terms of this distinction, then, the qualification 'as we understand it' relativises our knowledge to a conceptual scheme, or – what amounts to the same thing for analytic philosophers – a language. Since different languages could 'divide the world up' differently (cut the dough into different shaped cookies), this distinction allows for the possibility that our ancestors were not wrong after all, since their discourse may have been true relative to their own conceptual scheme. It also qualifies the empiricist view that all knowledge derives from experience by relativising experience to a conceptual scheme, rather than treating it as raw data. Davidson, however, does not think knowledge derives from experience even in this qualified sense, and thus rejects empiricism altogether. In his view, knowledge does not derive from ideas, or even neural input, but rather just from the world.

As Rorty presents Davidson's argument (301–5), the crucial point is that holism makes it impossible to separate truth from meaning. The scheme–content distinction, as Rorty sees it, requires both an atomistic approach to meaning which splits sentences into their individual components and then relates the meaning of those components to the world, and an extratheoretical conception of truth such as a correspondence theory. This allows for the meanings of words to be fixed differently within different conceptual schemes, and hence for a foreign sentence to correspond to reality in a way that no sentence of our own could; it could be true, but mean something untranslatable. Davidson, however, takes a 'top-down' approach to meaning, according to which words have meaning 'only in the context of sentences and thus of a whole language' (303), and uses only the intratheoretical conception of truth employed by the field linguist. This undermines any notion of evaluating whether a foreign sentence is true apart from by translating it into our own language and then evaluating it on our own terms. In other words, if we want to know whether a foreign sentence is true, we must translate it to find out what it means, and then decide its truth-value as we would any other sentence; for example, if we translate the sentence as meaning that snow is white, then it is true, and if we translate it as meaning that snow is green, then it is false. Thus Davidson's approach to meaning and truth allows for no prospect of a foreign sentence being true but untranslatable; whether it is true is simply a matter of whether its translation is true.

The obvious objection to this is that our translation may not actually capture the meaning of the foreign sentence; it may simply be
the best approximation available within our conceptual scheme.
However, Davidson argues that to even begin to interpret a foreign
language, we must assume that its speakers believe roughly the
same as we do. As he puts it, 'Charity is forced on us; whether we
like it or not, if we want to understand others, we must count them
right in most matters' (Davidson 1984: 197). The reasoning here is
that we will not be able to find a coherent pattern in the noises they
emit unless we assume that they are talking about the world as we
understand it, i.e. a world of objects causally interacting with them
and us. This is because the field linguist knows the conditions in
which foreign sentences are uttered, but does not know what they
mean, or whether they are being used to express true or false beliefs.
Only by assuming that they are generally expressing true beliefs –
i.e. beliefs the field linguist might also express in those circumstances – can the noises be correlated with environmental conditions.
So, for instance, if they say 'Il pleut' whenever it rains, then the
linguist will assume they are talking about the rain, and if the translation 'it's raining' can be accepted without massive adjustments
elsewhere, then the translation is done; a translation which had
them denying this obvious fact about the environment, or else
failing to register it, would simply be a bad translation.

According to Davidson's holistic approach to meaning, then,
interpreting foreign speakers involves trying to establish an equilibrium which rationalises their behaviour, minimises their inexplicable practices, and makes their beliefs consistent with each other
and broadly in line with our own; there are no facts about individual
meanings or beliefs to be respected at the outset, but no interpretation could be adequate unless it established such an equilibrium.
This means that if a language can be translated, its speakers must
believe largely what we do. If it cannot be translated, however, then
we are in no position to make assertions about what its speakers
mean or what they believe; as Davidson puts it, 'Given the underlying methodology of interpretation, we could not be in a position to
judge that others had concepts or beliefs radically different from our
own' (ibid.: 197). Thus there is no intelligible perspective from
which we can assert the existence of alternative conceptual schemes:

the world as we understand it is the world as they understand it too. It is just the world. Moreover, given that foreigners must be basically right about the world, and that they could say the same about us, Davidson reaches the conclusion that – as he put it in a later treatment – it is 'impossible correctly to hold that anyone could be mostly wrong about how things are' (Davidson 1986: 317).

In 'The World Well Lost', Rorty reads Davidson's argument as exposing the artificiality of the philosophical tradition, a tradition which makes us take seriously the idea that other cultures might talk about the world in unrecognisable ways, when it is entirely obvious that they could only talk about roughly the same things as us, and that all talk of 'alternative conceptual schemes' would drop by the wayside as soon as we actually met them. This elicits some of Rorty's best sarcasm, as he imagines a visit from an alien who fails to notice we even have a language:

> How sad that two cultures who have so much to offer each other should fail to recognise each other's existence! What pathos in the thought that we, time-travelling among our Neanderthal ancestors, might stand to them as the Galactic stands to us![10]
>
> (Rorty 1982: 9)

When we return to the real world, however, Davidson's argument reminds us that the vast majority of our beliefs must have always been the same:

> It makes us realise that the number of beliefs that change among the educated classes of Europe between the thirteenth and the nineteenth centuries is ridiculously small compared to the number that survived intact.
>
> (Ibid.: 13)

We may differ with our ancestors about refined matters like morality or physics, but we agree about how to get around in the world, that is, about how to tell an arm from a leg from a butterfly from a tree, etc. Since all language-users have mainly true beliefs, then, human beings must have been basically right about the world from the very first moment they started talking about it.

In Section 6, Rorty responds to the objection that Davidson's argument rests upon an implausible verificationalism: that he is inferring that there are no alternative conceptual schemes solely on the basis of our inability to verify that there are any. Thus it might be thought that all Davidson has really shown is that in order to interpret speakers of another language, we must regard them as mainly believing what we believe, but that this shows neither that they actually do share our beliefs, nor that our beliefs are right.

Rorty's response is to generalise the strategy he adopted earlier in distinguishing an ordinary and philosophical sense of reference: there are actually ordinary and philosophical senses of most of the key philosophical terms, such as 'truth', 'goodness', and 'world'. The ordinary sense is the 'homely and shopworn' (307) one used in everyday life, for example, 'good' is whatever 'answers to some interest' (307) and 'true' is 'what you can defend against all comers' (308); such terms are indefinable simply because their uses are so multifarious. The philosophical senses, however, were specifically designed to be indefinable in terms of anything worldly: they are Platonic ideals which escape 'the context within which discourse is conducted' (309), and hence provide models we can approximate to but never live up to. The only way to pick up these senses is to learn about the history of philosophy, thereby indoctrinating ourselves into linguistic practices that allow us to take seriously questions about, for instance, whether a universally applauded act is actually good, or whether I know I am awake. It is this sense of 'good' to which Moore's naturalistic fallacy applies, and to which there are equivalent fallacies (such as Putnam's regarding 'true') for other philosophical senses. They are the senses Socrates helped to invent by asking the great and the good of Athens for definitions of terms like 'greatness' and 'goodness', and then proceeding to dismiss all their suggestions as inadequate.

Rorty, however, thinks that culture has now reached the point where we can give up on otherworldly guidance, and hence on philosophical senses, in order to just make do with ordinary senses. That a view can be defended 'against all comers' is the best we can ever realistically say for it; to go on to claim that it is objectively true is 'like the village champion, swollen with victory, predicting that he can defeat any challenger, anytime, anywhere' (Rorty 2000a: 56).

The sense in which Davidson is saying that most of our beliefs must be true, then, is in the ordinary sense of 'true'. He is a verificationalist about truth only in the philosophical sense, for given the lack of any possible evidence that speakers of another language could be saying something true but untranslatable, he simply ignores this sense of 'truth', along with the philosophical sense of 'world' which goes with it.

As mentioned earlier, Rorty sees this development within a world-historical context, and we are now in a position to see how this very big picture looks in outline:

> Kant inherited from Descartes both the Mirror of Nature idea and the aim of providing science with the absolute guarantees God had once provided. To achieve this aim, he separated out the world itself from our conception of the world in order to claim Cartesian certainty about our subjective contributions to the latter. The problem was that this left the objective side of our conceptual scheme – the world itself – epistemically irrelevant ('The Myth of the Given'). So Hegel made do without it, and replaced Kant's single set of Categories with alternative conceptual schemes developing over the course of history. Since he remained within the Cartesian framework, however, this suggested that the world itself was changing, thus making Hegel 'a patsy for realistic reaction' (Rorty 1982: 16). Dewey reinterpreted Hegel's historicism naturalistically, seeing progress not in terms of increasing proximity to objective truth, but rather as problem solving in pursuit of our chosen political goals such as happiness, freedom and diversity. It took the linguistic holism of Sellars and Quine, however, to show that experience simply cannot dictate the most rational way to make progress towards the objective truth, since there is always a choice to be made about how to adjust our beliefs. This meant conceptual schemes could not provide the epistemic guarantees they were designed for. Davidson then drove the final nail into the coffin by undermining the distinction between the world itself and our conception of the world, and hence abandoning the philosophical senses of 'world' and 'true' altogether.

As Rorty sees it, then, our 'ambition of transcendence' (Rorty 1998: 109) has recently become intellectually untenable, and so it is time for us to give it up; his own role within the story is simply to get that message across.

We can now also see why Rorty thinks the issue between impure and pure philosophy of language is metaphilosophical, and why he denies that Davidson is an idealist (or a realist).[11] The reason is that Rorty sees Davidson as turning his back on the traditional problems of philosophy, and originating a new and untainted intellectual activity: he is simply not dealing with the philosophical senses which motivate impure philosophy of language and which divide realists from idealists. Thus his argument that most of our beliefs must be true is not an anti-sceptical argument, according to Rorty, because Davidson is not talking about the philosophical sense of 'true'. In that sense of 'true', we obviously cannot know that most of our beliefs are true – life might be a dream – but even if it is a dream, most of our beliefs must still be true in the ordinary sense of 'true'. This is the only sense of 'true' Davidson is talking about, since it is the only one of any use to the field linguist (see Rorty 1991a: 133).

This still sounds suspiciously like the traditional idealist view that we cannot sensibly talk about anything beyond our ideas, however, and Rorty has made the connection himself, saying that 'the old pragmatist chestnut that any specification of a referent is going to be in some vocabulary' and 'Berkeley's ingenuous remark that "nothing can be like an idea except an idea"' are both 'merely misleading ways of saying that we shall not see reality plain, unmasked, naked to our gaze' (Rorty 1982: 154). The difference, however, is that idealists such as Berkeley went on to give a philo-sophical account of the 'world' in the ordinary sense. Consider, for example, Berkeley's statement that,

> The only thing whose existence we deny is that which philosophers call Matter . . . in doing of this there is no damage done to the rest of mankind, who, I dare say, will never miss it.
>
> (Berkeley 1980: *Principles* §35)

This is just like Rorty's rejection of the 'world' in the philosophical sense. But whereas Berkeley also wants to say that the 'world' which the 'rest of mankind' are concerned with is ultimately composed of ideas, Rorty just wants to join Davidson and the rest of mankind in not having a view on ultimate matters.

9

SCIENCE AND PLURALISM
(*PMN*, CHAPTER 7)

EPISTEMOLOGY AND HERMENEUTICS

(§1)

Hegel thought the aim of philosophy was to make us feel 'at home' in the world by showing us how to think about the world as something which makes complete sense, with nothing left incomprehensible, alien or strange. He also thought of history as a process in which human reason has been progressing towards this goal of perfect comprehension. Rorty's understanding of the historical movement of thought from Kant to Davidson is very much within this Hegelian framework. He thinks that now the 'philosophical senses' have lost their intellectual viability, we should be able to see through the otherworldly guidance they once seemed to offer, thereby dismissing traditional philosophical problems as simply the result of, 'hypostatizing the Platonic *focus imaginarius* – truth as disjoined from agreement – and allowing the gap between oneself and that unconditional ideal to make one feel that one does not yet understand the conditions of one's existence' (340). Part Three of *PMN* is all about making sense of the new and more homely intellectual landscape which Rorty wants to usher in. This task splits into two components: drawing out the full ramifications of rejecting objective truth, and working out what to do with philosophy. Thus in Chapter 7, Rorty's concern is with the break-down of the cultural barriers which epistemology once upheld, particularly the barrier between science and other forms of inquiry, and then in Chapter 8, he turns to the question of what use society can make of the philosophical profession, given that there already is one, and that it has an impressive canon of great thinkers and great texts to its credit.

This is the best known, most accessible, and most influential part of *PMN*; it is almost certainly the reason why the book was so successful outside of professional philosophy. In particular, the reason is that in Chapter 7, Rorty discusses Thomas Kuhn's philosophy of science, and draws – in no uncertain terms – the conclusion that there is no deep difference between science and non-science: Kuhn had historicised and socialised natural science, there is no objective truth anyway, and so a new democracy between academic subjects was required. This message was understandably popular with academics in the humanities and social sciences, and Rorty added the reassurance that scientists would not care anyway, though philosophers certainly would; Kuhn's ideas were bound to 'trouble the deeper unconscious levels of the trained philosophical mind' (338). This was news to Kuhn himself, who thought of his work as contributing to philosophy, rather than as helping to undermine it, and as a consequence he was apparently quite angry about being made a hero of *PMN*, something which is all the more intriguing considering that Rorty and Kuhn were colleagues at Princeton while *PMN* was being written. Anyway, Rorty to his credit does not seem to have cared much that his admiration for Kuhn was unrequited, because the whole of this final part of the book is written in a very self-consciously Kuhnian mode, and he has called Kuhn 'the most influential philosopher to write in English since the Second World War' (Rorty 1999: 175).

The other major new player in Part Three is Hans-Georg Gadamer, from whom Rorty adopts the concept of hermeneutics; Gadamer himself adopted it from his teacher Heidegger. Rorty does not discuss Gadamer until Chapter 8, but he employs the concept from the outset, calling Chapter 7 'From Epistemology to Hermeneutics'. It puts something of a damper on proceedings, then, to learn that Rorty abandoned hermeneutics almost immediately after *PMN*, that he wishes he had 'never mentioned hermeneutics' (Knobe 1995:

61), and that he now lists Gadamer's hermeneutics as just another ill-advised attempt to devise a new philosophical method (Rorty 1999: xx). Nevertheless, all this really shows is that Rorty later decided that Gadamer was an inappropriate ally. The real problem with Rorty's use of the term 'hermeneutics' is presentational. In fact, he almost seems to have realised this at the time, because before saying, 'I am not putting hermeneutics forward as a "successor subject" to epistemology', he reminds us of his earlier presentational lapse of judgement by saying 'I was not suggesting that Quine and Sellars enable us to have a new, better, "behaviouristic" sort of epistemology' (315). Fair enough on both counts, but then 'epistemological behaviourism' and 'From Epistemology to Hermeneutics' were always going to suggest otherwise, and the latter probably explains how *PMN* acquired its persistent but false reputation for being anti-Analytic and pro-Continental Philosophy.

The term 'hermeneutics' (from Hermes, the messenger God) started to take on its modern meaning in relation to biblical exegesis: taking a hermeneutic approach to reading the Bible meant reading it and making sense of it for yourself, rather than taking official Church interpretations for granted. The philosopher Wilhelm Dilthey (1833–1911) made the term his own, developing a conception of hermeneutics as a distinct methodology appropriate to the *Geisteswissenschaften*, as opposed to the *Naturwissenschaften*. These are the German words for 'the humanities' and 'the natural sciences' respectively, and Rorty is following a tradition in always leaving them untranslated. The reason for this is that the German implies an equality between two *Wissenschaften* (sciences), and has overtones of the Hegelian distinction between spirit ('Geist') and nature, though this tradition does seem rather ironic given that *Geisteswissenschaften* was originally coined as a translation of J.S. Mill's term 'the moral sciences'. In any case, Dilthey thought that the *Geisteswissenschaften* – in particular history and sociology – should not be modelled on or judged according to the standards of the *Naturwissenschaften*, but should rather be treated as an autonomous field of inquiry with its own distinctive methodology. Whereas natural science aimed to provide causal explanations of phenomena, the *Geisteswissenschaften* were sciences of meaning which aimed to interpret and understand phenomena; the hermeneutic method was to provide an objective way of studying the significance of things.

The hermeneutic method, as it has been understood ever since Heidegger adopted it from Dilthey, is essentially the method of immersion: we immerse ourselves into the phenomenon to be understood (a text, an exotic culture, an historical epoch, etc.) in order to understand it from the inside out. This means not starting out with fixed preconceptions about what needs to be understood, but rather building up familiarity and then systematising the understanding we acquire later on. So, for example, to understand the religious practices of Papua New Guinean tribesmen hermeneutically, you might go to live with them, rather than turn up with a clipboard, and to understand why Caesar crossed the Rubicon hermeneutically, you might find out all you can about his life and circumstances in order to try to see the decision from his perspective, rather than just assessing the decision in military and political terms. A crucial feature of this approach is the so-called 'hermeneutic circle', which is the idea that you cannot understand the whole until you understand the parts, and you cannot understand the parts until you understand the whole. The only way to break into the circle, then, is to 'play back and forth between guesses' (319), as Rorty puts it, the hope being that you will eventually pick up a 'new angle on things' (321). What you do not do, if you are being hermeneutic, is start from some unquestionable starting point or foundation and build up from there. Rather, you just jump in and try to get into the swing of things, just as you might join a conversation before having any clear idea what the topic is.

Rorty tries to do three things at once with the term 'hermeneutics': relate it to Gadamer, relate it to Kuhn, and relate it to his own anti-philosophical agenda. As regards the first, Rorty draws on the idea of a hermeneutic method – or lack of method[1] – which we have just been outlining, and contrasts it with the foundationalist methodology employed by traditional epistemology. As regards the second, Rorty aligns the distinction between hermeneutics and epistemology with Kuhn's distinction between 'revolutionary' and 'normal' science (to be discussed below). And as regards the third, Rorty aligns hermeneutics with linguistic holism. In his attempt to maintain the very intricate balance required to unite these three elements, it often looks as if Rorty is contradicting himself. To avoid this impression, the reader needs to distinguish between two senses of 'epistemology' (distinguished only in the index). The first sense is 'epistemology as theory of knowledge', i.e. the sense used hitherto in *PMN*. The second sense is 'epistemology as commensuration', a new sense introduced to contrast most directly with hermeneutics in the second of the above senses. Thus whenever Rorty is engaged in his usual talk about the 'demise of epistemology' (315), then 'epistemology' should be read in the first sense, but whenever he seems to be envisaging a legitimate role for epistemology as a counterpoint to hermeneutics, then 'epistemology' should be read in the second sense.[2]

The two senses come together as follows. Epistemology (theory of knowledge) is the attempt to set up an ahistorical, neutral framework within which all discourses are commensurable. Rorty defines commensurability, one of Kuhn's key concepts, as meaning: 'able to be brought under a set of rules which will tell us how rational agreement can be reached on what would settle the issue on every point where statements seem to conflict' (316). To set up a framework which made all discourses commensurable, then, would mean that all disagreements could in principle be rationally resolved. The reason for wanting such a framework, of course, is the familiar Rortian theme that we want external constraint: we want arguments to be settled by the word of God, or by its updated equivalent, the objective truth. This would rubber-stamp our own views, silence dissent – for there is no comeback against something outside the conversation – and allow those who refuse to play by the 'set of rules' to be dismissed as irrational. In order to find common ground between discourses as diverse as those of the Papua New Guinean healer and the Swiss consultant, however, this framework needed to be extremely general, and that is why Rorty thinks the Mirror of Nature notion of experience came to dominate epistemology.

Rorty takes himself to have already shown that the Mirror of Nature cannot provide universal commensuration, and also that psychology, impure philosophy of language, and other forms of naturalised epistemology cannot either. This, he says, seems to have the disturbing consequence that some disputes simply cannot be rationally resolved, since there is no common ground on which they could be resolved; think, for instance, of the sort of disputes that take place between scientifically minded people and religious fundamentalists. It also seems to constitute an acceptance of relativism, according to which justification, knowledge and truth must be relativised to different incommensurable discourses. In short, it seems that by abandoning the notion of 'the philosopher as guardian of rationality' (317), we thereby abandon the hope of achieving consensus between disparate groups through any means except force.

Rorty thinks this apparent threat to rationality is illusory, since once the arguments for linguistic holism persuade us to think of 'culture as a conversation rather than as a structure erected upon foundations' (319), we should no longer think of rationality as requiring commensuration, only a willingness to engage with other discourses in the hope of finding resolutions or at least compromises. We do not need an overarching framework to unite disparate discourses; we just need hermeneutic engagement. A philosopher within such a culture might be able to play a useful role as,

> the informed dilettante, the polypragmatic, Socratic intermediary between various discourses. In his salon, so to speak, hermetic thinkers are charmed out of their self-enclosed practices. Disagreements between disciplines and discourses are compromised or transcended in the course of the conversation.

> (317)

The step 'from epistemology to hermeneutics', then, is from an unrealistic insistence on putting disputes into commensurable language so that they can be resolved mechanistically – according to an 'algorithm' (322 and ff.; Kuhn 1970: 200) – towards the more realistic but haphazard approach to resolving disputes of throwing ourselves into new discourses, opening ourselves to new perspectives, and hoping that some means of resolution will present itself. The role Rorty imagines the philosopher playing within this new culture, then, it not that of a specialist, of a professional with a *Fach*, but rather just that of the 'jack of all trades' intellectual who can smooth over the boundaries between disciplines by talking to both sides; note that we now have a second positive suggestion for the future of philosophy on the table.

Rorty's hermeneutic conception of rationality as being 'willing to pick up the jargon of the interlocutor rather than translating it into one's own' (318), seems *prima facie* at odds with the Davidsonian view he has just been defending in the previous chapter: before he was arguing that foreign discourses can always be translated, since everyone must have largely the same beliefs, whereas now he seems to be insisting on ineliminable differences that cannot be translated. This tension is resolved by remembering that Rorty want to distinguish 'sharply' between translatability and commensurability; he criticises Davidson for equating them (302). Rorty's concern here is with the fact that although we will always be able to translate foreign discourses, and in doing so will find that the vast majority of the translated beliefs accord with our own, there may still be some beliefs we do not share. It is these beliefs, then, which Rorty is suggesting should not be automatically translated into commensurable beliefs we regard as false; rather we should first try to 'pick up the jargon of the interlocutor' to understand why they hold those beliefs, even if we do ultimately reject them. This is how the Terrans and Antipodeans interacted with each other back in Chapter 2; that they could translate each other's languages was taken for granted, and the focus was on their attempts to hermeneutically engage each other over their incommensurable discourses about minds and brains.

In an allusion to Gadamer, Rorty elaborates on the distinction between epistemology and hermeneutics by describing the hermeneutic conception of knowledge as, 'a matter of φρόνησις [*phronēsis*] rather than ἐπιστήμη [*epistēmē*]' (319). This is one of numerous distinctions the Greeks made between types of knowledge, the contrast in this case being between the practical knowledge of *phronēsis*, and the technical knowledge of *epistēmē*. The concept of *phronēsis*, as Gadamer adapts it from Aristotle, has overtones of moral, social and historical awareness; it is the sort of knowledge which allows you to discriminate right from wrong, assess relative importance, exercise tact, and be able to empathise with other points of view. Gadamer thinks that this sort of knowledge is denigrated in the modern world in favour of the factual knowledge delivered by science, namely *epistēmē*. The reason for this, as Rorty sees it, is that we assume that, 'knowledge in the strict sense – ἐπιστήμη [*epistēmē*] – must have a λόγος [*logos*]' (319), *logos* being the term which was translated from the original text of the Bible as 'the Word' in the phrase, 'In the beginning was the Word'. Rorty's thinking, then, is that once we give up on the idea of an authority or *logos* backing up our claims to knowledge – be it the word of God or the objective truth – then there can be no more reason to think of the *Geisteswissenschaften* as producing a second-rate sort of knowledge in comparison with the *Naturwissenschaften*.

Thus Rorty's goal is to break down the traditional picture of hermeneutics as appropriate to the *Geisteswissenschaften*, where the aim is to produce *phronēsis*, and epistemology as appropriate to the *Naturwissenschaften*, where the aim is to produce *epistēmē*. Instead, he argues, the difference between hermeneutics and epistemology is 'purely one of familiarity' (321); note that he has now switched to the second sense of 'epistemology' (epistemology as commensuration). As Rorty sees it, then, when a study achieves consensus about what is and is not relevant, and about what needs to be done to prove something or solve a problem, then it can be described epistemologically. This means that it can be described by stating what is and is not known, and by stating the rules of evaluation used to settle disagreements. When the discourse is unfamiliar and conflicts with the consensus, however, then we must describe it hermeneutically, by trying to make it our own before describing it.

The significance Rorty sees in this is that there is no more reason to think that commensurability should be achievable within the *Naturwissenschaften* than within the *Geisteswissenschaften*; whether epistemology or hermeneutics is the right approach to take simply depends on how well settled the study is. To underline this point, Rorty claims that, 'At certain periods, it has been as easy to determine which critics have a "just perception" of the value of a poem as it is to determine which experimenters are capable of making accurate observations and precise measurements' (322). The connection between Rorty's two senses of 'epistemology', then, is that epistemology (theory of knowledge) was the attempt to construct a universal and ahistorical framework to render all discourses commensurable, and the reason this attempt failed was that epistemology (as commensuration) is only possible for particular discourses at particular times, namely whenever a discourse has continued long enough to become the unchallenged *status quo*.

KUHN AND THE GALILEO–BELLARMINE CONTROVERSY

(§2)

Kuhn's *The Structure of Scientific Revolutions* is a very heady mix of history and philosophy, which succeeded in removing the intellectual hegemony once enjoyed by the straightforward realist view of scientific progress as 'finding out more and more about the same objects' (275); realists have had to develop much more sophisticated positions since Kuhn. Kuhn set out to show that developments within science could only be properly understood within their historical context, science being no different in this respect from any other area of culture. He went about this by providing a series of detailed descriptions of what actually happened at key stages in the history of science, all of which cast doubt on the idea that science has progressed through a series of rational responses to experimental evidence, with old theories abandoned when observations counted against them, and new theories adopted in order to best accommodate the data. Instead, Kuhn recounts case after case from the history of science in which the scientists involved either obstinately maintained their allegiance to old theories with more or less blatant disregard for the evidence, or else adopted new theories in circumstances in which they apparently had much better reasons for sticking with the old ones. Kuhn also maintained that many of these crucial developments depended upon factors such as 'idiosyncrasies of autobiography', 'personality', and 'nationality', a particularly memorable example being 'the sun worship that helped make Kepler a Copernican' (Kuhn 1970: 152–53): not the sort of thing you would expect to influence a major scientist in deciding whether the Earth revolves around the Sun or *vice versa*.

The basic elements of Kuhn's philosophy of science are the following. Science becomes mature, rather than simply disjointed speculation, with the development of a paradigm, which is a 'core of solved problems and techniques' centring around some exemplary text, or set of experiments laid out in a textbook (ibid: 43). So, for example, the Roman astronomer Claudius Ptolemy's *Almagest*, which used the principles of Aristotelian science to provide a system for understanding the observable movements of the Sun, Moon and planets around an unmoving Earth, was the basis for well over a thousand years of astronomy. With the backdrop of the basic principles and concepts it provided, subsequent astronomers were able to build up a consensus about research aims, methods, and standards of evaluation, allowing astronomy to proceed as what Kuhn calls 'normal science'. Research in times of normal science is commensurable (literally 'co-measurable'), with common standards of evaluation which make scientific work routine, professional, and systematic, thereby allowing a body of knowledge to be steadily accumulated. Normal science comes to an end when anomalies have built up to such an extent that scientists lose faith in their ability to resolve them: they stop regarding the anomalies as unsolved puzzles, and start regarding them as indications of a fault with the paradigm. This state of crisis precipitates a scientific revolution, in which one paradigm is abandoned in favour of another, as for example Ptolemaic astronomy was abandoned in favour of Copernicus's heliocentric alternative from the sixteenth century onwards.

Kuhn uses the word 'revolution' for two reasons. The first is that the new paradigm allows normal science to start over again, the idea being that science evolves in cycles rather than making cumulative and steady progress towards the objective truth. The second is that Kuhn thinks of a paradigm shift as akin to a political revolution, in the sense that such revolutions occur when the normal mechanisms of political change have been exhausted, leaving no recourse for resolving political discontent except the overthrow of the whole system by abnormal means (ibid.: 92). Such transitions from one paradigm to another cannot be achieved by rational persuasion, according to Kuhn, because different paradigms are incommensurable: there are no common standards of evaluation for deciding between paradigms, because paradigms determine standards of evaluation. Consequently, inter-paradigm disputes inevitably take place at cross-purposes, with the opposing sides talking right past each other. For a paradigm shift to occur, then, rational deliberation can never be enough. What is required is more akin to a religious conversion, i.e. a transformation 'made on faith' (ibid.: 158), influenced by all sorts of idiosyncratic factors, and tending to involve a sudden moment of 'illumination' (ibid.: 123).

Kuhn likens conversion to a new paradigm to the sort of gestalt change that occurs when viewing optical illusions; he uses the example of the duck-rabbit illusion, where the double loop on the diagram is either a duck's bill or a rabbit's ears, depending on how you look at it. Kuhn thinks of scientific revolutions as bringing about this sort of 'shift', 'switch' or 'transformation of vision' (ibid.: 111). This leads him to claim that 'after a revolution scientists work in a different world' (ibid.: 135), and that scientists faithful to different paradigms can 'see different things when they look from the same point in the same direction' (ibid.: 150), just as one person can see a duck and another a rabbit when looking at the same diagram. Kuhn himself experienced a gestalt switch of just this sort while preparing a course on Aristotelian physics early on in his career. As he immersed himself in the subject, he became increasingly perplexed by the question of how men who in their own time counted among the world's greatest minds, could have managed to make what seemed to him to be fairly elementary mathematical mistakes (Kuhn was an accomplished physicist as well an historian and philosopher). Everything changed, however, when Kuhn 'learned to think like' an Aristotelian physicist: once he could see the world through Aristotelian eyes, their reasonings made perfect sense to him (Kuhn 1977: xii).[3]

Rorty's use of Kuhn is fairly straightforward, and he will not stray far from these ideas for the remainder of the book. To spell out the fundamental points of contact, Rorty thinks that Kuhn undermines both the Enlightenment's notion of science as the 'paradigm of knowledge, to which the rest of culture had to measure up' (322), and also epistemology (theory of knowledge) as the subject which underwrites the status of science. Kuhn does this by showing that science does not progress rationally according to a 'previously statable algorithm' (336), but rather only according to a '*post factum* and Whiggish one' (324), i.e. one which is fabricated in the history books written by the winning side. Since rationality and progress are always relative to a paradigm, and cannot span incommensurable paradigms, epistemology (theory of knowledge) is impossible: there

can be no ahistorical framework which renders all possible paradigms commensurable, and thus allows them to be compared.
Commensuration is always limited and only exists in periods of
normal science. Moreover, since past science cannot be made
commensurable with our own, the only way to understand it is
hermeneutically. So, for example, trying to understand why people
once thought that the Sun revolved around the Earth is no different
in principle from trying to understand why people once thought
that certain women should be burnt at the stake: both require trying
to break into an alien belief system.

Where Rorty parts company with Kuhn is over his 'idealist-
sounding' claims, i.e. his claims about seeing new worlds. Rorty calls
these 'incidental remarks' which 'philosophers pounced upon' (324)
– despite the fact that Kuhn would have been hard pressed to make
them much more prominent within his book.[4] As usual, what Rorty
really means to say is just that Kuhn can be 'purified', and to this
effect, he dismisses the gestalt-switches which so impressed Kuhn
(which inspired his work in the first place) as just a trivial consequence of familiarity: scientists working within different paradigms
simply make different non-inferential responses to the same
sensory stimulations. Kuhn wanted to deny that a paradigm shift is
just a transition to a new interpretation of the same world, on the
grounds that there is no neutral language in which the world could
be said to have stayed the same. But this was an overreaction, Rorty
thinks, because there was no need to deny the possibility of such a
language (e.g. the language of sensory stimulations), so long as it is
made clear that it would be useless for epistemological purposes.

This is a curious development. Rorty is appealing (on Kuhn's
behalf) to the notion of sensory stimulation in order to avoid the
charge of idealism, the reasoning being that since sensory stimulations are neutral between paradigms, their constancy throughout
paradigm shifts avoids any implication of the world itself changing.
We shall return to this later on, but for the time being it should be
noted that the Kuhnian 'idealism' which Rorty is trying to avoid
here is motivated by exactly the same reasoning that Rorty so often
uses to deny there is a 'way the world is'. This is because the reason
Kuhn says that scientists after a paradigm-shift see a different
world, rather than just see the world differently, is that he denies

that there is any perspective from which we can talk about the world independently of a paradigm. As Kuhn puts it, 'In so far as their only recourse to [the world of their research-engagement] is through what they see and do, we may want to say that after a revolution scientists are responding to a different world' (Kuhn 1970: 111). In other words, there is 'no skyhook'. In the case of the duck-rabbit illusion, there is a third way of describing what is being seen, namely as ink on paper, but Kuhn denies that there is any third way for scientists before and after a paradigm-shift; where there is only a duck or a rabbit, a transition between them is a transition to a different world.[5]

After introducing and purifying Kuhn, then, Rorty moves on to a discussion of the Galileo–Bellarmine controversy. This discussion (327–33) is something of a *tour de force*, so much so, in fact, that it has recently become the focus of a book, namely Paul Boghossian's *Fear of Knowledge*. As might be gleaned from the title, the anti-epistemological views of Rorty and others like him are the general target, but it is the discussion of Galileo and Bellarmine in particular which occupies the central chapters and which occasions some of Boghossian's best arguments. Although fairly stock Rortian replies can be made to some of what Boghossian says, he does nevertheless touch on a major tension within Rorty's thought, and so the most relevant parts of this critique will be considered once Rorty's view is on the table.

The backdrop is this. Galileo adopted and developed Copernican astronomy, making observations to confirm it with the new type of telescope he invented. For this he was accused of heresy, and went to Rome to defend himself. The Ptolemaic orthodoxy was defended for the Vatican by Cardinal (later Saint) Bellarmine, a very sophisti-cated thinker within the Aristotelian mould, who wanted Galileo to admit that Copernican astronomy was just a mathematical device, useful for simplifying astronomical calculations perhaps, but not really a description of physical reality. If Galileo was saying that the Earth literally revolved around the Sun, Bellarmine argued, then his views would conflict with the holy scriptures. Galileo, for his part, argued that the scriptures should not always be interpreted so literally.

Rorty asks whether the scriptural considerations Bellarmine

invoked against Copernican astronomy were 'illogical and unscientific'. His answer is 'no' – 'a negative answer is implied by the argument of the present book' (328–29) – for the reason that Bellarmine and Galileo were in the process of determining what counts as logical and scientific. Until these values had been 'hammered out' (330), there simply was no perspective from which Bellarmine could be accused of being unscientific. Bellarmine had excellent scriptural evidence for thinking the heavens were Ptolemaic, and Galileo had excellent observational evidence for thinking the heavens were Copernican. Since they were operating within different paradigms, however, they disagreed about the standards of evidence to be employed. Galileo and other new scientists were trying to limit the scope of scripture; they believed in God, but they wanted to keep religion and science separate, with those parts of scripture conflicting with science to be construed non-literally. Bellarmine and other churchmen, on the other hand, were trying to limit the scope of the New Science; they could see its power, but they thought it would have to be construed non-literally whenever it conflicted with the word of God. From our present day perspective, of course, it could hardly seem more obvious that looking through a telescope is a good source of evidence in astronomy and reading the Bible is not. However the only reason for this, according to Rorty, is that Galileo 'won the argument' and we are his 'heirs' (330–31).

Rorty's view, then, is that there was no fact of the matter which determined that Galileo's position was justified and Bellarmine's was not. This is because there is no wider frame of reference (or 'grid') to render both positions commensurable, and decide in favour of Galileo. The achievements of new scientists like Galileo led to the development of a new frame of reference in the Enlightenment which imposed sharp distinctions between science and religion, politics, and other areas of culture. Relative to this frame of reference, then, Bellarmine was indeed being irrational. But since rationality is always relative to a paradigm, the original paradigm shift which brought about this state of affairs was no more or less rational than comparable shifts which have taken place in politics and art: 'what could show that the Bellarmine-Galileo issue "differs in kind" from the issue between, say, Kerensky and Lenin, or that between the Royal Academy (*circa* 1910) and Bloomsbury?' (331).[6] Philosophy developed as the attempt to use the Mirror of Nature idea to provide the wider context needed to set science apart from other areas of culture, thereby backing up the autonomy of science. Nowadays, however, we no longer need the 'ideology which . . . protected the rise of modern science' (333), and so can maintain our loyalty to Enlightenment values without thinking of science as uniquely rational.

In Boghossian's terminology, Rorty's principal claim is that there is no absolute justification, only justification relative to an 'epistemic system'. Galileo and Bellarmine can only give 'norm-circular' justifications of their beliefs: they can only justify them according to their own evidential norms. So Galileo uses his telescope and is justified according to his epistemic system, and Bellarmine reads his Bible and is justified according to his epistemic system, but there is no absolute justification according to which one epistemic system can be justified over the other (Boghossian 2006: chapter 5).

Boghossian's first argument (ibid.: 84–87) turns on the idea that for there to be even relative justification, we have to accept some statements of absolute justification. This is because an epistemic system consists of general principles which are themselves 'just more general versions of particular epistemic judgements'. So, for instance, Galileo's judgement that seeing the moons of Jupiter through his telescope justifies him in believing that Jupiter has moons, is just a particular application of the general principle that seeing something provides good *prima facie* justification for believing it is there. If there is no absolute justification, then any general principle of this kind must be false, and so all epistemic systems must be 'made up out of uniformly false propositions'. Nevertheless, we still have to accept or endorse an epistemic system in order to judge that our beliefs are relatively justified: for Galileo to judge that his belief about the moons of Jupiter is justified relative to his epistemic system, he must at least accept that system. But if we must accept false general statements about what is absolutely justified – i.e. the ones constitutive of epistemic systems – it makes no sense to insist that we must reject false particular statements about what is absolutely justified. So Rorty's view is 'incoherent': he wants us to reject all claims of absolute justification, and yet in order to think of our beliefs as even relatively justified requires us to accept the claims to absolute justification constitutive of our epistemic system.

Rorty can respond by appealing to his pragmatic conception of justification, according to which saying that a claim is justified is saying that it is useful. Since usefulness is always usefulness relative to some purpose or another, and Galileo and Bellarmine had different purposes – a point which Rorty emphasises throughout his discussion – Rorty can distinguish their epistemic systems without appealing to absolute justification. So, for example, Galileo's observations justify his belief about the moons of Jupiter relative to his epistemic system, but not absolutely (not for Bellarmine, for instance), and accepting an epistemic system amounts to accepting certain general principles, such as the principle that for certain purposes, seeing something makes it useful to believe that it is there. Galileo's purposes might be said to include, for argument's sake, the ability to manipulate and control the environment; other purposes might include 'the impact of science on theology' or 'the future of life on earth' (327). In accepting different epistemic systems, then, Galileo and Bellarmine do not need to accept any epistemic absolutes, only epistemic principles which are useful for their different purposes. Thus Rorty's position is not incoherent, because the general claims constitutive of an epistemic system are simply claims to usefulness relative to a purpose. There is no reason these general claims should be false, and accepting them is perfectly compatible with rejecting all claims to absolute justification – Rorty would say 'context-free justification' (Rorty 1999: 34) – which from Rorty's perspective amount to nothing more than idly boasting that our beliefs can be justified to any audience whatsoever.

Boghossian's second argument (Boghossian 2006: 89–91) turns on the idea that epistemic systems cannot be 'on a par as far as their correctness is concerned' because each one 'will have a possible alternative that contradicts it'. So, for instance, according to Bellarmine's epistemic system, what it says in the Bible is sufficient justification for believing in Ptolemaic astronomy, and according to Galileo's epistemic system, it is not the case that what it says in the Bible is sufficient justification for believing in Ptolemaic astronomy. If there is no absolute justification, however, then Rorty must agree that it is not the case that what it says in the Bible is sufficient justification for believing in Ptolemaic astronomy, thereby conceding that there are indeed facts which favour some systems over others.

Rorty's view that justification is usefulness in the way of belief, relative to some set of purposes, again provides a response. This is that since Galileo and Bellarmine have different purposes, their views cannot be represented as neat contradictory pairs: Bellarmine thinks believing the Bible is useful for his purposes, but Galileo thinks that it is not the case that believing the Bible is useful for his distinct purposes. Rorty's own view that it is not the case that there is any source of evidence which is useful for all purposes whatsoever is different again, and favours neither Bellarmine nor Galileo's system.

Boghossian's third argument (ibid.: 103–5) targets the presumption that Galileo and Bellarmine are in fact employing different epistemic systems, since in Boghossian's view, they are actually having a much more mundane sort of dispute within the same epistemic system. As he makes the point,

> Yes, the Cardinal consults his Bible to find out what to believe about the heavens, rather than using the telescope; but he doesn't divine what the Bible itself contains, but rather reads it using his eyes. Nor does he check it every hour to make sure that it still says the same, but rather relies on induction to predict that it will say the same tomorrow as it does today. And, finally, he uses deductive logic to deduce what it implies about the make-up of the heavens.
>
> (Ibid.: 103)

Boghossian's idea, underpinning his discussion from the outset, is that we have a stock of ordinary and fundamental epistemic principles, rooted in observation, induction, and deduction, to which it is very difficult to imagine any genuine alternative. Since Bellarmine relies on them to find out that the stars are above him, that he has two hands, that the Bible supports Ptolemaic astronomy, etc., it would be uncharitable to interpret his refusal to employ them in astronomy as evidence of an alternative epistemic system, for such a system would be incoherent. Thus Bellarmine must be employing our epistemic system, but think that the Bible trumps observation because it is the word of God. So there is no clash of epistemic systems, then, just 'a dispute, within a common epistemic system, about the origins and nature of the Bible' (ibid.: 105).[7]

The difficulty in finding a suitable response for Rorty to make to this argument, is that the line Boghossian is taking here seems to be very similar to the Davidsonian line Rorty himself was taking back in Chapter 6. Davidson's view, as we said before, is that 'we could not be in a position to judge that others had concepts or beliefs radically different from our own' (Davidson 1984: 197). But in that case, how can Galileo and Bellarmine disagree so radically? If both must be basically right about the world, how can they disagree about whether *looking* is a good source of evidence? The obvious Davidsonian response is that they cannot: they must have a much more limited disagreement of the kind Boghossian suggests. After all, the field linguist has to look in order to gather evidence, and he or she must assume that the people being interpreted do the same; even a Bellarminean field linguist would have to agree. But then if Galileo and Bellarmine are using the same kinds of evidence to talk about the same world – a world which they both must have mainly true and justified beliefs about – then surely Bellarmine was wrong even by his own lights.[8]

The hub of Rorty's problem here is that there is a tension between the views of Davidson and Kuhn which it is not clear he has managed to transcend. On a natural reading, Davidson and Kuhn are opposites: Davidson's view is that there are no conceptual schemes, and Kuhn's view is that there are alternative and incommensurable conceptual schemes. This is certainly how Davidson read the situation, for he explicitly targeted Kuhn throughout 'On the Very Idea of a Conceptual Scheme'. And Kuhn also seems to have read the situation in something like this manner, for in his first book, *The Copernican Revolution*, he showed no qualms about using the terminology of changing 'conceptual schemes' to describe the transition between Ptolemy and Copernicus.[9] Of course, Rorty is a specialist in forging unlikely alliances between philosophers. But when you see him trying to ignore the fact that Davidson was targeting Kuhn, trying to pretend that Kuhn's 'idealist-sounding' claims were 'incidental', and worst of all, making a very ill-considered (albeit one-off) attempt to equate 'normal discourse' with 'conceptual scheme' (346–47), then you really do wonder whether he has bitten off more than even he can chew.[10]

The reason Rorty thinks of Davidson and Kuhn as allies is plain enough. It is that he sees in their work two powerful and influential routes to undermining the distinction between science and non-science, both of which are partially motivated by the 'no skyhook' thought (Rorty 1999: 35–36). But they are nevertheless different routes, and it is no mean feat to wrap them up together. Davidson rejects the scheme–content distinction full stop. There is no neutral content and organising scheme, just a plain old world which indifferently makes both scientific and non-scientific sentences true. But Kuhn, who does not share Davidson's concern about alternative conceptual schemes, focuses instead on neutrality. For Kuhn, there can be no neutral data, because when paradigms change the 'data themselves' change (Kuhn 1970: 126, 135). Thus scheme and content move together – schemes do not change against a backdrop of unchanging neutral content – and so there is no yardstick with which to contrast paradigm shifts in science and non-science. These two different positions suggest two different reactions to the Galileo–Bellarmine controversy. The Kuhnian reaction is that Galileo and Bellarmine saw different worlds, or at least employed different epistemic systems, and so did not have enough in common for one to be right and the other wrong. The Davidson reaction, on the other hand, is that they had almost everything in common, and hence Galileo was right.

As we saw above, Rorty thinks he can unite Davidson and Kuhn by interpreting the disagreement between Galileo and Bellarmine as confined to a very limited area of incommensurable discourse, i.e. just astronomy. But this simply cannot work for reasons Boghossian brings out, namely that the overwhelming agreement between them is bound to be enough to show that Bellarmine was wrong. There are Kuhnian responses to be made to this line of argument, of course, but Rorty cannot make them because he has already agreed with Davidson. Even insisting that justification is always relative to a purpose will not help this time, because the fact that Galileo and Bellarmine had the same purposes for observation in the vast run of cases is bound to be enough to make the case that Bellarmine was indeed being 'unscientific and illogical'.

This tension between Rorty's Davidsonian and Kuhnian commitments stem ultimately from a tension within his fundamental project. As was stated at the outset of this book, Rorty's two preoccupations are philosophy and truth. The difficulty, however, is in reconciling an anti-philosophical stance to a denial of objective truth, given that it is very hard to see what the latter is supposed to be if not a philosophical view. Davidson goes nicely with the anti-philosophical stance, allowing Rorty to say that there is just one ordinary way of understanding the world, and that we should just ignore philosophical senses, scepticism, objective truth, conceptual schemes, and all other exotica of no concern to the field linguist. Kuhn, by contrast, goes nicely with the denial of objective truth, allowing Rorty to say that since there can be any number of different incommensurable ways of understanding the world, useful for different purposes, there simply cannot be a single objective truth about the world. But Rorty cannot have it both ways; he cannot ignore the objective truth along with the rest of philosophy, while providing substantive Kuhnian reasons why there cannot be one.

By trying to have it both ways, Rorty inevitably finds himself dragged down into philosophical debates of his own making. After all, philosophers were bound to line up to refute the view that there is no objective truth, for it has the extreme consequence – strongly implied if not stated – that if we had been the heirs of Bellarmine, then the Sun would revolve around the Earth, just as had we been the heirs of the Royal Academy, then post-impressionist paintings would be fit only to hang in lunatic asylums. Now maybe that is right; maybe that only seems absurd because we cannot imagine a world in which Bellarmine won the argument. But the point, surely, is that this is exactly the sort of highly speculative and socially useless philosophical position which Rorty is supposed to yawn at. You would have thought that an anti-philosophical pragmatist would want to marginalise his critics, rather than provoke them. But then, maybe denying objective truth is more important to Rorty than metaphilosophy: maybe he really is some kind of updated idealist.

FINDING AND MAKING

(§§3–4)

Rorty proposes a re-alignment of the subject–object distinction away from the mental–physical distinction and towards the herme-neutic–epistemological (epistemology as commensuration) distinc-tion. The traditional assumption, Rorty thinks, is that we can only be fully objective when describing the physical world. This is because the physical world is found rather than made, and so how we describe it has nothing to do with taste or opinion, and is rather just a matter of finding a correspondence to what is already there. We ought to be able to get an algorithm for rational agreement in science, then, because the world forces our agreement: if our words correspond to the world, we are right, and if they do not, we are wrong. With politics and art, on the other hand, we are dealing with something that human beings have made or imposed upon the world, and hence which is to some degree mind-dependent. Accord-ing to the traditional view, then, debates about human rights or the value of a painting are not settled by a correspondence to reality; we cannot find somebody's human rights as we might find their red blood cells, and a complete physical description of two paintings will not tell us which one is best. Thus we cannot get an algorithm for rational agreement outside of science, because whereas in science there is an objective truth we are simply trying to fall into line with, outside of science we have to actively decide what counts as true by reaching intersubjective agreements.

Rorty's suggestion is that we cut out the metaphysical middle-man by correlating objectivity and subjectivity directly with the ease or difficulty with which we can reach intersubjective agree-ment. Thus we should forget about trying to metaphysically explain this difference in terms of correspondence, objective truth, and the mental–physical distinction, and make do with the bland historical observation that in the development of any area of culture, there tend to be periods of consensus we can be epistemological about, punctuated by periods of disarray we can only be hermeneutic about. The idea that science is somehow exempt from this trend is simply Enlightenment propaganda which Kuhn managed to put behind us. Consequently, all that needs to be said about objectivity and subjectivity is that commensurable discourse is objective, and incommensurable discourse is subjective. This means that science has no special claim to objectivity: with a paradigm firmly in place, politics and art can be just as objective as science. Moreover, subjectivity concerns personal idiosyncrasy only to the extent that bringing in subjective considerations is refusing to play by the rules; if you fail to bring others around to your way of thinking then you are 'kooky', but if you succeed you are 'revolutionary' (339).

From the perspective of Rorty's new conception of objectivity and subjectivity, the distinction between 'finding' and 'making' is just terminological. When talking about physics, for example, we can either be 'romantic' with Kuhn and talk about 'making a new world' or else 'classic' with his opponents and talk about 'describing the same world in a new way' (344). The sole reason Rorty prefers the classic idiom is that a physical 'genre of world-story' is 'definatory of the West' (345). As he puts it,

> Physics is the paradigm of 'finding' simply because it is hard (at least in the West) to tell a story of changing physical universes against the background of an unchanging Moral Law or poetic canon, but very easy to tell the reverse sort of story.
>
> (344–45)

Our kind of story originated back in fifth-century BC Greece, when Democritus said, 'By convention sweet, by convention bitter, by convention hot, by convention cold, by convention colour: but in reality atoms and void' (Kirk *et al.* 1983: 410). In Rorty's view, however, physical descriptions are no more or less 'conventional' than any other. Thus we are wrong to think that scientific progress is different from other sorts of cultural progress because the physical stuff it describes was there long before we evolved out of it. Physical nature is not an unavoidable backdrop to human development. Rather, it is just that we happened to take up Democritus's idea as a useful plot device for telling the story of human progress.

Here is an argument against Rorty's view that the only reason we hold science apart from the rest of culture is that there is greater consensus in science, a consensus which aesthetics or morality could just as easily have enjoyed had history turned out differently. The argument is as follows. Suppose we were able to show our ancestors the future of science and art. So, for example, we show people in the twelfth century some of the achievements of thirteenth-century art and science, and we also show them some of the achievements of twentieth-century art and science. Will they notice any difference between the progress of science and the progress of art? It seems that they will: they will immediately recognise that major progress has occurred in science between the thirteenth and twentieth centuries, but they may not be able to recognise the difference between thirteenth- and twentieth-century art as progress at all. They will hardly be able to miss the fact that twentieth-century medicine and 'cannons' are a lot better than thirteenth-century ones, and yet they are probably going to be considerably more impressed by Cimabue and Giotto than by Matisse and Picasso. The same point can be made for moral and political progress: by their chivalrous and undemocratic lights, it may seem that things have actually gone downhill. And yet they are hardly going to be able to think the same about science once we show them their unborn babies, blow something up, or take them flying.

The difference here is that science feeds into technology, and it is hard to see why much if any historical background or cultural empathy should be required to recognise technological achievement. No doubt our imaginary twelfth-century spectators would be able to make much more sense of both thirteenth-century art and science than twentieth-century art and science, but whereas their inability to make sense of twentieth-century science would not prevent them from appreciating the results, their inability to make sense of twentieth-century art would indeed, it seems, prevent them from appreciating the results. This difference cannot be explained in terms of consensus, because the twelfth-century observers need know nothing about that at all. And neither can it be a matter of post-Enlightenment prejudice, or even post-Democritian prejudice for that matter: the ancient Egyptians would surely have been just as impressed by the science and just as baffled by the art. Thus scientific progress really does differ from other sorts of cultural progress, for the reason that science issues in technological progress which could be recognised by almost any culture.

Rorty's mistake, it seems, is to assume that if scientific progress is not guided by the objective truth and is not uniquely rational, then there cannot be any principled distinction between science and other forms of inquiry. This does not follow, however, because there could be another way to explain the difference between science and non-science. That there is a genuine difference to be explained is strongly suggested by the fact that science produces an increased capacity for manipulating the environment which is recognisable irrespective of cultural background; perhaps Rorty is right that we should not say that the objective truth forces intersubjective consensus upon us, but we could still try to find something else to say.[11]

Rorty's preferred option of denying that there actually is any difference, and moreover claiming that it was arbitrary that physics rather than aesthetics or politics became our 'paradigm of "finding"' (344), is both counterintuitive and deeply revisionary. It has the consequence that if our intellectual history had developed differently, we could just as easily have come to think that we live in an aesthetic (or moral, or political) rather than a physical universe, in which case we would presumably believe that aesthetic reality predated human existence, and that when the human race dies out, rocks and trees will lose their size, shape and mass, but retain their aesthetic properties. This view is utterly bewildering to even begin to think through, but that is no objection to Rorty; he will say that this is only to be expected given that we are the heirs of Democritus. What is an objection, however, at least from the perspective of Rorty's project, is that it is quite patently a philosophical view. It is a view which he must have arrived at through *a priori* reasoning, a view which has implications that cut right across disciplinary boundaries, and a view which anybody outside of academic philosophy (or other subjects strongly influenced by philosophy) would find extremely difficult to take seriously. It is also a view at odds with Rorty's Davidsonian commitments, unless of course people who think the universe is aesthetic rather than physical could have mostly the same beliefs as us.

After arguing that the *Naturwissenschaften* have no special claim to objectivity on the grounds that they describe a world we found rather than made, Rorty next considers the opposite objection to his pluralism, which is that the *Geisteswissenschaften* should be accorded special status because they deal with subjectivity and human creativity. In particular, Rorty is concerned to undermine the view that humans are more difficult to understand than things because we are creative language users, freely deciding how to describe ourselves and the world around us, and always at liberty to change our descriptions. According to this view, the *Geisteswissenschaften* deal with a level of understanding and significance which could never be reduced to the kind of predictive explanation provided by the *Naturwissenschaften*, so that even if some scientist of the future had a full physical account of the sounds emitted by a human being, based on a molecule for molecule blueprint of their body, this would not reveal the meaning of those sounds, and hence would not provide any understanding of what was being said. The objection to this, made by those who think science can explain everything, is that so-called 'understanding' is just primitive predictive explanation, and that the defenders of the irreducibility of the *Geisteswissenschaften* are just trading on the fact that science is simply not yet advanced enough to fully explain human behaviour; if we had a 'language of unified science' (348), then we would indeed be able to understand linguistic meaning in terms of the sounds and inscriptions people produce. 'Both sides are quite right' (347), according to Rorty.

His thinking is that since we do not actually have a 'language of unified science', we cannot do without the hermeneutic understanding of the *Geisteswissenschaften* simply for practical reasons. This has nothing to do with any principled difference between humans and objects, for Rorty does not think there is any. The difference is just one of familiarity and consensus: we can all agree about how to describe objects, but there is no similar agreement about how to describe people. The situation is complicated by the fact that humans describe themselves, and may do so in incommensurable ways. However, these self-descriptions need not be taken into account; with 'particularly stupid, or psychotic' (349) or 'particularly dull and conventional' (352) people, it may pay to wave aside their self-descriptions and treat them like objects. Likewise, the non-human world may sometimes be so baffling – Rorty's example is the migration of butterflies – that it pays to 'anthropomorphize' it (352),

202 SCIENCE AND PLURALISM

to treat it as having a preferred way of being described we have yet to uncover. The only real difference is how confident we are that we have the right vocabulary. At the present time, we are more confident when describing the non-human world, but the situation might well reverse: 'In a sufficiently long perspective, man may turn out to be less δεινός [wondrous] than Sophocles thought him, and the elementary forces of nature more so than modern physicists dream' (352).[12] Thus there is nothing more to the spirit–nature distinction than the hermeneutic–epistemology (as commensuration) distinction, and no more reason to use hermeneutics on people than objects: we should just use whatever works. However, having rehabilitated the spirit–nature distinction, Rorty ultimately decides that it is probably best to abandon it altogether, simply because it is too bound up with the history of philosophy and the Mirror of Nature idea. All forms of inquiry should simply be treated equally.

10

THE POWER OF STRENGENESS

(*PMN*, CHAPTER 8; CONCLUSION)

GADAMER AND BAD FAITH

(§1)

Rorty is an anti-essentialist: he does not think things are essentially physical and only accidentally of aesthetic, moral, or economic value, and he does not think things are essentially mental or spiritual either. This is because he denies that there is any ultimate context of the sort required to make sense of the assertion that one way of describing a thing is more fundamental or essential to it than all others. There are only limited contexts set by changing circumstances and purposes; as Dewey once put it, 'Anything is "essential" which is indispensible to a given inquiry and anything is "accidental" which is superfluous' (Dewey 1938: 138). Rorty begins his last chapter, then, with the suggestion that it is essentialism which is the overarching prejudice we need to overcome for the sake of cultural progress; the Mirror of Nature was just a subservient idea. According to the essentialism which is 'common to Democritus and Descartes' (357), it is of the essence of human beings to seek to acquire knowledge by discovering essences, as for instance in the search for fundamental particles in physics, or for first principles in philosophy. This picture of 'man-as-essentially-knower-of-essences' (364) generates a conception of inquiry as the search for truth, where to know the truth about something is to know its essence. Rorty's plan is to sketch an alternative by combining Gadamer's hermeneutics with some themes drawn from Existentialism.

The main importance Rorty sees in Gadamer's hermeneutics is that it offers an alternative conception of inquiry which allows us to 'distance' (358) ourselves from essentialism by placing the search for truth within a wider context. This is a context in which edification rather than knowledge is the 'goal of thinking' (359), and the search for truth is 'just one among many ways in which we might be edified' (360). In a turn of phrase that was to be much repeated in subsequent years, Rorty provides Gadamer's conception of edification with an Existentialist twist by saying that, 'redescribing ourselves is the most important thing we can do' (358–59). Thus Rorty wants people to stop worrying about truth and start worrying about edification, where edification is a project of self-creation and unceasing development, accomplished by finding ever new and more interesting ways to describe ourselves, others, and the world around us. Unlike the search for the objective truth, this project has no terminating point; it is an 'infinite *striving*' (377) in which the aim is to keep finding new descriptions to expand our horizons and incorporate new points of view. We succeed not by reaching or even approaching a goal, but rather by never allowing ourselves to settle upon one view of the world or ourselves, and instead always looking to change or expand that view. Fact accumulation is only one among many ingredients within this process of edification, but it was blown out of all proportion by the essentialist tradition.

There are two main ways edification is to proceed. The first is through hermeneutically engaging with incommensurable discourses employed by different academic disciplines, different cultures, different historical periods, or any combination thereof; even imaginary aliens can have their uses, as we have seen. And the second is the 'poetic' (360) activity of devising new incommensurable discourses (trying to ensure we are not just being kooky, of course). The aim in both cases is, 'to take us out of our old selves by the power of strangeness, to aid us in becoming new beings' (360). Rorty wants this to be the new impetus for inquiry after the demise of objective truth, one which is self-consciously internal to inquiry, rather than provided by an imaginary external goal. This impetus is required to prevent culture from freezing over, and is to be achieved by continually throwing spanners into the works to interrupt normal discourses. As Richard Bernstein has put it, 'Rorty is calling for the "invention" of incommensurable vocabularies – ever new forms of dissensus, not epistemological consensus' (Bernstein 1991: 62). Thus the drive to progress becomes the drive against intellectual complacency, since progress will grind to a halt if we assume we already understand, or even that we are already on the right track.

Rorty uses ideas drawn from Jean-Paul Sartre's version of Existentialism to explain the need to supplement or even disrupt normal and commensurable discourses with abnormal and incommensurable ones. Sartre distinguished two types of existence, the human existence of being 'for-itself' (pour-soi), and the being 'in-itself' (en-soi) of objects (351 and ff.). The difference is that humans have free will, and so have to choose for themselves how they are going to be; nobody is born a bright and quick-tempered socialite, or a sullen and introverted misfit, for these are ways of being that must be chosen, albeit in a rather more complex way than we might choose a shirt. An object, however, has no say over what it is like at all. Sartre expressed this difference by saying that for people, 'existence precedes essence' (Sartre 1974: 28): we find ourselves born into a certain situation, and must choose what we are going to be like, the implied contrast being with the traditional theological picture in which God considers all possible essences in order to decide which ones to bring into existence (cf. Leibniz 1985). Since we must choose our being, and are thus responsible for it, Sartre argued that we are prone to 'bad faith', which is the condition of trying to flee from the burden of freedom by pretending that we have a fixed essence akin to the being of the in-itself, i.e. a nature which determines how we will act in any given situation, rather as the nature of a coin determines its trajectory of fall when dropped.

Rorty equates the threat posed by the normalisation of discourse with the threat of bad faith: if a discourse becomes too entrenched, we will think that we know ourselves as we essentially are, when in actual fact we are not essentially any way at all. That is, we will stop thinking of our descriptions as just descriptions, and start thinking of them as having some special attachment to reality, a misinterpretation which obscures our capacity to continually re-describe the world, and thereby to edify ourselves. For Rorty, however, this point has more general application than it does for Sartre. Criticising Sartre for reinforcing the traditional spirit-nature distinction (361–62), Rorty extends the Existentialist point so as to deny that there are any fixed essences at all; the point has no special application to people, as it does in Sartre. Thus Rorty would regard it as just as much a case of bad faith to attribute fixed and unchangeable characteristics to a rock as to a person. Each is just as much a case of us trying to 'slough off responsibility' (376) for our freedom to describe and re-describe, by pretending that one privileged description is forced upon us by the God-substitute of objective truth.

How much any of this has to do with Gadamer is a moot point. Rorty twice mentions Gadamer's key concept of *wirkungsgeschichtliches Bewusstsein* (359, 363), which translates as 'effective-historical consciousness'. The concept of 'effective history' is designed to capture the idea of history as an active force in the present, one which determines both what we are and what it is possible for us to think, since the languages in which we understand ourselves have been developing for thousands of years to express the ways of life of innumerable people who came before us. For Gadamer, this means that any individuality we possess is vastly outweighed by our ordinariness, an ordinariness revealed within our historically determined prejudices and automatic presuppositions. As he puts it, 'the prejudices of the individual, far more than his judgments, constitute the historical reality of his being' (Gadamer 1989: 277). Gadamer's project, then, is to counteract the 'prejudice against prejudice' (ibid.: 270) which entered into culture in the Enlightenment, by placing our preoccupation with truth and method within the wider and more fundamental context of prejudice and tradition. To achieve 'effective-historical consciousness' would be to self-consciously understand ourselves and the world in a manner that is determined by history and tradition; that is the aim of hermeneutic engagement with history.

What does this have to do with the pluralism and experimentalism Rorty proposes as an antidote to intellectual bad faith and cultural stasis? Well, there are certainly major overlaps, the three biggest being the following. First, Gadamer and Rorty both want to place our interest in hard facts within a social context, dispelling the notion of science as autonomous, disinterested and objective. Second, Gadamer and Rorty both reject any notion of history as an inert repository of facts, and want to use history to change the way we understand ourselves. And, third, they both oppose the Enlightenment split between facts and values, which leads us to depreciate values as non-rational or even non-cognitive, and thus to treat science as an area in which the values of our society are irrelevant.

There are also some major differences, however. For a start, pluralism is simply not part of Gadamer's agenda. He does not want to argue that all academic subjects are on a par, only that all knowledge must not be modelled on science, and that science must not be regarded as autonomous and ahistorical. Although Rorty agrees with these views, Gadamer's motivation for putting them forward has little to do with undermining objective truth and philosophy, or indeed with worries about abnormal discourse being closed off. Rather, Gadamer is motivated by the rather graver thought that the discoupling of science from *phronēsis* has led to a situation in which society is being led by technology rather than *vice versa*, a sentiment quite understandable in light of the fact that *Truth and Method* was first published at about the same time that people first acquired the technological means to destroy all life on Earth. These sorts of concern about science are simply not part of Rorty's agenda, however. He is, after all, a tactical physicalist: although Rorty does not believe in ontology and does not believe physical descriptions have any privilege among 'the potential infinity of vocabularies in which the world can be described' (367), he does nevertheless want to call himself a physicalist.

An equally stark contrast between Rorty and Gadamer is presented by their differing attitudes to philosophy, for as Georgia Warnke has persuasively argued against Rorty's claim to Gadamer as an ally, Gadamer himself envisaged a vitally important role for philosophy within society, namely that of, 'integrating our knowledge within a cohesive whole, of aiding public consensus on common aims and purposes and thus giving direction to the scientific and technological apparatus' (Warnke 1987: 163). In light of such contrasts, it can seem that the overlap between Rorty and Gadamer is something of a coincidence, and that Gadamer's views just happened to suit Rorty's very different purposes. Certainly, it would be hard to exaggerate the difference in tone between these two thinkers. On one occasion, for example, Rorty explained Heidegger's originality as a philosopher as 'the result of some neural kink' (Rorty 1988). This explanation was perfectly acceptable to Rorty, for it fitted the purposes he had at the time of writing, but Gadamer would have regarded it as crass and scientistic in the extreme, and hence antithetical to everything he stood for.

To criticise Rorty for a presenting a misleading picture of Gadamer, however, runs the risk of missing the point in this context. This is because Rorty has been using this section to argue for a conception of edification that calls for the imaginative weaving together of incommensurable discourses, and that is exactly what he has just done: he has managed to combine Gadamer, Sartre, and Kuhn into a stable and coherent whole. Not only is this a show of some intellectual virtuosity, but it is also a good example of two of Rorty's main virtues: he takes risks and he practises what he preaches.

VARIETIES OF PHILOSOPHY AND RELATIVISM

(§§2–3)

Rorty now applies his conception of edification specifically to philosophy, providing a limited taxonomy of different types of philosophy. The two distinctions he makes are between systematic and edifying philosophy, and normal and revolutionary philosophy. The normal–revolutionary distinction is the familiar Kuhnian one between those who work within a paradigm and those who instigate a new one; it is the systematic-edifying distinction which is the new development.

Rorty introduces systematic philosophy as the type of philosophy which 'centers in epistemology' (366), but this turns out to be a red herring, since by the end of the book he is speculating about 'a new form of systematic philosophy . . . which has nothing whatever to do with epistemology' (394).[1] The real unifying factor is actually 'universal commensuration' (368): systematic philosophy is the sort of philosophy which aims to produce a framework to unify all discourses, thereby allowing any claim from any area of culture to be evaluated objectively. Epistemology (as theory of knowledge) is simply the means to universal commensuration that has dominated Western philosophy. Systematic philosophy proceeds by using the latest triumph of reason – Rorty gives examples such as Aquinas's use of Aristotle, Descartes's use of the New Science, and Carnap's use of Fregean logic – as the basis of a general theory of knowledge. This theory is supposed to allow judgement to be passed on other areas of culture, and to provide a method for tackling the perennial philosophical problems. When apparent progress towards these aims inevitably grinds to a halt, however, then revolutionary philosophers emerge. These philosophers are still systematic because they regard the incommensurability of their new discourses as just a 'temporary inconvenience' (369); they still have the same overarching aims, and want philosophy back on the 'secure path of a science' (372) as soon as possible, with their new discourses thereby normalised and institutionalised.

Edifying philosophers, by contrast, are revolutionary philosophers who develop abnormal, incommensurable discourses as a deliberate reaction against systematic philosophy, without wanting their discourses to ever become normalised. Edifying philosophy is thus 'intrinsically reactive' (366), whereas systematic philosophy is intrinsically constructive. Edifying philosophers do not react against the normal philosophy of their day because they think the current paradigm is impeding progress, which is the motivation for revolutionary systematic philosophers. Rather, they react because they reject the aims of systematic philosophy; they do not want universal commensuration, and they do not think there are any perennial philosophical problems to solve. This is because they are anti-essentialists, historicists, and holists: they do not think the world has any essence for us to describe accurately, they regard currently state-of-the-art descriptions of the world as simply more descriptions that will pass away with time, and they think that descriptions are meaningful only because of the way they relate to the rest of language, not because of the way they relate to the world.

The overall aim of edifying philosophy is neatly captured in Dewey's phrase 'breaking the crust of convention' (379), since edifying philosophers want to disrupt systematic philosophy in order to counteract the intellectual bad faith of thinking that we can 'know ourselves by knowing a set of objective facts' (373). Rather than trying to close off conversation by finding definitive answers to questions about ourselves and the world, then, the edifying philosopher aims to keep reinvigorating the conversation by finding new descriptions capable of making the world seem fresh all over again; they want to elicit a 'sense of wonder that there is something new under the sun' (370). It is for this reason that as soon as the systematic philosopher formulates a crystal clear and apparently incontrovertible position, the edifying philosopher will try to confuse matters, and more generally, as soon as any way of describing the world starts to look obvious and unavoidable, the edifying philosopher will look for a way of avoiding it. This kind of agenda is to be found in many of the French philosophers of Rorty's generation, especially Jacques Derrida, who once described his aim in philosophy as 'to keep open the width of language' (Derrida 1995).

Overall, then, there are three types of philosopher (normal edifying philosophy is a contradiction in terms), which are the following:

Revolutionary Edifying Philosophers
Revolutionary Systematic Philosophers
Normal Systematic Philosophers

Wittgenstein and Heidegger belong to the first type, Russell and Husserl belong to the second type, and Sellars, Quine, Davidson, and Kuhn presumably belong to the third type, along with the rest of the herd of professional philosophers.[2] So where does Rorty fit in? We should be told. The only two options would seem to be that Rorty is a revolutionary edifying philosopher, or that Rorty is not a philosopher at all. Maybe the former is right, because Rorty has certainly been trying to create edifying discourses throughout *PMN*. However the combination of his metaphilosophical stance and the fact that he made an institutional break with philosophy not long after the book was published might be thought to suggest that he had the latter in mind.

In Section 3, Rorty takes on the charge that he is a relativist, which was prescient given that this charge has followed him ever since *PMN*. Rorty has always denied that he is a relativist, and his denials grow ever more jaded with each passing year.[3] He is quite right to keep at it, however, because although there are many different forms of relativism of varying degrees of sophistication (e.g. Kölbel 2002; see also O'Grady 2002), he is certainly not a relativist in any ordinary sense, and it is this ordinary sense which has the negative connotations intended by his critics. In the ordinary sense, a relativist is somebody who believes that different groups of people have different truths, and that consequently there can be no way of saying who is right; the Papua New Guinean healer has his medicine and the Swiss consultant has her medicine, and neither one is better than the other; 'better' only means something relative to a culture, or an historical era, or to some other grouping of people. Rorty does not believe anything like this, however, and would have no qualms whatsoever about saying that the Swiss consultant has the better medicine. This is because he thinks that we (meaning 'the heirs of Galileo') are right.

This point is potentially confusing because Rorty certainly does think that justification is always relative to an audience, and that the distinction between justification and truth is trivial. However his denial that there is any perspective from which we can make sense of absolute justification means that he writes from the perspective of a particular audience, i.e. the contemporary West. Thus he writes in full acceptance of our standards of justification, and more controversially, thinks non-Western cultures would be better off if they adopted our standards too. As Susan Haack once put it, Rorty is a 'tribalist' (Haack 1993: 192) rather than a relativist, though Rorty himself prefers to use the term 'ethnocentrism' (Rorty 1991a: 21–34).[4] So, to return to the medicine example, Rorty's view would be that if we engaged in hermeneutic dialogue with Papua New Guinean tribesmen, we could eventually render their medical discourse commensurable with our own, and subsequently decide in favour of our medicines. Of course, they could do the same with us, but Rorty (employing our standards of justification) will just say that they are wrong. The point is that he has no less confidence in our beliefs than someone who thinks they can be absolutely rather than just ethnocentrically justified; the dispute is about how this confidence is to be explained. Rorty thinks only 'norm-circular' justification of our beliefs is possible, but that the success we have achieved with those beliefs speaks for itself, whereas his opponents think that the success itself must be explained in terms of absolute justification. The typical relativist, however, would regard both views as equally guilty of the chauvinistic assumption that what we think is better than what other people think.

Rorty is not a relativist in any ordinary sense, then, and in actual fact, Rorty's view opposes the most widespread forms of relativism, since it allows for truths about morality and art to be on a par with truths about physics. Nevertheless, there is obviously some element of relativism to his thought, given that he continually emphasises the relativity of justification to audiences. This is best captured by describing his view as committed to a kind of counterfactual relativism: Rorty thinks that we could have adopted different standards of justification. Thus even though Galileo was right and Bellarmine was wrong, history could have turned out differently. This must be the case, according to Rorty, because our standards of justification are not determined by an ahistorical, objective truth, but rather by the contingent twists and turns of an historical conversation that could have gone differently. That is why Rorty emphasises the point that there is no sense in which Bellarmine was wrong before Galileo won the argument, and likewise no way anyone could have known Bellarmine was being irrational at the time.

Rorty thinks the reason that his refusal to offer 'uniquely individuating conditions' for 'truth or reality or goodness' (374) attracts charges of relativism, is due to a confusion between causation and representation. Uniquely individuating conditions are expected because philosophers presuppose the philosophical rather than the ordinary senses of 'truth', 'reality' and 'goodness', i.e. the senses in which they refer to hypostatised universals. When attempts to provide individuating conditions for hypostatised universals are inevitably blocked by a naturalistic fallacy, however, philosophers treat physical reality differently from moral truth. That is, they may be prepared to accept that our inability to discover the individuating conditions for the one true moral code is a good reason for thinking that there is no one true moral code, but abandoning the view that there are unitary and definitive answers to moral dilemmas is not equated with relativism. Our inability to discover the individuating conditions for the one true physical reality (the way the world is), on the other hand, is just as good a reason for thinking that there is no one true physical reality, and yet someone like Rorty who draws this parallel conclusion does get accused of relativism. The reason, Rorty thinks, is that his critics are assuming that the notion of a one true physical reality which our representations approximate is required to explain the fact that the world exerts causal pressure on us. He thinks this is a mistake.

To understand this point, it is again helpful to consider the passage from Brandom which we used before (Chapter 6 above), this time cited in full:

> Normative relations are exclusively intravocabulary. Extravocabulary relations are exclusively causal. Representation purports to be *both* a normative relation, supporting assessments of correctness and incorrectness, *and* a relation between representings within a vocabulary and representeds outside of that vocabulary. Therefore, the representational model of the relation of vocabularies to their environment should be rejected.
>
> (Brandom 2000: 160)

In Rorty's view, then, the only way in which language relates to the world is causal; language-world relations are 'exclusively causal'. This means looking at the interaction between language and the world as the field linguist does, namely as the causal interaction of a series of marks and noises with changes in the environment. Once normative relations between language and the world are rejected, and we realise that normative relations are exclusively conversational, then philosophical questions about whether our languages are representing things correctly can no longer arise, and the relation between language and the world becomes as unproblematic as any other causal relation. The Myth of the Given can thereby be seen as the result of confusing conversational relations within language, with causal relations between language and the world.

After *PMN*, Rorty further developed his causal account of the relation between language and the world in Darwinian terms. As he was to put it, the world can indeed 'cause us to hold beliefs' and 'decide the competition between alternative sentences', but only 'once we have programmed ourselves with a language' (Rorty 1989: 5–6). Despite the causal pressure exerted by the world, however, there is 'no way of transferring this non-linguistic brutality to *facts*' (Rorty 1991a: 81). Thus even though when Galileo looked through his telescope, there was a 'brute physical resistance – the pressure of light waves on Galileo's eyeball', there were nevertheless 'as many *facts* . . . brought into the world as there are languages for describing that causal transaction' (ibid.: 81). For Bellarmine with his Aristotelian programming, and Galileo in the process of re-programming himself – and subsequently all of his heirs – this causal impact established very different facts.

The initial linguistic programming of human beings was the result of natural selection; we evolved to use 'certain features of the human throat, hand, and brain' to co-ordinate group actions by 'batting marks and noises back and forth'. These marks and noises, however, have, 'no more of a *representational* relation to an intrinsic nature of things than does the anteater's snout or the bowerbird's skill at weaving' (Rorty 1998: 48; see also Rorty 1999: 64–66). Language is thus an adaptation to the environment, a set of tools for dealing with the causal pressures exerted by the environment, rather than a way of mirroring it. We are 'animals clever enough to take charge of our own evolution' (Rorty 1998: 174), but it is also true that cultural evolution 'takes over from biological evolution without a break' (Rorty 1999: 75), and thus there are important parallels between 'stories about how the elephant got its trunk and stories about how the West got particle physics' (Rorty 1998: 152).

The reason Rorty thinks he is accused of being a relativist, then, is that 'absence of description is confused with a privilege attaching to a certain description' (375). In other words, his critic is confusing the fact that causal pressures impose themselves upon us regardless of how we describe them, with the idea that causal pressures impose themselves upon us under a certain description. So, to use the example of stepping on a nail, the confusion is between the causal effect being imposed upon us, and the causal effect being imposed upon us under a certain description, namely as pain. The critic thereby confuses Rorty's claim that there are no 'uniquely individu-ating conditions' for physical reality, with the claim that even the causal pressures exerted upon us by physical reality are relative to descriptions, i.e. there are only causal pressures as a result of our describing the world in a certain way, rather as a moral relativist might claim that there are only right and wrong actions as a result of our describing the world in a certain way.

To find Rorty making a claim about how reality is in the absence of descriptions comes as something of a bolt from the blue. The reason is obvious: if there are description-independent causal pressures, then there is a way the world is independently of what we say about it (cf. Guignon and Hiley 2003: 31–32; Hall 1994: 91–93). Rorty cannot even deny that these causal pressures have no preferred way of being described, because he has already told us what their preferred way of being described is: they are 'causal pressures'. He can still claim that these causal pressures are describable in any number of different ways (compatible with them being causal pressures of course), and also that the causal pressures themselves will not determine how we do this. But this simply has the effect of rendering them unknowable (except, once more, for the fact that they are causal pressures). As Rorty himself has put it, 'once you have said that all our awareness is under a description, and that descriptions are functions of social needs, then "nature" and "reality" can only be names of something unknowable – something like Kant's "Thing-in-Itself"' (Rorty 1999: 49).[5] Presumably, the same could be said of 'causal pressures', and indeed, some pages later Rorty is arguing that the supposed '*intrinsic causal powers*' and 'sheer brute *thereness*' (ibid.: 56) of things is as description-relative as anything else. Yet in another essay of the same year, he can be found saying of causal pressures that: 'These pressures will be described in different ways at different times and for different purposes, but they are pressures none the less' (ibid.: 33). Since Rorty clearly does not want to commit himself to the existence of unknowable causal pressures by making them description-independent, but he does want to claim that causal pressures exist however we describe the world, the question arises of how his position is to be rendered coherent.

The best option is to construe Rorty as taking our own current vocabulary for granted, and making the historical claim that the causal pressures we know about have always been thought of as causal pressures, as well as the prediction that they always will be.

This allows him to combine his view that awareness is always under a description with his purely causal account of the relation of language to the world, without thereby making any claim about how things are apart from our ways of describing them. Rorty can still claim that the accusation of relativism depends on confusing causal pressures being exerted upon us with causal pressures forcing us to describe things in a particular way. He would, however, have to drop his talk of 'nonlinguistic brutality', and causation as a 'non-description-relative relation' existing in 'absence of description' (375). But conceding that causal pressure itself is relative to our 'programming' seems a much better option for him than making claims which jeopardise his anti-essentialism and linguistic holism according to which, 'the distinction between things related and relations is just an alternative way of making the distinction between what we are talking about and what we say about it' (Rorty 1999: 56). Such pragmatist views simply leave no room to accommodate the metaphysical realist's intuition that causation is a 'non-description-relative relation'; Rorty seems to have thought that he could have it both ways, but was mistaken.

TOMORROW IS THE QUESTION

(§§4–5)

Rorty's next aim is to show that the edifying philosophy he is advocating is compatible with the physicalism he defended earlier in the book. These commitments appear to be at odds, because whereas edifying philosophy aims to counteract the objectifying tendencies within culture, physicalism might easily be interpreted as the ultimate manifestation of such tendencies, on the grounds that it converts reality into a conglomeration of objects described by one normalised area of discourse, namely physics. Certainly, this is a common interpretation amongst continental philosophers, who might well sympathise with Rorty's advocacy of edification, but who have tended to regard physicalism as both a form of scientism, and a sign that analytic philosophy never properly absorbed Kant's transcendental turn. From the opposite perspective, many analytic philosophers would probably be unable to take Rorty's continental borrowings seriously unless convinced that they were compatible with physicalism. Rorty attempts a reconciliation, then, by trying to show that countering the self-deception of scientism and other forms of objectification does not require a rejection of physicalism. And as a twist in the tale – to be expected in a book by Rorty – this reconciliation turns out to be Kantian.

Rorty's main target is the idea developed by Frankfurt School philosophers Karl-Otto Apel and Jürgen Habermas, that countering 'objectivistic illusions' (381) requires the adoption of a new and explicitly social transcendental standpoint, as opposed to the transcendental standpoint of traditional German idealism. In varying ways, these philosophers have tried to identify the rules and conditions which are presupposed by communication; these are 'transcendental' conditions because they claim universal validity and make communication possible, just as Kantian pure concepts and forms of intuition claim universal validity and make cognition possible, but they are rooted only in the shared interests arising from human social existence, and hence are supposed to be free from metaphysical baggage. Through transcendental reflection, then, it is hoped that we can resist the intellectual bad faith of thinking that the world dictates the objective truth to us, and proceed in full cognisance that the results of our inquiries are inevitably shaped by the presuppositions we bring to them.

Rorty sees this as an unfortunate attempt to take a systematic and constructive approach to edification, and thus as an attempt to normalise creativity. For Rorty, there is no need to isolate the conditions of theory-construction to remind us that our theories are just theories, since this end can be achieved through historicist reflection and edifying philosophy: we need only remind ourselves of the continual displacement of normal discourses throughout history, and of our potential for abnormal discourse. Moreover, the approach is worse than just unnecessary, for it is itself a form of the objectification it ostensibly aims to curtail. The reason is that to look for universal presuppositions of inquiry that can cross over the boundaries between paradigms, is to try to view our creation of paradigms in the normal way we view the world from within a paradigm. For Rorty, by contrast, a transition between paradigms is a Darwinian lunge forwards which can only be rationalised Whiggishly after the event. Any attempt to find universal conditions governing our invention of new vocabularies for describing and re-describing the world is ultimately an attempt to, 'make the sense of the world consist in the objective truth about some previously unnoticed portion or feature of the world' (387). Thus in looking for the transcendental presuppositions of all discourses, we look for something 'previously unnoticed' by our normal discourses, but nevertheless objective and determinate. This is 'the philosopher's special form of bad faith', namely the attempt to substitute 'pseudo-cognition for moral choice' (383).

The reason Rorty says 'moral' choice, is that he thinks the route out of bad faith is provided not by Kant's distinction between the empirical and transcendental standpoints, but rather by Kant's distinction between the empirical and moral (or more generally, practical) standpoints. In 'The Canon of Pure Reason', one of the closing sections of the *Critique of Pure Reason*, Kant lists three questions: 'What can I know?', 'What ought I to do?', and 'What may I hope?' (Kant 1933: A805/B833). Kant takes himself to have already answered the first question, and uses this section to broach the second two as a prelude to his subsequent work. The principal point he makes in this section is that knowledge alone will not answer questions about what we ought to do with our lives, or what significance we ought to read into them, questions for which Rorty provides his own equivalents, such as 'What is the point?' (383). Nevertheless, we can still have genuine and even necessary beliefs about such matters from a moral standpoint, so long as our theoretical knowledge does not actually conflict with our moral beliefs. Thus we can believe that we are free, or that God exists, on the practical but nevertheless rational grounds that having such a belief is a presupposition of our moral choices. I cannot say '*It is* morally certain that there is a God, etc.', Kant argues, for there is no fact about empirical reality which forces this belief upon me, but I can say 'I *am* morally certain, etc.' if I am inclined to this belief, it is able to structure and guide to my actions, and there is nothing theoretical to be said against it (ibid.: A829/B857).

This idea that knowing objective facts about the world will not determine the significance we find in it – will not provide it with a sense or a moral – is for Rorty an amplification of the point he has been pressing throughout *PMN*, namely that justification must be strictly separated from causation. The world will not tell us how to interpret it, and hence will not tell us what practices of justification to adopt; it can only cause us to hold beliefs after we have adopted such a practice. Adopting a new practice of justification is a matter of moral choice in the sense that we are deciding to accept an 'unjustifiable but unconditional moral claim' (384) about how we ought to act. In Rorty's Kuhnian and historicist terms, however, the Kantian view that freedom cannot be reduced to nature means only that at certain times there is a lack of consensus about practices of justification, and that we consequently have to make a consensus, that is, we have to create new discourses for describing the world and agree to abide by the norms they generate. This is not an agreement with the world, but an agreement between human beings, one which will govern the future actions and interactions of those who adopt the discourse. We are, however, always free to choose new discourses, and the sense in which this is a moral choice sheds new light on Rorty's phrase 'redescribing ourselves is the most important thing we can do'.

The specifically philosophical form of bad faith, then, is to make an attempt at 'straddling the gap between description and justification' (385), by trying to find an algorithm for moral choice. The antidote, Rorty thinks, is to view our normal discourses 'bifocally', that is, as both practices we believe in, and as practices which were adopted for contingent reasons. Thus we can accept the facts discovered in science with a clear conscience, so long as we bear in mind that scientific practice is just one way of making sense of the world that was chosen for contingent historical reasons, and that the objective facts delivered by natural science are on a par with those of any normal discourse. Art criticism, or even philosophy, could in principle tell us objective facts of no lesser status than those discovered in physics; Rorty once said that it is mere courtesy which prevents philosophers from describing present-day Cartesian dualists as factually ignorant (Rorty 1998: 248). Once this is seen, then, there is no reason for philosophers who recognise the bad faith inherent in objectification to reject physicalism. Moreover, Rorty thinks physicalism actually helps to keep bad faith at bay, since it removes any temptation to think of human beings as metaphysically unique beings whose capacity for abnormal discourse requires systematic description from a transcendental standpoint.[6]

Rorty's statement of what his physicalism amounts to, however, is unfortunately just as puzzling as usual. Of his five bold statements (387–88), only the third and fifth are unproblematic, for they simply reiterate his view that physics is just another normal discourse, and that knowing all the truths of physics would not obviate our moral choice about what sense to make of the world. The first, second and fourth, however – especially the second – are problematic. The first statement amounts to an endorsement of the causal closure of the physical domain, something most philosophers accept whether they are physicalists or not (it only rules out interactionist dualism). This would be unproblematic (although unargued) had Rorty not earlier said that causation is 'non-description-relative'; here we have another reason for dropping that earlier claim. The fourth statement says that the irreducibility of other discourses to 'atoms-and-the-void science' does not devalue them; physics is not being accorded any privileged status. This claim is unproblematic in itself, but is potentially misleading. The reason is that given Rorty's other commitments, there can be no principled reason why all other discourses should not be reduced to physics. Rorty thinks universal commensuration would be a cultural disaster, but he cannot rule it out, and so what he has called his 'non-reductive physicalism' should not be assimilated to Davidson's, which does indeed depend on a principled difference between physical and other discourses.[7]

The second statements says,

> Nobody will be able to predict his own actions, thoughts, theories, poems, etc., before deciding upon them or inventing them. (This is not an interesting remark about the odd nature of human beings, but rather a trivial consequence of what it means to 'decide' or 'invent'.)

Imagine I am wired up to a cerebroscope with a screen which shows me its predictions. There is a blue and a red button, and I am about to decide which one to press. The machine predicts that I will press the red button. Now if I proceed to press the red button, I will still have decided to do so, since I did so freely without being coerced by anyone; this is the sort of Humean compatibilist point Rorty has in mind. However, it also seems that I could decide to prove the machine wrong and press the blue button instead. Since the cerebroscope presumably cannot be wrong – my awkwardness would have entered into its physical calculations – this must be illusory. And yet this just seems to show that the machine cannot actually make a prediction unless it predicts that I will go along with whatever it predicts. But why not? Even if I am awkward, I am still a just a physical thing whose motions it should be able to predict. The case is more baffling still with Rorty's poetry example: once I have read the poem on the screen I cannot invent it (Rorty is right about that), but then unless I invent it, how is the cerebroscope going to predict it? However these 'conundrums' are to be resolved, if indeed they are, Rorty certainly should not be raising them.

The final section of the book looks to the future. Before doing so, however, Rorty provides a final recasting of his fundamental criticism of traditional philosophy, by saying that the philosopher's 'urge to break out into an ἀρχή [archē, meaning 'first principle'] beyond discourse' (390) is motivated by the desire to lock our practices of justification onto something more solid than transient conversation. The term archē was first employed in this sense by the Milesian Cosmologists, traditionally regarded as the originators of philosophy, and so Rorty is reminding us that his 'attempts to deconstruct the image of the Mirror of Nature' need to be placed within the much wider context of 'the history of European culture' (390): modern philosophy was just the 'most explicit' manifestation of our search for a non-human foundation for human consensus. Rorty earlier made this same point in terms of the presumption of a *logos* backing up our claims, which is what Derrida called 'logocentrism'. Thus *PMN* has been described as, 'an analytical philosopher's critique of what Derrida calls the logocentrism of Western philosophy' (Culler 1982: 152). Rorty's approach to deconstructing this aspect of culture is considerably less avant-garde than Derrida's, however, and is rooted in history of a fairly conventional kind. As he puts it, his aim in *PMN* has been to describe philosophy as an historical episode, thereby contributing to the wider goal of allowing us to see the religious urge for an ahistorical basis for commensuration as itself an 'historical phenomenon' (392).

Now we already know that Rorty wants a future free of the Mirror of Nature, but does he also want a future free of philosophy? In considering his final reflections on this matter, it is worth bearing in mind the well known statement by the philosopher Etienne Gilson, that, 'the first law to be inferred from philosophical experience is: Philosophy always buries its undertakers' (Gilson 1950: 306). It is worth bearing this in mind, because Rorty certainly did; he goes out of his way to establish his belief in the future of philosophy in these closing pages, and always seems a little indignant whenever critics overlook the fact (e.g. Rorty 1998: 47, ftnt 16). Nevertheless, it is surely fair to say that up until this point, a much more negative conclusion certainly looked to be on the cards.

Let us review facts. Until Chapter 6, Rorty did not have a good word to say for philosophy. He then introduced Davidsonian semantics as an unobjectionable pursuit, though nevertheless a case of philosophy converting itself into a 'boring academic specialty' (385). In Part Three edifying philosophy was introduced, which is a type of philosophy Rorty really does approve of. Nevertheless, since edifying philosophy is a reaction to systematic philosophy, and Rorty wants the search for universal commensuration to come to an end, it seems to follow that he should also want edifying philosophy to come to an end. Edifying philosophy may be an admirable reaction to the bad faith of systematic philosophy, but if the ultimate goal is for culture to get over its need for non-human guidance, then surely we would be better off if there was no longer any need for edifying philosophy. We will always need edification to create abnormal discourses, of course, but there is no reason for edification to be a type of philosophy; only if systematic philosophy were to continue would we need specifically philosophical edifying discourses, but Rorty hopes that it will not. So the logic of his position does seem to be that of a philosophical undertaker.

What Rorty actually says, however, is just that philosophy needs to abandon all vestiges of the Mirror of Nature paradigm which Kant used to create an autonomous academic subject with a professional self-image. This means that philosophers can no longer adjudicate areas of culture – praising physics and maligning homeopathy, for instance – on the pretence of 'knowing something about knowing which nobody else knows so well' (392). Without the Mirror of

Nature, philosophy has no special subject-matter, no special method, and not even a unique point of view. Rorty nevertheless rejects 'the claim that there can or should be no such profession' (393), though he seems considerably more sure about the 'can' than the 'should'. The profession will go on, he says, because people will continue to read the 'great dead philosophers', and universities will need people to teach them. Philosophers can also contribute some 'useful kibitzing' between subjects, though the only reason Rorty can think of for why philosophers should be better suited to this role than any other sort of academic, is that the professional philosopher's background in the history of philosophy allows them to spot 'stale philosophical clichés' (393). It is as if someone were to write a critique of chemistry which ended with the claim that even though there are no chemicals, and chemistry has no special method, universities will nevertheless continue to employ chemists, and so they should make themselves useful by acting as a go-between for other disciplines, and by trying to make sure that nobody falls into the trap of doing any chemistry.

The conclusion takes on a more positive aspect, however, in light of Rorty's anti-essentialism and historicism. After all, Rorty would not regard chemicals as an ahistorical subject matter either. As he said in his classic paper, 'Philosophy as a Kind of Writing: An Essay on Derrida',

> All that 'philosophy' as a name for a sector of culture means is 'talk about Plato, Augustine, Descartes, Kant, Hegel, Frege, Russell . . . and that lot.' Philosophy is best seen as a kind of writing. It is delimited, as is any literary genre, not by form or matter, but by tradition – a family romance involving, e.g., Father Parmenides, honest old Uncle Kant, and bad brother Derrida.
>
> (Rorty 1982: 92)

If we think of philosophy in this way, namely as a tradition of writing woven around a certain family tree, then we can see Rorty's conclusion in a new light: he wants a radically new plot development. This needs to be an almost clean break, since traditional philosophy had little going for it, but Rorty does not want to rule out the possibility of the great philosophy texts becoming the basis for something useful in the future, if interpreted in novel enough ways. To this effect, he has made numerous positive suggestions about future directions for philosophy, not all consistent but not particularly meant to be either. This is just icing on the cake, however, for Rorty's position is overwhelmingly negative, and even though he clearly has some sympathy for the view that the best possible outcome would be for society to become entirely post-philosophical, he is sufficiently haunted by Gilson not to commit himself.[8]

CONCLUSION OF THIS BOOK

In Chapter 9 above, I said that there is a tension within Rorty's fundamental project between his negative metaphilosophy and his denial of objective truth. This is because on the one hand, Rorty wants to walk away from philosophy, thereby simply forgetting about a dialectical cul-de-sac which proved its social irrelevance long ago, and yet on the other hand, Rorty wants to deny objective truth, thereby making some surprising and revisionary claims about the world on the basis of *a priori* reflection. The separation between these two strands of his thought struck me with some force one day when I was trying to give a coherent exposition of one of his positions, balancing all the various commitments, considering possible objections, etc.: it suddenly occurred to me that I had lost track of what was supposed to be so different about Rorty. It felt as if I could have just as easily been writing an exposition of any of the great philosophers, and the idea that this was somebody with serious doubts about philosophy seemed to have gone completely out of the window. If you start thinking through his views on language and causation, commensuration, physicalism, the equality between science and the humanities, bad faith and objectification, and other related topics, then I think you will see what I mean.

What brings the two strands together for Rorty is his Hegelian vision of the future, since he regards criticising philosophy and criticising objective truth as both ways of contributing to the completion of the secularisation process begun in the Enlightenment; as he has quite candidly put it, pragmatists like himself are engaged in 'a long-term attempt to change the rhetoric, the common sense, and the self-image of their community' (Rorty 1998: 41). Rorty takes this mission very seriously – Putnam thinks that 'Rorty hopes to be a doctor to the modern soul' (quoted at ibid.: 44) – and although he is always exceptionally self-depreciating whenever he talks about himself, his work exudes a sense of importance which avoids self-importance only because of his style of grand narration, a style which involves displacing his own views into the mouths of others.

Completing the secularisation process is important, Rorty thinks, because once we stop worshipping idols like Gods, Marxist utopias, rationality, physical particles, etc., then we will be able to concentrate more fully on each other and achieve a heightened sense of human solidarity. As he once definitively put it,

> Our identification with our community – our society, our political tradition, our intellectual heritage – is heightened when we see this community as ours rather than nature's, shaped rather than found, one among many which men have made. In the end, the pragmatists tell us, what matters is our loyalty to other human beings clinging together against the dark, not our hope of getting things right.
>
> (Rorty 1982: 166)

The question to ask, however, is whether this future culture is one in which people have forgotten about philosophy because it was socially useless, or whether it is one in which people have forgotten about philosophy because one kind of philosophy won through.

The suspicion, then, is that Rorty's metaphilosophy may just be a ploy to refute metaphysical realism once and for all, since by announcing that the philosophical game is over, the realist is thereby refused the right of reply. Rorty's frustration with the perennial to and fro between realism and idealism might simply be anxiety that his own favoured variety of post-Quinean idealism will not stay in fashion forever. I have continually returned to the charge that Rorty is an updated idealist, because it is prevalent and persistent among his critics. It is not hard to see why either, for all of Rorty's key moves are idealist: his endorsement of the British idealist slogan that 'only thought relates', his (social) coherentism and unrestricted holism, and his endorsement (but reinterpretation) of 'Berkeley's ingenuous remark that "nothing can be like an idea except an idea"'.

Moreover, little familiarity with Rorty's writings is required to spot the marked difference between the way he criticises realists and idealists. There is no 'way the world is' – full stop – but idealists (who he routinely lists alongside pragmatists) make themselves a 'patsy for realistic reaction', or else commit some other tactical error that requires them to be ticked off. And as if this did not already amply explain the idealist tag, Rorty occasionally says things like this: 'My hunch is that the twentieth century will be seen by historians of philosophy as the period in which a kind of neo-Leibnizian panrelationism was developed in various different idioms' (Rorty 1999: 70). Neo-Leibnizian Panrelationism is certainly one way to describe the combination of linguistic holism and anti-essentialism which Rorty has developed in *PMN*.

My own view, however, is that Rorty is quite obviously not an idealist. The reason is that he is a critic of the Mirror of Nature: he does not even believe in ideas, so he was hardly going to make them the basis of his thinking. Moreover, the vague notion that Rorty is something called a 'linguistic idealist' is even sillier: how could reality be language-constituted? What would that even mean? So Rorty is not an idealist. Rather, I think that Rorty has developed a new metaphysical position, metaphysical pluralism. He only seems pro-idealist because he was heavily influenced by idealist philosophers, and because the default status of realism within contemporary culture made it his obvious main target.

Rorty would probably not mind being called a pluralist, but he would not like the prefix 'metaphysical'. Nevertheless, he believes all of the following:

1 We can only ever know about the world under some description or another.
2 The world has no preferred way of being described, so how we describe it is down to us.
3 Any privilege attaching to one way of describing the world over another is always the result of a human decision.

As far as I can see, this adds up to a position which is both metaphysical, because it is a view about all of reality which is not based on any empirical research, and pluralistic, because it denies that reality is mind-dependent, mind-independent, neutral, or that it has any other preferred way of being described. It also seems to involve an ahistorical claim, because presumably the world will never be able to force one sort of description upon us; there is modal force to Rorty's position. Moreover, in a convoluted sort of way, I think that it probably even 'straddles the gap between description and justification', since Rorty believes that his metaphysical pluralist description of the world promises the moral benefits of greater solidarity.

Rorty would probably say that he holds no such position, and that he is simply trying to say abnormal things which are currently useful for the purpose of breaking the crust of convention. However, I tend to think that Rorty only appeals to social usefulness when it suits him. Is it really socially useful to think that there is a Myth of the Given? Or that there is 'no skyhook'? Is it not rather that causal impact alone cannot justify a belief, and that we cannot compare our descriptions to the world itself? Surely Rorty would think these were philosophical errors even if empiricism and metaphysical realism had somehow clocked up impressive social track-records. Imagine, for instance, that there was overwhelming evidence (from cerebroscopes, perhaps) that widespread belief in an objective truth would make the world a better place, perhaps for the reason that removing all hope of an after-life would discourage warfare: would that persuade Rorty that there is a 'way the world is' after all? I very much doubt it, because he seems to be a convinced metaphysical pluralist. The real give-away in *PMN* comes, I think, when he is working out what to say about paradigm-shifts in science, given that the West chose physical description as the backdrop for its stories of change. Rorty's solution is that any description can be used to provide the prerequisite constancy, sense-data reports if needs be, because although the world must always be there under some description, no particular type of description is required. Thus we find Rorty quite blatantly engaged in an activity metaphysicians have always engaged in, namely plugging a gap in his system; no social pay-off is even remotely in sight.

Rorty also thinks social utility justifies his highly implausible neo-Wittgensteinian philosophy of mind, but this is even less credible (cf. Rorty 1998: 98–121). The main justification is that if we believe that subjectivity is adequately accounted for by the social practice of incorrigibility, then we will not concern ourselves with the mind–body problem anymore. However, freeing up the talents of a handful of academic specialists does not seem like much of a social pay-off, and the existence of subjective states is no threat to Rorty's secularisation process anyway, so long as they are not used as the basis of an empiricist epistemology. There are, however, easily foreseeable social disadvantages to Rorty's view, the most obvious one being an increase in cruelty to animals; whether the overall consequences from changes to medical ethics would be good or bad is hard to evaluate. And anyway, did Rorty draw up a cost-benefit analysis to decide what it would be most useful for him to say about the mind? Did he really determine his position by thinking about the good of society? I very much doubt it. It seems to me, rather, that the only motivation there has ever been for neo-Wittgensteinian conceptions of mind is that they dissolve sceptical problems and make physicalist ontology unproblematic, both of which are issues which Rorty is officially not supposed to care about. Of course, he might simply be persuaded by the arguments. But he should not be, because the historical deconstruction was inconclusive, and the Antipodean thought-experiment was unsuccessful.

Rorty would not recognise 'highly implausible' as a criticism: he sees himself as bravely embracing paradox to get rid of troublesome intuitions. However, he misses a crucial point whenever he takes this sort of line. The point is that you do not decide to be revolutionary, it just happens that way. Galileo did not want to say something abnormal and counterintuitive. Rather he had a big idea, he saw things in a new light, and what he had to say was considered counterintuitive by others, though presumably his own intuitions told him it was right. The same is true of edifying philosophers like Nietzsche and Heidegger; they broke the crust of convention because they saw something wrong with received opinion and came up with an alternative. It seems very unlikely that they were trying to be counterintuitive, and even if they were, this has nothing to do with why their work was good. Thus Rorty's encouragement of abnormal discourse is at best unnecessary, because people will come up with new ideas anyway, and at worst an incitement to talking trash. Implausibility is a quality control which the best ideas manage to overcome; it is not a badge of honour.

To answer my own question, then, I do not think the future intellectual climate Rorty is imagining is one where everyone has forgotten about philosophy because it was socially useless. Rather, I think it is one in which everyone has become a metaphysical pluralist, and that the only real connection between Rorty's position and social usefulness is that Rorty is convinced, for no particularly good reason, that this would be a better world. If we were all metaphysical pluralists, he thinks, we could unite in the shared cause of devising the most socially useful and interesting ways of describing the world, we would never try to abdicate responsibility for our descriptions, and we would never feel that continuing to redescribe the world was pointless. Maybe so. Metaphysical pluralism is an appealing position, and *PMN* makes a brilliant case for it. Nevertheless, it is simply misleading for Rorty to suggest that his position enjoys some sort of special status on the grounds that its projected usefulness obviates the need to overcome contrary intuitions. After all, unless Rorty can overcome our contrary intuitions, then the people in his future society may well stop being metaphysical pluralists as soon as they read Descartes's *Meditations* or Kant's *Critique*. Merely forgetting our intuitions can never be enough while these books are around to remind us of them, for unlike scholastic accounts of angels and the Holy Eucharist, these books only need mundane objects like tables and chairs to get you thinking their way. And besides, deciding to forget your intuitions is just as ineffectual as deciding to be revolutionary.

I prefer the other strand of Rorty's thinking: Rorty the metaphilosopher who knows all the moves better than anyone and yet refuses to make one. This purified Rorty is not simply rejecting foundationalist philosophy, as if he thought some other approach were needed; that is why he spends so much time criticising naturalised epistemology. Rather, he is claiming that foundationalism *is* philosophy. He thinks that since this is the idea which academic philosophy was built around, and since it has failed, then there simply is no neutral subject to fall back on. In other words, philosophers think they have a subject but they do not: they have a literature built up around an unsuccessful attempt to smooth over the intellectual transition from Aristotelianism to the age of modern science. This is a powerful thought, especially when Rorty is screaming across the page at you that the very idea of a general theory of knowledge is self-evidently absurd. 'Whoever wanted one?', he asks, and his answer is that some defenders of the New Science wanted one hundreds of years ago.

This thought came across particularly well in the review Rorty wrote of John McDowell's *Mind and World*, one of a number of important works in contemporary philosophy which have attempted to meet Rorty's challenge. In McDowell's case, Rorty was impressed: 'He has rehabilitated empiricism' (Rorty 1998: 150), he declared, only to immediately go on to question why anyone would want to do something like rehabilitate empiricism. And that is what Rorty does best: surprising, reactive philosophy. Edifying philosophy, if you like, which he consistently puts across with more energy than anyone else can manage. Whether or not his metaphilosophical scepticism is justified is another matter, but it is certainly the perfect foil to that tendency towards overconfidence within the subject which generates bad philosophy.

NOTES

1 RORTY

1 This is the sense in which I shall use 'objective truth' throughout this book. Rorty sometimes confuses matters by talking as if he has no problem with objective truth, but in such cases he means truth against a backdrop of contingent consensus or linguistic 'programming' (see Chapters 9 and 10 below).

2 Soames said this in response to a very high-handed review, in which Rorty is apparently amused that anyone would consider vagueness an important topic of debate, neglecting the fact that he himself once did; see his discussion of Peirce on vagueness in 'Pragmatism, Categories, and Language' (Rorty 1961a).

3 Despite it being his favourite Dewey quote, Rorty never provides the reference. The passage I think he has in mind is when Dewey wrote,

> The function of art has always been to break through the crust of conventionalized and routine consciousness. Common things, a flower, a gleam of moonlight, the song of a bird, not things rare and remote, are means with which the deeper levels of life are touched so that they spring up as desire and thought. The process is art.
>
> (Dewey 1954: 183)

But that is art, not philosophy. Another reference I found was to breaking 'the crust of the cake of custom' (Dewey 1922: 170), but again Dewey was not talking about philosophy. However, back in 1967 (Rorty 1967a: 36), Rorty did refer to Friedrich Waismann saying that 'What is characteristic of philosophy is the piercing of that dead crust of tradition and convention, the breaking of those fetters which bind us to inherited preconceptions, so as to attain a new and broader way of looking at things' (Waismann 1956: 483).

4   Some philosophers make a distinction between 'materialism' and 'physicalism', but Rorty does not. I prefer 'physicalism' (nobody believes that only matter exists anymore), and hence will use that term except when referring to 'eliminative materialism' (nobody ever says 'eliminative physicalism'), or archaic positions, or when commenting on quotations about 'materialism'.

5   'Richard Rorty: The Man who Killed Truth', directed by Carole Lochhead, BBC4 (UK television), Tuesday 4 November, 2003.

2 THE MIRROR OF NATURE

1   This quotation is of course completely out of context; Ayer should have taken a more systematic approach to the text, because Chapter 11 of *Appearance and Reality* presents a powerful critique of phenomenalism, Ayer's own position.

3 THE ORIGINS OF THE MIRROR

1   Rorty seems to be unsure throughout *PMN* whether to call intuitions that he does not like 'intuitions' or 'so-called intuitions', but according to the article he wrote about intuition, they count as 'Intuitive Acquaintance with Concepts' (Rorty 1967b: 204, 208–9).

2   'Intentional' and 'Representational' are used as synonyms in analytic philosophy, though they are often contrasted in continental philosophy; see Sartre 1970 for the idea of intentionality as an *antidote* to representational content.

3   See especially Locke 1979: IV.3.§6 and Yolton 1984 for a discussion of the debates which Locke's ideas precipitated. Physicalism in the twentieth century was inspired by psychologists such as E.G. Boring (Boring 1933) and has been completely dominated by concerns about phenomenal properties (esp. pain), a concern which shows no sign of abating (see Chalmers 1996).

4   For Dewey, philosophical ideas are always to be understood in terms of the needs of the society that originated them. For Heidegger, according to Rorty's interpretation at least, there is a self-deceptive motivation underlying attempts to 'substitute a "technical" and determinate question' for the 'openness to strangeness which initially tempted us to begin thinking' (9); for Heidegger ruminating on the importance of 'wonder' to philosophy, see Heidegger 1994: Chapter 5.

5   Julia Annas, for instance, argues that the Stoic notion of *hēgemonikon* 'can be thought of, not too misleadingly, as the mind, and the Stoic

theory of the soul as a theory of our mental life' (Annas 1992: 64). For an excellent overview of Stoic and Epicurean concepts of mind, see Macdonald 2003, pp. 71–87.

6   In the preface to *Appearance and Reality*, Bradley thought that it would be fun to show the reader some of the jottings he had made in his note-books when confused or stuck in the course of writing his book. One such jotting was 'Metaphysics is the finding of bad reasons for what we believe upon instinct' (Bradley 1908: xiv), and it has been quoted as if it were intended as a serious metaphilosophical statement ever since.

4 THE ANTIPODEANS

1   Place was actually British, as is Smart. Place tried and failed to convert Smart to the identity theory during the years he spent at Adelaide, but Smart – who never left Australia – eventually came around to it, influenced in part by reading American philosopher Herbert Feigl's similar theory published two years after Place's. The second wave of physicalists continued the Antipodean connection: David Armstrong is an Australian, Keith Campbell is a New Zealander, and David Lewis was an American on the Australian scene. In the introduction to Clive Borst's widely used anthology, which included Rorty's 1965 paper, Borst uses the term 'antipodean' (Borst 1970: 19), which is probably what gave Rorty the idea.

2   Another idea in the background of the Antipodean discussion is Gustav Bergmann's conception of an 'ideal language', a language in which it is possible to do everything we currently do with language, except for raise philosophical questions; see Rorty 1967a: 6 and ff.

3   Rorty might respond that the Terrans would describe this period in Antipodean terms, and hence not as a period of unconsciousness. Nevertheless, they must either remember looking around and talking Antipodean, or else nothing at all.

4   N.B. In the last sentence of p. 77, where Rorty also makes this point, 'former' and 'latter' have been printed the wrong way around.

5   These include the following: (1) The Antipodeans know vastly more than us: consider the difference between what you know from seeing a tree, and what an Antipodean would know, given that seeing a tree reveals to them the exact configuration of their own brain. Learning Antipodean would be no easy matter. (2) Their appearance–reality distinction (i.e. the distinction between right and wrong) cannot be the same as ours, because ours allows us to look at optical illusions without getting anything wrong. (3) The Antipodean's ability to talk interchangeably about their brain states or the state of the world suggests a particularly bizarre concealed metaphysic, namely the one Russell held when he wrote, 'I should say that what the physiologist sees when he looks at a

brain is part of his own brain, not part of the brain he is examining'
(Russell 1927: 383).

6 There are irrelevant discrepancies between how Principle P is formulated in each of its three appearances (pages 84, 93, and 100) which
should have been edited out long ago.

7 Basic expositions of Kripke's argument can be found in any decent introduction to the philosophy of mind. The 'Brandt–Campbell objection'
(83–86, 93, 118) is as follows. Suppose the physicalist says that pain is
how C-fibre stimulation appears to the possessor of the C-fibres. They
must then grant that this appearance is an 'imperfect apprehension' of
C-fibre stimulation, just as the visual appearance of water is an imperfect apprehension of H_2O. This means, however, that it is the imperfect
apprehension which is the pain, and not the C-fibre stimulation, since
any physical state can be misidentified and pain cannot be. Identifying
the imperfect apprehension with another physical state does not help,
because then we are forced to posit yet another state of imperfect apprehension, and so on *ad infinitum*. So the only way to stop the regress is by
positing a phenomenal property for which no appearance–reality
distinction can be made; as Rorty puts it, 'It is as if man's Glassy
Essence, the Mirror of Nature, only became visible to itself when slightly
clouded' (86).

8 Rorty based his account of incorrigibility on the ideas of Wilfrid Sellars
(Sellars 1997: 90–117).

9 Rorty defended this procedure in his 'Incorrigibility' paper (Rorty 1970:
418).

10 The main problem is that Rorty's characterisation of Behaviourism in
this section is incompatible with what follows in Section 4. The following
are also important to know about for the reader who wants to follow the
text: (1) There is no good reason for Rorty's reversion to the original
Terran dilemma on p. 91 after having narrowed down the options to the
Antipodean Materialist and the Terran Other positions on p. 88; (2)
When Rorty says 'If we adopt this principle [(P)], then, oddly enough, we
can no longer be skeptics: the Antipodeans automatically have raw feels'
(93–94), he must have meant to add: *if we accept that the Antipodeans
make incorrigible reports*; (3) On p. 95, when he says that the 'paradox'
the Materialist faces is enough to 'drive us right back to (P)', he must
have forgotten that the Materialist position is supposed to presuppose
(P).

11 Rorty's sudden interest in plausibility when discussing behaviourism
does not cohere very well with his official position: surely Ryle ought to
be commended for 'breaking the crust of convention'.

12 David Chalmers makes exactly this criticism of topic-neutral analysis
(Chalmers 1996: 23); the whole plot of his book is based on splitting the
concept of mind in two, as per Rorty's 'gerrymandering' tactic.

5 THE ORIGINS OF PHILOSOPHY

1 Russell's *History* must have infuriated Rorty when he first read it. It accords the highest importance to philosophy, presents it as an ancient subject, and concludes with Russell's announcement that his new logical philosophy has finally made the subject scientific. Moreover, it contains a chapter about Dewey, replete with condescending comments on pragmatism and American philosophy in general.

2 To take just one example: Locke set out to refute Plato's idea of innate knowledge (Locke 1979: Book I), and Leibniz set out to revive it (Leibniz 1973: *Discourse on Metaphysics*, §26).

3 Rorty himself suggests that Pyrrhonian scepticism is the problem which 'Descartes thought he had solved' (139).

4 Kant would dispute this, as would most contemporary Kantians, since the critical system is supposed to provide an account of causation, rather than presuppose it. Nevertheless, Rorty certainly touches on a raw nerve: Kant needs the claim that we are 'affected by objects' (Kant 1933: A19), but since he cannot allow this 'affecting' to count as causation, he has to say that we are applying a category without determinate meaning, namely the unschematised category of ground to consequent. As generations of critics have noted, this sounds suspiciously like causation in all but name.

6 LINGUISTIC HOLISM

1 It was in effect Sellars's transformation of the Kantian distinction between the world as it is for us and the world as it is in itself; see DeVries 2005: 7–15 and 149–61.

2 It is not even altogether clear that a Kantian intuition counts as a given in Sellars's sense, since, unlike the sensory givens of empiricism, a Kantian intuition is neither an independent epistemic unit, nor uninterpreted. However, since the interpreting does not take place in Sellars's 'logical space of reasons', and since Kant's intuitions (as well as his *a priori* concepts) are supposed to have an epistemic significance that goes beyond the social domain, Sellars would probably want to classify them as givens, though the sense in which a Kantian intuition is given (passively received) clearly underdescribes the Sellarsian notion.

3 Compare Sellars: 'It is in the very act of *taking* that he [the sense-datum theorist] speaks of the *given*' (Sellars 1997: 117; see also p. 77).

4 This is a very old complaint against pragmatism – see Lovejoy 1908 – and so it is hard to believe that Rorty was actually bothered by it; presumably he just thought that his audience would be more receptive to 'epistemological behaviourism'. Nevertheless, in his 1979 presidential address to the APA (reprinted as Rorty 1982: Chapter 9; see also Rorty 1990), Rorty discusses three definitions of pragmatism and endorses the third one – pragmatism as anti-representationalism and

linguistic holism – so he must have changed his mind almost immediately after sending *PMN* to the publishers.

5 See, for example, his comments on machine pain (123), and the approving quote from Putnam (189); Putnam's 1964 paper (reprinted as Putnam 1975a) strongly influenced Rorty's thinking on these matters.

6 As far as I am aware, only a handful of Western philosophers – Cartesians and Wittgensteinians – have ever managed to genuinely believe that animals and babies (or just animals) are not conscious.

7 For an interesting discussion of the issues between Rorty and Quine, see Føllesdal 1990.

8 Rorty's view that ontological conclusions should not be drawn from linguistic holism derives from Sellars (Sellars 1997: 33).

9 It is also called non-truth-functionality, as well as – confusingly and unnecessarily – intensionality (as opposed to intentionality, which is the feature of mental states discussed in Chapter 3 above). Chisholm argued that non-extensional language was only required for describing mental states (Chisholm 1957: Chapter 11), thereby bolstering Quine's distrust of the mental. For a much earlier treatment by Rorty of the issues surrounding extensionality, see Rorty 1963.

7 NATURALISED EPISTEMOLOGY: PSYCHOLOGY

1 Wittgenstein and Ryle were only opposed to certain conceptions of psychology, however: the overall impression Ryle creates in Chapter 10 of *The Concept of Mind* ('Psychology') is favourable, and Wittgenstein was apparently much influenced by James's *Principles of Psychology* (Passmore 1968: 592). It was their followers such as Norman Malcolm who best conformed to the cliché.

2 Contemporary physicalism of course has more to say than just 'reality consists in whatever physicists say it consists in', but this captures the heart of the view; see, for example, Levine 2001: Chapter 1. For contemporary eliminativism, see Churchland 1981.

3 I.e. Quine's naturalised *account of human knowledge*, despite the fact that Rorty said quite clearly in the last chapter that Quine and Sellars were not trying to 'substitute one sort of account of human knowledge for another', but were rather trying to 'get away from the notion of "an account of human knowledge"' (180). Sellars also had a positive account of human knowledge (see DeVries 2005: 123–41).

4 Quine is reputed to have said that there are two types of philosophy professor: the sort that are interested in philosophy and the sort that are interested in the history of philosophy. Rorty mentioned this in the obituary he wrote for Quine (Rorty 2001).

5 Cremonini, an associate of Cardinal Bellarmine, famously refused to look through Galileo's telescope because he thought the Bible was a

better source of evidence about the stars in the sky; see Chapter 9 below for more on Galileo and Bellarmine.

6   The only legitimate criterion for picking one part of the causal chain to be the input rather than another, according to Rorty, is convenience in drawing up an account of cognitive processing (245–46).

7   In C: CDCEE – DEDFF – EGCFE – DCBC. Ryle introduced the example (Ryle 1963: 216–17).

8 NATURALISED EPISTEMOLOGY: LANGUAGE

1   Dummett thinks that philosophy has 'only just very recently struggled out of its early stage into maturity' but is now ready to become a collective enterprise with agreed upon methodologies and criteria of success (Dummett 1978: 454–58). In other words, it has finally reached the Kantian 'secure path of a science'.

2   For a discussion of the connections between traditional idealism and Dummett's anti-realism, see Green 2001: Chapter 3, esp. 105–24.

3   Dummett nevertheless thinks that Davidson's approach is inadequate; for an early response, see 'Frege's Distinction between Sense and Reference' in Dummett 1978: 116–44, esp. pp. 123 and ff. See also Green 2001: Chapters 1 and 5, esp. pp. 17–19.

4   For a concrete and easy to follow example of the kind of theory of meaning which philosophers like Davidson have in mind, see Hookway 1988: 151–53.

5   This use of 'Whiggish' comes from Herbert Butterfield's 1931 book The Whig Interpretation of History, which begins,

> What is discussed is the tendency in many historians to write on the side of Protestants and Whigs, to praise revolutions provided they have been successful, to emphasize certain principles of progress in the past and to produce a story which is the ratification if not the glorification of the present.

Another of Butterfield's books, The Origins of Modern Science, exerted a great influence on Thomas Kuhn (Kuhn 1957: 283). Thanks to G.A.J. Rogers for this reference.

6   If you are interested in following the development of Rorty's views on truth, try reading 'Pragmatism, Davidson and Truth' in Rorty 1991a, followed by 'Introduction' and 'Is Truth a Goal of Inquiry?' in Rorty 1998, followed by Rorty 2000b.

7   The exposition of this argument in PMN is somewhat cryptic, so it is best read in conjunction with the two other papers where Rorty presented it more fully: 'Realism and Reference' (Rorty 1976) and 'Is there a Problem about Fictional Discourse?' (in Rorty 1982).

8 Rorty's argument has been unduly neglected, but there are nevertheless two excellent critical discussions of it by Michael Devitt (Devitt 1996: 203–19) and David Houghton (Houghton 1990). Neither of them state Rorty's position entirely accurately, however: according to Devitt, Rorty agrees that 'the causal theory applies' (op. cit.: 216) in cases of 'really talking about', which is not correct, and according to Houghton, Rorty thinks that 'really talking about something implies its existence' (op. cit.: 161), which is also not correct.

9 Davidson occasionally renounced pragmatism (e.g. Davidson 1984: xxi), but, given Rorty's understanding of pragmatism as a thesis about justification, he was unquestionably a pragmatist; there were only subtle reasons for his unease with the term (Davidson 2005: 7–10).

10 The Neanderthals were not our ancestors but our cousins: we share an ancestor with them in *Homo heidelbergensis*.

11 Many think that Rorty misrepresents Davidson, and he certainly does to some extent; good points are made by Farrell 1994: 117–22, for instance. However, Rorty did succeed in persuading Davidson not to call his account of truth either a correspondence or a coherence theory (Davidson 2005: 39), and Davidson never objected particularly strongly to Rorty's interpretations, despite having many opportunities to do so over the years. Probably their biggest disagreement was over the metaphilosophical significance of Davidson's work, for Davidson certainly did not think that the philosophical interest of his work was 'largely negative' (261). If anything, he thought that Tarski had placed philosophy 'on the secure path of a science', whereas Rorty prefers to 'regard Tarksi as founding a new subject' (Rorty 1982: 18).

9 SCIENCE AND PLURALISM

1 Rorty's denial that hermeneutics is a 'method' (which needs to be read in light of his discussion of Gadamer in Chapter 8) is awkward and not very consistently applied; at one point he calls hermeneutics 'guess-work' and quotes Kuhn calling it a 'method' on the same page (323).

2 Rorty does not explicitly distinguish two senses of 'epistemology' in the text, and gives no indication of recognising any tension in the way he uses the word. I will prominently superimpose the distinction, however, because without it a number of passages in Part Three do not make sense.

3 A crucial factor was that Kuhn realised the Aristotelians meant something different when they talked about 'motion' and 'change'; this makes his gestalt switch seem slightly less mysterious.

4 In later years, Kuhn explicitly aligned his work with Kant's transcendental idealism (see Bird 2000: 123–30).

5 This is one of Kuhn's arguments for his position that we see a different world rather than see the world differently, *contra* Paul Boghossian's

suggestion that Kuhn made a simple conflation (Boghossian 2006: 123).

6 Roger Fry (of the Bloomsbury group) organised an exhibition of Post-Impressionist paintings that enraged the Royal Academy of Arts, which at that time favoured traditional styles and themes. Kerensky led the Provisional Government which ruled Russia after the February stage of the 1917 Revolution, before Lenin's Bolsheviks took over in the October stage; Kerensky wanted to keep Russia in the First World War and was a democrat, whereas Lenin pulled Russia out of the War and was not a democrat.

7 By all accounts, Galileo did not actually have any doubts about the Bible being the revealed word of God (this is *ca.* 1610 we are talking about). Rather he had doubts about the very unconvincing passages that were supposed to show God's support for Ptolemy; the most convincing reference (which is not saying much) is at Psalms 104:5, and the others are Psalms 93:1 and Ecclesiastes 1:5.

8 Since the Davidsonian view that Rorty endorses applies to beliefs, he cannot respond by distinguishing between 'background beliefs' and 'standards of evidence' (Rorty 1995: 151, 224–25, ftnt 6): Bellarmine must have mostly the same background beliefs as Galileo. Moreover, since Galileo and Bellarmine must both have mainly true beliefs, they must also both have mainly justified beliefs, since 'the only point in contrasting the truth with the merely justified is to contrast a possible future with the actual present' (Rorty 1999: 39).

9 For instance, Kuhn says that,

> each new conceptual scheme embraces the phenomena explained by its predecessors and adds to them. But, though the achievements of Copernicus and Newton are permanent, the concepts that made those achievements possible are not ... As science progresses, its concepts are repeatedly destroyed and replaced.
> (Kuhn 1957: 264–65)

A paradigm is not the same as a conceptual scheme, of course, but we could say that a paradigm *provides* a conceptual scheme.

10 A normal discourse cannot be a conceptual scheme if there are no conceptual schemes and there is normal discourse.

11 It might be possible to explain the difference by linking technological progress to perennial human desires – not being ill, giving birth safely, travelling quickly and easily, etc. – but Rorty would probably want to insist that even these desires could change.

12 Rorty is referring to the line in Sophocles's play *Antigone* which is traditionally translated as 'Many wonders there be, but naught more wondrous than man'.

10 THE POWER OF STRANGENESS

1   Rorty cannot have meant epistemology-as-commensuration, because he says that the hypothetical 'new form of systematic philosophy' would make normal philosophy possible, and normal philosophy presupposes epistemology-as-commensuration. So he must have meant theory of knowledge.

2   Rorty says that all four of these philosophers are 'systematic' (7), and although he does not actually say that they are 'normal' rather than 'revolutionary', they could hardly be said to have initiated new paradigms comparable to Analytic Philosophy or Phenomenology. Either way, a clear consequence of Rorty's taxonomy is that Kuhn, like all systematic philosophers, must have secretly hankered after universal commensuration, which surely cannot be right.

3   Rorty tried a new tactic in the Introduction to *Philosophy and Social Hope*, claiming that 'Relativist' is an inevitable label for his opponents to use against him and for him to repudiate, just as 'Platonist' is an inevitable label for him to use against his opponents and for them to repudiate. It is not clear this helps, however, because the extent to which this defuses his opponent's charge exactly matches the extent to which it defuses his own denial.

4   The word 'ethnocentrism' derives from ἔθνος [*ethnos*], which basically means 'people', although one of its connotations for the Greeks was indeed 'tribe'.

5   Kant said 'things-in-themselves'; 'Thing in itself' was Bradley's formulation, adopted on the grounds that an unknowable reality could not be known to consist in a plurality of things (Bradley 1908: 129).

6   Michael Williams has argued that there is a tension between Rorty's endorsement of irony in *Contingency, Irony and Solidarity* and his antiphilosophical stance in *PMN* (Williams 2003). I agree, but the tension was already there in *PMN*, since 'irony' in Rorty's sense is the same as looking at our practices 'bifocally'.

7   Davidson's position was that every instance of a causal relation must be subsumed by a strict law, and that events only instantiate strict laws under physical descriptions. Thus, Davidson was a non-tactical physicalist; as Frank Farrell rightly points out, Rorty goes with the 'Anomalous' but leaves out the 'Monism' (Farrell 1994: 126).

8   A good selection of Rorty's positive proposals for the future of philosophy can be found in the following: 'Introduction: Pragmatism and Philosophy' and 'Philosophy as a Kind of Writing: An Essay on Derrida' in Rorty 1982, 'Introduction: Pragmatism and Post-Nietzschean Philosophy' and 'Deconstruction and Circumvention' in Rorty 1991b, and 'Philosophy and the Future' in Saatkamp ed. 1995. A comparison between Rorty 1967a and the 1984 paper 'Deconstruction and Circumvention' reveals a continuing sympathy for the view that it would be better for philosophy to come to an end.

BIBLIOGRAPHY

BY RORTY

Rorty's main philosophical works consist of two monographs and six collections of papers.

The monographs are:
(1979) *Philosophy and the Mirror of Nature*, Princeton, NJ: Princeton University Press.
(1989) *Contingency, Irony, and Solidarity*, Cambridge: Cambridge University Press.

The collections are:
(1982) *Consequences of Pragmatism*, Minneapolis: University of Minnesota Press.
(1991a) *Objectivity, Relativism and Truth: Philosophical Papers, vol. 1*, Cambridge: Cambridge University Press.
(1991b) *Essays on Heidegger and Others: Philosophical Papers, vol. 2*, Cambridge: Cambridge University Press.
(1998) *Truth and Progress: Philosophical Papers, vol. 3*, Cambridge: Cambridge University Press.
(1999) *Philosophy and Social Hope*, London: Penguin.
(2007) *Philosophy as Cultural Politics: Philosophical Papers, vol. 4*, Cambridge: Cambridge University Press.

The above do not include any of Rorty's early (pre-1972) works, of which the most notable are:

(1965) 'Mind–Body Identity, Privacy, and Categories', *Review of Metaphysics*, 19: 24–54; reprinted in Borst (ed.) (1970), pp. 187–213.

(1967a) 'Introduction: Metaphilosophical Difficulties of Linguistic Philosophy', in R. Rorty (ed.) *The Linguistic Turn*, Chicago, IL: University of Chicago Press.

(1970) 'Incorrigibility as the Mark of the Mental', *Journal of Philosophy*, 67: 399–429.

The second edition of the 1967 philosophy of language anthology which Rorty edited, *The Linguistic Turn*, contains 'afterwords' written in 1977 and 1992.

OTHER CITED WORKS BY RORTY:

(1961a) 'Pragmatism, Categories and Language', *Philosophical Review*, 70: 197–223.

(1961b) 'Recent Metaphilosophy', *Review of Metaphysics*, 15: 299–318.

(1963) 'Empiricism, Extensionalism and Reductionism', *Mind*, 72: 176–86.

(1967b) 'Intuition', in P. Edwards (ed.) *The Encyclopedia of Philosophy, vol. 4*, New York: Macmillan and Free Press, 204–12.

(1976) 'Realism and Reference', *The Monist*, 59: 321–40.

(1988) 'Taking Philosophy Seriously', *The New Republic*, April 11: 32–33.

(1990) 'Introduction: Pragmatism as Anti-Representationalism', in J. Murphy, *Pragmatism: From Peirce to Davidson*, Boulder, CO: Westview.

(1992) 'Twenty Five Years After', in R. Rorty (ed.) *The Linguistic Turn*, Chicago: University of Chicago Press.

(1995) 'Response to Susan Haack', in Saatkamp (ed.) (1995), pp. 149–53 and 223–26.

(1997) 'Introduction' to Sellars (1997).

(2000a) 'Response to Jürgen Habermas', in Brandom (ed.) (2000), pp. 56–64.

(2000b) 'Response to Bjørn Ramberg', in Brandom (ed.) (2000), pp. 370–77.

(2001) 'An Imaginative Philosopher: The Legacy of W.V. Quine', *Chronicle of Higher Education*, February 2.

(2005) 'How Many Grains Make a Heap?', *London Review of Books*, January 20: 12–13.

ABOUT RORTY

For readers of *PMN*, the most important collections of papers are:
Brandom, R. (ed.) (2000) *Rorty and his Critics*, Oxford: Blackwell.
Guignon, C. and Hiley, D. (eds) (2003) *Richard Rorty*, Cambridge: Cambridge University Press.
Malachowski, A. (ed.) (1990) *Reading Rorty*, Oxford: Blackwell.
Malachowski, A., (ed.) (2002), *Richard Rorty*, 4 volumes, London: Sage.
Saatkamp, H. (ed.) (1995) *Rorty and Pragmatism*, Nashville, TN: Vanderbilt University Press.

The Brandom and Saatkamp volumes include replies by Rorty. Malachowski's Sage set is a large selection of articles, reviews, and book extracts from a wide variety of sources: if you have access to it, you may not need anything else. Volume 4 contains a complete Rorty bibliography up until 2001. For additional secondary literature, the first place to turn is the selected bibliography in the Guignon and Hiley volume, though completists will want to consult:
Rumana, R. (2002) *Richard Rorty: An Annotated Bibliography of Secondary Literature*, Amsterdam: Rodopi.

The best work on Rorty is to be found in the above collections, but there are also some monographs. Two very short introductions are provided by:
Calder, G. (2003) *Richard Rorty*, London: Weidenfeld & Nicolson.
Rumana, R. (2000), *On Rorty*, Belmont, CA: Wadsworth.

Full-length critical treatments are provided by:
Hall, D. (1994) *Richard Rorty: Poet and Prophet of the New Pragmatism*, Albany, NY: State University of New York Press.
Malachowski, A. (2002) *Richard Rorty*, Chesham, UK: Acumen.

Though full of information about Rorty, analytic readers should be warned that these both employ the very flamboyant 'Rorty squared' (Hall's coinage) approach. More straightforward is the unjustly obscure:
Vaden House, D. (1994) *Without God or his Doubles: Realism, Relativism and Rorty*, Leiden, The Netherlands: E.J. Brill.

OTHER WORKS

Annas, J. (1992) *Hellenistic Philosophy of Mind*, Berkeley, CA: University of California Press.

Apel, K-O. (1980) *Towards a Transformation of Philosophy*, trans. G. Adey and F. Fisby, London: Routledge.

Aristotle (1984) *Complete Works of Aristotle: Revised Oxford Translation, vol. 2*, ed. J. Barnes, Princeton, NJ: Princeton University Press.

Armstrong, D. (1968) *A Materialist Theory of the Mind*, London: Routledge.

Ayer, A.J. (1971) *Language, Truth and Logic*, Harmondsworth, UK: Penguin.

Baldwin, T. (2001) *Contemporary Philosophy: Philosophy in English since 1945*, Oxford: Oxford University Press.

Berkeley, G. (1980) *Philosophical Works*, ed. M. Ayers, London: Dent.

Bernstein, R. (1980) 'Philosophy in the Conversation of Mankind', *Review of Metaphysics*, 33: 745–75.

Bernstein, R. (1991) *The New Constellation*, Cambridge: Polity Press.

Bird, A. (2000) *Thomas Kuhn*, Chesham, UK: Acumen.

Blackburn, S. (2005) *Truth*, London: Allen Lane.

Boghossian, P. (2006) *Fear of Knowledge*, Oxford: Oxford University Press.

Boring, E. (1933) *The Physical Dimensions of Consciousness*, New York: The Century Company.

Borradori, G. (ed.) (1994) *The American Philosopher: Interviews*, Chicago, IL: University of Chicago Press.

Borst, C. (ed.) (1970) *The Mind–Brain Identity Theory*, London: Macmillan.

Bradley, F.H. (1908) *Appearance and Reality*, London: Swan Sonnenschein and Co.

Brandom, R. (1994) *Making it Explicit*, Cambridge, MA: Harvard University Press.

Brandom, R. (2000) 'Vocabularies of Pragmatism: Synthesizing Naturalism and Historicism', in Brandom (ed.) (2000), pp. 156–83.

Brentano, F. (1973) *Psychology from an Empirical Standpoint*, trans. A. Pancurello, D. Terrell, and L. McAlister, London: Routledge.

Broad, C.D. (1925) *Mind and its Place in Nature*, London: Routledge.

Burnyeat, M. (1992) 'Is an Aristotelian Philosophy of Mind Still Credible?', in M. Nussbaum and A. Rorty (eds) *Essays on Aristotle's* De Anima, Oxford: Clarendon.

Burtt, E. (1932) *The Metaphysical Foundations of Modern Physical Science*, London: Routledge.

Butterfield, H. (1931) *The Whig Interpretation of History*, London: G. Bell and Sons Ltd.

Butterfield, H. (1949) *The Origins of Modern Science: 1300–1800*, London: G. Bell and Sons Ltd.

Carnap, R. (2003) *The Logical Structure of the World and Pseudoproblems in Philosophy*, trans. R. George, Peru, IL: Open Court.

Chalmers, D. (1996) *The Conscious Mind*, Oxford: Oxford University Press.

Chisholm, R. (1957) *Perceiving: A Philosophical Study*, Ithaca, NY: Cornell University Press.

Choy, V. (1982) 'Mind–Body, Realism and Rorty's Therapy', *Synthese*, 52: 515–41, reprinted in Malachowski (ed.) (2002), vol. 2, pp. 31–51.

Churchland, P.M. (1981) 'Eliminative Materialism and the Propositional Attitudes', *Journal of Philosophy*, 78: 67–90.

Comte, A. (1974) *The Essential Comte*, ed. S. Andreski, trans. M. Clarke, London: Croom Helm.

Cornman, J. (1968) 'On the Elimination of "Sensations" and Sensations', *Review of Metaphysics*, 22: 15–35.

Crane, T. (2001) *Elements of Mind*, Oxford: Oxford University Press.

Crane, T. (2003) *The Mechanical Mind*, 2nd edn, London: Routledge.

Culler, J. (1982) *On Deconstruction*, Ithaca, NY: Cornell University Press.

Davidson, D. (1984) *Inquiries into Truth and Interpretation*, Oxford: Oxford University Press.

Davidson, D. (1986) 'A Coherence Theory of Truth and Knowledge', in E. LePore (ed.) *Truth and Interpretation: Perspectives on the Philosophy of Donald Davidson*, Oxford: Blackwell, pp. 307–19.

Davidson, D. (1990) 'Afterthoughts, 1987', in Malachowski (ed.) (1990), pp. 134–37.

Davidson, D. (2005) *Truth and Predication*, Cambridge, MA: Harvard University Press.

Dennett, D. (1991) *Consciousness Explained*, Boston: Little, Brown.

Derrida, J. (1995) 'Personal Statement', in Pyke (1995), arranged alphabetically.

Descartes, R. (1985) *The Philosophical Writings of Descartes, vol. II*, trans. J. Cottingham, R. Stoothoff, and D. Murdoch, Cambridge: Cambridge University Press.

Devitt, M. (1996) *Realism and Truth*, 2nd edn, Princeton, NJ: Princeton University Press.

DeVries, W. (2005) *Wilfrid Sellars*, Chesham, UK: Acumen.

Dewey, J. (1910) *The Influence of Darwin on Philosophy and Other Essays*, New York: Henry Holt.

Dewey, J. (1917) *Creative Intelligence: Essays in the Pragmatic Attitude*, New York: Henry Holt.

Dewey, J. (1922) *Human Nature and Conduct: An Introduction to Social Psychology*, New York: Modern Library.

Dewey, J. (1930) *The Quest for Certainty*, London: George Allen and Unwin.

Dewey, J. (1938) *Logic: The Theory of Inquiry*, New York: Holt, Rinehart and Winston.

Dewey, J. (1954) *The Public and its Problems*, Athens, OH: Swallow Press.

Donagan, A. (1966) 'Wittgenstein on Sensation', in G. Pitcher (ed.) *Wittgenstein: The Philosophical Investigations*, Garden City, NY: Doubleday Anchor, pp. 324–51.

Donnellan, K. (1966) 'Reference and Definite Descriptions', *Philosophical Review*, 75: 281–304.

Dummett, M. (1978) *Truth and Other Enigmas*, London: Duckworth.

Epicurus (1993) *The Essential Epicurus*, trans. E. O'Connor, New York: Prometheus Books.

Farrell, F. (1994) *Subjectivity, Realism and Postmodernism*, Cambridge: Cambridge University Press.

Feyerabend, P. (1962) 'Explanation, Reduction and Empiricism', in H. Feigl and G. Maxwell (eds) *Minnesota Studies in the Philosophy of Science*, 3: 43–52.

Feyerabend, P. (1963) 'Materialism and the Mind–Body Problem', *Review of Metaphysics*, 17: 49–66.

Fodor, J. (1966) 'Could There Be a Theory of Perception', *Journal of Philosophy*, 63: 375–95.

Fodor, J. and LePore, E. (1992) *Holism: A Shopper's Guide*, Oxford: Blackwell.

Føllesdal, D. (1990) 'Indeterminacy and Mental States', in R. Barrett and R. Gibson (eds) *Perspectives on Quine*, Oxford: Blackwell, pp. 98–109.

Fosl, P. (1999) 'Note to Realists: Grow Up', *The Philosophers' Magazine*, 8: 40–42.

Gadamer, H-G. (1989) *Truth and Method*, 2nd edn, trans. J. Weinsheimer and D. Marshall, New York: Continuum.

Gallagher, K. (1985) 'Rorty's Antipodeans: An Impossible Illustration?', *Philosophy and Phenomenological Research*, 45: 449–55; reprinted in Malachowski (ed.) (2002), vol. 2, pp. 67–73.

Giaquinto, M. (1996) 'Non-analytic Conceptual Knowledge', *Mind*, 105: 249–67.

Gilson, E. (1950) *The Unity of Philosophical Experience*, New York: Scribners.

Goodman, N. (1972) 'The Way the World Is', in his *Problems and Projects*, Indianapolis, IN: Bobbs-Merrill.

Green, K. (2001) *Dummett: Philosophy of Language*, Cambridge: Polity Press.

Green, T.H. (1874) 'Introduction', in T. Green and T. Grose (eds) *A Treatise of Human Nature* by David Hume, London: Longmans, Green and Co.

Gross, N. (2003) 'Richard Rorty's Pragmatism: A Case Study in the Sociology of Ideas', *Theory and Society*, 32: 93–148.

Guignan, C. (1983) *Heidegger and the Problem of Knowledge*, Indianapolis, IN: Hackett.

Guignon, C. and Hiley, D. (2003) 'Introduction: Richard Rorty and Contemporary Philosophy', in Guignon and Hiley (eds) (2003), pp. 1–40.

Haack, S. (1993) *Evidence and Inquiry: Towards Reconstruction in Epistemology*, Oxford: Blackwell.

Habermas, J. (1972) *Knowledge and Human Interests*, trans. J. Shapiro, London: Heinemann.

Habermas, J. (2000) 'Richard Rorty's Pragmatic Turn', in Brandom (ed.) (2000), pp. 31–55.

Hacking, I. (1980) 'Is the End in Sight for Epistemology?', *Journal of Philosophy*, 77: 579–88.

Hegel, G.W.F. (1977) *The Phenomenology of Spirit*, trans. A. Miller, Oxford: Oxford University Press.

Hegel, G.W.F. (1991) *Elements of the Philosophy of Right*, ed. A. Wood, trans. H. Nisbet, Cambridge: Cambridge University Press.

Heidegger, M. (1962) *Being and Time*, trans. J. Macquarrie and E. Robinson, Oxford: Basil Blackwell.

Heidegger, M. (1973) *The End of Philosophy*, trans. J. Stambaugh, New York: Harper and Row.

Heidegger, M. (1994) *Basic Questions of Philosophy*, trans. R. Rojcewicz and A. Schuwer, Bloomington, MN: Indiana University Press.

Hookway, C. (1988) *Quine*, Cambridge: Polity Press.

Hornsby, J. (1990) 'Descartes, Rorty and the Mind–Body Fiction', in Malachowski (ed.) (1990), pp. 41–57.

Houghton, D. (1990) 'Rorty's Talk-About', in Malachowski (ed.) (1990), pp. 156–70.

Humphrey, N. (1992) *A History of the Mind*, London: Chatto and Windus.

Huxley, T.H. (1887) *Hume*, London: MacMillan and Co.

James, W. (1995) *Pragmatism*, New York: Dover.

Jay, M. (1993) *Downcast Eyes: The Denigration of Vision in Twentieth-Century French Thought*, Berkeley, CA: University of California Press.

Kant, I. (1933) *Critique of Pure Reason*, trans. N. Kemp Smith, London: Macmillan.

Kant, I. (1996) 'An Answer to the Question: What Is Enlightenment?', in his *Practical Philosophy*, trans. and ed. M. Gregor, Cambridge: Cambridge University Press, pp. 11–22.

Kim, J. (1988) 'What is "Naturalized Epistemology?"', in *Philosophical Perspectives: Epistemology*, 2: 381–405.

Kirk, G., Raven, J., and Schofield, M. (eds) (1983) *The Presocratic Philosophers*, 2nd edn, Cambridge: Cambridge University Press.

Knobe, J. (1995) 'A Talent for Bricolage: An Interview with Richard Rorty', *The Dualist*, 2: 56–71.

Kölbel, M. (2002) *Truth without Objectivity*, London: Routledge.

Kripke, S. (1972) 'Naming and Necessity', in G. Harman and D. Davidson (eds) *Semantics of Natural Language*, Dordrecht: Reidel, pp. 253–355.

Kuhn, T. (1957) *The Copernican Revolution*, Cambridge, MA: Harvard University Press.

Kuhn, T. (1970) *The Structure of Scientific Revolutions*, 2nd edn, Chicago, IL: University of Chicago Press.

Kuhn, T. (1977) *The Essential Tension*, Chicago, IL: Chicago University Press.

Leibniz, G. (1973) *Philosophical Writings*, trans. G. Parkinson and M. Morris, London: J.M. Dent.

Leibniz, G. (1985) *Theodicy*, trans. E. Huggard, Peru, IL: Open Court.

Levine, J. (2001) *Purple Haze: The Puzzle of Consciousness*, Oxford: Oxford University Press.

Levinson, A. (1987) 'Rorty, Materialism, and Privileged Access', *Noûs*, 21: 381–93; reprinted in Malachowski (ed.) (2002), vol. 1, pp. 111–21.

Loar, B. (1997) 'Phenomenal States', in N. Block, O. Flanagan, and G. Güzeldere (eds) *The Nature of Consciousness*, Cambridge, MA: MIT Press.

Locke, J. (1979) *An Essay Concerning Human Understanding*, ed. P. Nidditch, Oxford: Clarendon Press.

Lovejoy, A.O. (1908) 'The Thirteen Pragmatisms', *Journal of Philosophy, Psychology and Scientific Methods*, 5: 5–12.

Löwith, K. (1991) *From Hegel to Nietzsche*, trans. D. Green, New York: Columbia University Press.

Lucretius (1951) *The Nature of the Universe*, trans. R. Latham, Harmondsworth, UK: Penguin.

Lycan, W. (1987) *Consciousness*, Cambridge, MA: MIT Press.

Macdonald, P. (2003) *History of the Concept of Mind*, Aldershot, UK: Ashgate.

McDowell, J. (1994) *Mind and World*, Cambridge, MA: Harvard University Press.

McGinn, C. (1991) *The Problem of Consciousness*, Oxford: Blackwell.

McKeon, R. (1990) 'Philosophical Semantics and Philosophical Inquiry', in Z. McKeon (ed.) *Freedom and History and Other Essays: An Introduction to the Thought of Richard McKeon*, Chicago: University of Chicago Press.

Matson, W. (1966) 'Why Isn't the Mind–Body Problem Ancient?', in P. Feyerabend and G. Maxwell (eds) *Mind, Matter and Method: Essays in Philosophy and Science in Honor of Herbert Feigl*, Minneapolis, MN: University of Minnesota Press, pp. 92–102.

Moore, G.E. (1903) *Principia Ethica*, Cambridge: Cambridge University Press.

Nagel, T. (1998) 'Conceiving the Impossible and the Mind–Body Problem', *Philosophy*, 73: 337–52.

Neurath, O. (1981) 'Protocol Sentences', in O. Hanfling (ed.) *Essential Readings in Logical Positivism*, Oxford: Basil Blackwell, pp. 161–68.

Nietzsche, F. (1967) *The Will to Power*, trans. and ed. W. Kaufmann, trans. R. Hollingdale, New York: Random House.

Nietzsche, F. (1990) *Twilight of the Idols* and *The Anti-Christ*, trans. R. Hollingdale, London: Penguin.

Niznik, J. and Sanders, J. (eds) (1996) *Debating the State of Philosophy: Habermas, Rorty and Kolakowski*, Westport, CT: Praeger.

O'Grady, P. (2002) *Relativism*, Montreal: McGill-Queen's University Press.

Passmore, J. (1968) *A Hundred Years of Philosophy*, Harmondsworth, UK: Penguin.

Patterson, S. (2000) 'How Cartesian Was Descartes?', in T. Crane and S. Patterson (eds) *History of the Mind–Body Problem*, London: Routledge.

Peirce, C.S. (1932) *Collected Papers, Volume 5*, eds C. Hartshorne and P. Weiss, Cambridge, MA: Harvard University Press.

Pettegrew, J. (ed.) (2000) *A Pragmatist's Progress? Richard Rorty and American Intellectual History*, Lanham, MD: Rowman and Littlefield.

Place, U.T. (1956) 'Is Consciousness a Brain Process?', *British Journal of Psychology*, 47: 44–50.

Plato (1961) *The Collected Dialogues of Plato*, eds E. Hamilton and H. Cairns, Princeton, NJ: Princeton University Press.

Popper, K. (1968) *The Open Society and its Enemies, vol. 2*, London: Routledge.

Prado, C. (1987) 'Objectivity, Science, and Relativism', in his *The Limits of Pragmatism*, Atlantic Highlands, NJ: Humanities Press, pp. 87–111; reprinted in Malachowski (ed.) (2002), vol. 2, pp. 233–53.

Putnam, H. (1975a) 'Robots: Machines or Artificially Created Life?', in his *Mind, Language and Reality: Philosophical Papers Volume 2*, Cambridge: Cambridge University Press, pp. 386–407.

Putnam, H. (1975b) 'The Meaning of "Meaning"', in his *Mind, Language and Reality: Philosophical Papers Volume 2*, Cambridge: Cambridge University Press, pp. 215–71.

Putnam, H. (1978) *Meaning and the Moral Sciences*, London: Routledge.

Putnam, H. (1987) *The Many Faces of Realism*, Peru, IL: Open Court.

Pyke, S. (1995) *Philosophers*, London: Zelda Cheatle Press.

Quine, W.V.O. (1953) 'Two Dogmas of Empiricism', in his *From a Logical Point of View*, Cambridge, MA: Harvard University Press.

Quine, W.V.O. (1960) *Word and Object*, Cambridge, MA: MIT Press.

Quine, W.V.O. (1969) 'Epistemology Naturalized', in his *Ontological Relativity and Other Essays*, New York: Columbia University Press.

Quine, W.V.O. (1990) 'Let me Accentuate the Positive', in Malachowski (ed.) (1990), pp. 117–19.

Quine, W.V.O. (1995) 'Personal Statement', in Pyke (1995), arranged alphabetically.

Reichenbach, H. (1951) *The Rise of Scientific Philosophy*, Berkeley, CA: University of California Press.

Robinson, H. (1991) 'The Flight from Mind', in T. Tallis and H. Robinson (eds) *The Pursuit of Mind*, Manchester: Carcanet Press, pp. 9–25.

Ruja, H. (1981) 'Review of *Philosophy and the Mirror of Nature*', *Philosophy and Phenomenological Research*, 42: 299–300.

Russell, B. (1927) *The Analysis of Matter*, London: Routledge.

Russell, B. (1991) *History of Western Philosophy*, London: Routledge.

Ryle, G. (1963) *The Concept of Mind*, Harmondsworth, UK: Penguin.

Sartre, J-P. (1970) 'Intentionality: A Fundamental Idea of Husserl's Phenomenology', trans. J. Fell, *Journal for the British Society of Phenomenology*, 1: 4–5.

Sartre, J-P. (1974) *Existentialism and Humanism*, trans. P. Mairet, London: Methuen.

Searle, J. (1983) *Intentionality*, Cambridge: University of Cambridge Press.

Searle, J. (1992) *The Rediscovery of the Mind*, Cambridge, MA: MIT Press.

Sellars, W. (1997) *Empiricism and the Philosophy of Mind*, Cambridge, MA: Harvard University Press.

Skinner, Q. (1981) 'The End of Philosophy?', *New York Review of Books*, March 19: 46–48.

Smart, J.J.C. (1959) 'Sensations and Brain Processes', *Philosophical Review*, 68: 141–56.

Soames, S. (2005) 'How Many Grains Make a Heap?', *London Review of Books*, March 3: 4.

Stern, R. (2002) *Hegel and the Phenomenology of Spirit*, London: Routledge.

Strawson, P.F. (1974) 'Self, Mind and Body', in his *Freedom and Resentment and Other Essays*, London: Methuen.

Stroud, B. (1984) *The Significance of Philosophical Skepticism*, Oxford: Oxford University Press.

Tye, M. (1995) *Ten Problems of Consciousness*, Cambridge, MA: MIT Press.

Urmson, J. (1960) 'Introduction', in J. Urmson (ed.) *The Concise Encyclopaedia of Western Philosophy and Philosophers*, London: Hutchinson.

Waismann, F. (1956) 'How I See Philosophy', in H. Lewis (ed.) *Contemporary British Philosophy*, London: George Allen and Unwin, pp. 445–90.

Warnke, G. (1987) *Gadamer: Hermeneutics, Tradition and Reason*, Cambridge: Polity Press.

Whitehead, A.N. (1978) *Process and Reality*, New York: The Free Press.

Williams, M. (2000) 'Epistemology and the Mirror of Nature', in Brandom (ed.) (2000), pp. 191–213.

Williams, M. (2003) 'Rorty on Knowledge and Truth', in Guignon and Hiley (eds) (2003), pp. 61–80.

Wittgenstein, L. (1953) *Philosophical Investigations*, trans. G.E.M. Anscombe, Oxford: Blackwell.

Woolhouse, R. (1988) *The Empiricists*, Oxford: Oxford University Press.

Yolton, J. (1984) *Thinking Matter: Materialism in Eighteenth Century Britain*, Oxford: Blackwell.

INDEX

abstract–concrete distinction 144
abstraction 114, 143–4
American Philosophical Association
    14
analytic philosophy 9–15, 19, 36–9,
    112–28, 140, 149–52, 171, 179, 216
analytic–synthetic distinction 34–5,
    37, 109, 112, 116, 121–6, 132, 159
Annas, J. 232n5
anti-realism 151–2, 162, 164
Apel, K-O. 217
appearance–reality distinction 50–1,
    80, 233n5, 234n7
archē 221
Aristotle 63–6, 183
Armstrong, D. 46, 61
art 190, 197–200, 219, 231n3
Ayer, A.J. 37–9, 150

bad faith 205–6, 210, 217–19, 222
behaviourism 74, 87–91, 94, 132, 136
Bellarmine, R. 189–96, 214, 236n5
Bergmann, G. 233n2
Bergson, H. 114
Berkeley, G. 143, 176, 225
Bernstein, R. 10, 205

bivalence 51–2
Boghossian, P. 189, 191–5
Bradley, F.H. 35, 37, 67, 114, 233n6,
    240n5
'brain switching' machine 78
Brandom, R. 121, 154, 213
Brandt-Campbell objection 234n7
Brentano, F. 45, 113
British Idealism 35–6, 104, 156, 225
Broad, C.D. 75
Burnyeat, M. 66

Canon of Pure Reason 218
Carnap, R. 11–12, 39, 133
Categories (Kant) 170, 175
causation 168–9, 212–16, 219–20
cerebroscopes 90, 220–1, 227
Chalmers, D. 234n12
change, problem of knowledge
    throughout 56–7, 59
commensurability 181–90, 194–8,
    201, 204–11, 220–2; and
    translatability 183
compresence of opposites 56–7
Comte, A. 114
conceptual analysis 126

conceptual schemes 148, 157–8, 162, 170–6, 194–6
Connection Principle 46–7, 50, 52
consciousness 25–7, 31, 55, 97–8, 107, 146; of animals and babies 69, 117, 128–31; as appearance 53, 66, 78–9; 'effective-historical' (Gadamer) 206; see also phenomenal consciousness
continental philosophy 14–15, 19, 114–15, 179, 216
conversation 120, 180–2, 210, 221
Copernican Revolution (Kant) 32–3, 101
Copernican vs. Ptolemaic astronomy 32, 186, 189–96
Copernicus, N. 32
Crane, T. 47

Darwin, C. 213–14, 217
Davidson, D. 4, 13, 147–9, 152–8, 168–77, 183, 194–6, 200, 210, 220, 222, 238n11, 240n7
deconstruction 20–1, 55–6
Democritus 198–200, 203
Derrida, J. 210, 221
Descartes, R. 27–8, 41–5, 51–2, 62, 66–70, 100–3, 135, 137, 148, 151, 175, 203
descriptionism 165–9
Dewey, J. 11, 21–2, 40, 53, 59–60, 71–2, 113, 118, 148, 175, 203, 209, 231n3
Dilthey, W. 179–80
Donagan, A. 90
Donnellan, K. 165
dualism 26–7, 74, 89–90, 97, 125; Cartesian 26–7, 41–4, 51–2, 67; Platonic 56–8; property 26–7, 42–3
Dummett, M. 150–3, 237n1

eliminative materialism see physicalism: eliminative materialism

empiricism 28–38, 102–6, 109, 117–19, 122, 141, 149–50, 154, 159, 170–1, 227, 230
Enlightenment 6, 187, 190–1, 197, 199, 206–7, 224
Epicurus 65
epiphenomenalism 82–3
epistēmē 28, 183–4
epistemic systems 191–5
epistemological behaviourism 128, 135
epistemological principle 90–4
epistemological turn 29, 101
epistemology: as commensuration 181, 184, 197, 202; as cultural adjudicator see philosophy: as judicial; as 'first philosophy' 29–30, 103, 151; foundationalism 16–18, 28, 39, 101, 127, 135, 138–40, 180–2, 229; naturalised (Quine) 135–41, 151, 155, 229; as theory of knowledge 28, 103–4, 120, 168, 181–8, 208–9, 228–30
essentialism 203–6, 209, 216, 223, 226
ethnocentrism 211, 240n4
existentialism 204–5
extensionality 133, 236n9

Fach 102, 182
fact–value distinction 207
'fake torture' machine 79–81
Feyerabend, P. 159–61
field linguist 155–6, 171–2, 176, 194–6, 213
Fodor, J. 142–4
forms see ideas: Platonic
foundationalism see epistemology: foundationalism
Frankfurt School 217
Frege, G. 113, 148, 151–2, 156, 165
functionalism 135, 145

Gadamer, H-G. 178–80, 183, 204, 206–8

Galileo Galilei 28, 68, 140, 189–95, 211–14, 228, 239n7
Gallagher, K. 84
Geistewissenshaften 179, 184, 201
Giaquinto, M. 123
Gilson, E. 222, 224
Green, T.H. 104–5, 117–18

Haack, S. 211
Habermas, J. 10, 217
Hacking, I. 59
Hartshorne, C. 12
Hegel, G.W.F. 12, 35–6, 114, 131–2, 148, 175, 177, 224
Heidegger, M. 20–2, 53, 110–11, 115, 178–80, 208, 210, 228, 232n4
hermeneutics 178–84, 188, 197, 201–6
historicism 36, 103, 109, 115, 149, 175, 178, 209, 217, 219, 221, 223
holism 114–41, 149, 154–61, 169–76, 180–2, 209, 216, 225–6
Homuncular Fallacy 142
Hume, D. 38, 221
Husserl, E. 114–15, 210
Huxley, T.H. 25

idealism 91, 114, 156–8, 176, 188, 194–6, 217, 225–6
ideas: innate 29–30, 35, 69, 118; Lockean 30–1, 57, 63, 104, 118, 143, 150, 154, 176; Platonic 56–62, 174
identity theory 74–7, 83, 94
incorrigibility 85–90, 138, 145–6, 228; logical vs. empirical 90, 95
indirect realism 31
indubitability 67–9, 87
infinite regress argument 141–5
intentionalism 46–7, 52; as theory of reference *see* descriptionism
intentionality 44–52, 66–7, 74, 132–3, 232n2
introspection 138

intuition–concept distinction 35–8, 107–17, 124–5, 170, 235n2
intuitions: Kantian *see* intuition–concept distinction; as language-game familiarity 55, 71, 232n1; and plausibility 66, 228–9, 234n11
irony 240n6

James, W. 77, 102, 114, 136
judgements (Kant) 33–5, 107–8
justification 28, 104, 108, 117–21, 139–47, 154, 162–5, 169, 219, 227, 238n9; absolute 174, 191–2, 211–12; norm-circular 191, 211; pragmatic 192–5

Kant, I. 2–6, 32–8, 100–19, 148–50, 160, 170, 175, 215–19, 222, 235n4
Kepler, J. 185
Kim, J. 139
knowledge: knowledge-of vs. knowledge-that 105–6; propositional conception of 108, 111
Kripke, S. 86, 161, 165–9, 234n7
Kuhn, T. 22, 178–89, 194–7, 208, 210, 219, 239n9

language-games 44
Leibniz, G. 48–9, 205, 226
Lillibulero 142–4
linguistic turn 35, 113
Locke, J. 28–32, 35–8, 47, 62, 67, 100–9, 117, 143
logical positivism 37–9, 44, 118, 121–2, 126, 149–51
logocentrism 221
logos 184, 221
Lucretius 65
Lycan, W. 51

McDowell, J. 15, 230
McGinn, C. 65
McKeon, R. 12

Magritte, R. 31
'mark of the mental' 44–52, 67–9, 95, 144
materialism see physicalism
Matson, W. 63–6
meaning 66–7, 89, 95, 124, 132–3, 171–6, 179, 201; philosophical vs. ordinary 174–7, 196, 212; theories of 49–50, 149–56, 237n4
metaphilosophy 3–4, 8, 15–16, 53–4, 73, 90, 96, 112–16, 125–8, 131, 148–58, 176, 196, 210, 224–30
metaphysical pluralism 226–30
metaphysics 17, 35–7, 61–2, 92, 94, 103, 125, 169, 217, 226
Milesian Cosmology 221
mind: family resemblance approach 47–50; immediacy of 31, 38, 45, 63, 117; as non-spatial 42, 49; as personhood 54–5, 72–3; as reason 54–5
mind–body problem 25–7, 41–99, 109, 136, 227–8; 'fast dissolution' 44–54, 66, 72, 74, 97; historical deconstruction 53–72, 97, 228
Moore, G.E. 162, 174
moral choice 218–20
mysticism 91
Myth of the Given 109, 112, 116–21, 131, 138, 154, 156, 175, 213, 227

Naturalistic Fallacy 162, 170, 174, 212
Naturwissenschaften 179, 184, 200–1
Neurath, O. 125–6
New Science 28–30, 59, 68–70, 72, 103, 140, 190, 209, 230
Nietzsche, F. 1, 7, 36, 56, 228
nominalism 61–2

objective truth 231n1; see also truth: as objective
ocularcentrism 60
ontology 91–2, 96–8, 125, 132–3, 136–7, 207, 228

ordinary language philosophy 126, 150

paradigm (Kuhn) 185–90, 195, 198, 209, 217, 227
Parmenides 148
Peirce, C. 170
Pessimistic Meta-Induction 163–5
phenomenal consciousness 44–53, 57, 63–7, 72–90, 97–8, 232n3, 234n7
phenomenalism 150
philosophical senses see meaning: philosophical vs. ordinary
philosophy: as ahistorical 2, 16–18, 29, 147, 152; as edifying 115, 204–6, 208–10, 216–17, 222, 228–30; future of 148–9, 182, 222–4, 240n8; as judicial 17, 160–1, 178, 222; as literature 5, 93, 95, 156, 229; normal–revolutionary distinction 208–10, 240n2; as science 2–3, 10, 114–15, 209, 237n1; as systematic 3, 113, 150–3, 209; systematic–edifying distinction 208–10, 222; as therapy 19–20, 53
philosophy of language: pure–impure distinction 147–58, 161, 168, 176
phronēsis 183–4, 207
physicalism 13, 26–7, 42, 49, 53, 65–6, 75–7, 94–9, 114, 137, 198, 216–21, 232n4&n3, 236n2; Australian 74–6, 83; eliminative materialism 4, 13, 72–3, 76–7, 83, 94–5, 137–8; tactical 73, 95–9, 137, 207
Place, U.T. 74–6, 89
Plato 55–60, 63–6, 110, 143, 148
'Platonic Principle' 91, 110
plausibility see intuitions
pluralism 197–202, 206–7; see also metaphysical pluralism

Popper, K. 36
postmodernism 14–15
pragmatism 11–13, 21–2, 92, 121, 125, 128, 132, 137, 149, 152, 158–61, 168, 170, 192, 196, 224–6, 235n4
'Principle P' 85–90, 97, 234n10
privileged access 25–6, 52–3, 72, 78, 86–9, 98
Protagoras 9
psychology 36, 114, 134–46, 236n1
Ptolemy, C. 186
Putnam, H. 161–70, 174, 225
Pyrrho, of Elis 102–3

Quine, W.V.O. 22, 112–16, 121–6, 132–5, 138–41, 150–1, 159, 175, 210, 225

rationalism 28–9, 33–5, 102, 109, 118
realism: metaphysical 7–8, 31, 151–2, 156–8, 164, 170, 185, 225–7; about universals 61
reductionism 121–3, 150, 159, 220
reference 95, 127, 149, 155, 158; causal theory of 161–9; philosophical sense of 166–9, 174; as 'really talking about' 167–9; as 'talking about' 166–9, 174
referentialism see reference: causal theory of
Reichenbach, H. 36
relativism 182, 210–16
religion 6–7, 21, 57, 101, 110, 135, 137, 186–7, 189–90, 221
representationalism 17–20, 27–8, 39–40, 102–3, 108, 113, 120–1, 140, 212–16; as Brentano's thesis see intentionalism
Robinson, H. 61–2
romantic–classic distinction 198
Russell, B. 35–6, 101, 113–14, 149, 151, 156, 165, 210
Ryle, G. 74, 89, 136, 141

Sartre, J-P. 205–8
scepticism 31, 139–40, 165, 168, 176, 228 (see also veil of perception problem); other minds 87, 91–4; Pyrrhonian 103
scheme–content distinction 170–6, 195
scholasticism 28, 104, 140
science 28, 91, 96, 101–3, 113–14, 136–41, 158–70, 175, 177–9, 183–202, 207, 216–17, 219–20, 227
Searle, J. 46, 81–2
Sellars, W. 96, 112–21, 124–9, 142, 175, 210, 235n2
sense-data 38, 118, 126, 138, 150, 159, 188, 227
Sextus Empiricus 103
Shakespeare, W. 60
Smart, J.J.C. 74–6, 233n1
Soames, S. 10, 126, 231n2
Socrates 174
solidarity 8, 225, 227
Sophocles 202
spirit–nature distinction 202, 206; see also Geistewissenshaften and Naturwissenschaften
Strawson, P.F. 42
Stroud, B. 139
subjectivity 5, 26–7, 44, 51, 57, 64–5, 74–5, 86, 89–90, 92, 98, 136, 175, 197–8, 201, 227–8
synthesis 34, 107–8

Tarski, A. 153–6
technē 28
technology 199–200, 207, 239n11
theory change, problem of 157–69
'theory of everything' 7, 169
things-in-themselves 32, 35, 215
thought-experiments 85
topic-neutral analysis 75–7, 94–5
transcendence 26, 57–8, 175
transcendental ego 107–8
transcendental idealism 32–5, 113, 115

truth: as correspondence 5–6, 157, 162, 171, 197; extra-theoretical vs. intra-theoretical 121, 162–9, 171; and justification 163, 211, 239n8; and meaning 171–6; as objective 5–9, 73, 91, 96, 110, 120, 125, 127, 156–61, 164, 169–70, 174–8, 181, 196–200, 204, 212, 217–18, 224, 227; and religion 6–8, 110, 134–5, 175, 181, 184, 206, 221; Rorty's position 163, 237n6; theory of (Tarski) 153; as usefulness 162
truth-conditions 153–6
Tye, M. 46

universals 55–62, 109; hypostatised 51–60, 143, 177, 212

veil of perception problem 31–3, 38, 50–1, 63, 65, 93, 103, 119, 156
verificationalism 37–8, 174–5
vision (as model for knowledge) 55, 58–61

Waismann, F. 231n3
Warnke, G. 207
'Whiggish' history 159, 187, 217, 237n5
Whitehead, A.N. 12
Williams, M. 102–3, 240n6
Wittgenstein, L. 13, 19–20, 44, 48–9, 53, 90, 115, 136, 141, 150–1, 168, 210, 227–8
World Well Lost, The 13, 148, 173